T0319886

Organizational Knowledge and Technology

I dedicate this book to my main source of inspiration,
my children Marco and Sara

Organizational Knowledge and Technology

An Action-Oriented Perspective on Organization
and Information Systems

Rodrigo Magalhães

*Consultant in Organization and Information Systems and Guest
Professor at the Catholic University of Portugal, Lisbon,
Portugal*

Edward Elgar
Cheltenham, UK • Northampton, MA, USA

Published by
Edward Elgar Publishing Limited
Glensanda House
Montpellier Parade
Cheltenham
Glos GL50 1UA
UK

Edward Elgar Publishing, Inc.
136 West Street
Suite 202
Northampton
Massachusetts 01060
USA

A catalogue record for this book
is available from the British Library

Library of Congress Cataloguing in Publication Data

Magalhães, Rodrigo, 1950–
    Organizational knowledge and technology: an action-oriented perspective
on organization and information systems/Rodrigo Magalhães.
        p.   cm.
    Includes bibliographical references and index.
    1. Information technology—Management. 2. Management information
systems. 3. Organizational behaviour. I. Title.
HD30.2.M347   2004
658.4'038'011—dc22

                                                            2003068788

ISBN 1 84376 282 X

Typeset by Manton Typesetters, Louth, Lincolnshire, UK
Printed and bound in Great Britain by MPG Books Ltd, Bodmin, Cornwall

Contents

List of figures   vii
List of tables and box   viii
Acknowledgements   ix

1   Introduction   1
2   Causes and consequences of information technology   16
3   Complexity and the new epistemological foundations of
     organization   41
4   Organizational paradigms: old and new   70
5   Strategy as managerial action   98
6   Evolving perspectives on IS/IT implementation   125
7   An action-based view of IS/IT strategic alignment   158
8   Notes on IS/IT strategic development   187
9   Conclusion   216

Bibliography   227
Index   247

Figures

1.1	Road map of the book	15
2.1	The web of causes and consequences of information/ organizational technology	21
2.2	The organizational growth cycle of IS/IT	28
2.3	Major IS/IT management activities and trends for the future	32
4.1	The three-dimensional organization	88
5.1	Outline of a theory of competitive positioning	104
5.2	Enacted cognition and structuration applied to managerial action	120
5.3	An action perspective on Clausewitz's theory of strategy	121
6.1	Methodological approaches to IS/IT implementation	132
6.2	Strategic change framework	134
6.3	Relative standing of Morgan's organizational metaphors	136
6.4	SAM: the interacting triangles	143
6.5	Socio-technical systems design	146
6.6	Structurational models of technology	148
6.7	The four perspectives of IS/IT implementation: a summary of key features	154
7.1	The Organizational Fit Framework (OFF) alignment model	161
7.2	A modified version of the Organizational Fit Framework (OFF) alignment model	164
8.1	The components of ISSD	189
8.2	The market value hierarchy	191
8.3	The logic of BSC: a strategy map	192
8.4	ISSD as a process of innovation	195
8.5	A managerial process approach to ISSD	198
8.6	Resources-based versus product-based views of information systems	202
8.7	The process of organizational competencies formation and application	203
8.8	Interlocking roles and learning loops of IS/IT governance	206
8.9	Modes and processes of knowledge creation	210

Tables and box

TABLES

2.1 Emerging trends in the organization and management of the IS function   34
2.2 Typical climate surrounding the IS/IT function in large organizations   36
3.1 Evolution of views in the cognitive sciences   55
3.2 Evolutionary levels of self-referential (social) systems   64
4.1 Differences between the notions of tacit and explicit knowledge   79
4.2 A comparative model of culture   83
4.3 The three-dimensional organization: concurring views from the literature   89
5.1 The historical search for organizational effectiveness   102
5.2 The resource-based approached compared with the neo-classical school of business economics   109
6.1 Perspectives on the implementation of information systems   130
6.2 IS/IT Infusion and Diffusion   135
7.1 Organizational context dimensions   170
7.2 IS/IT context dimension: IS/IT intent   173
7.3 IS/IT context dimension: IS/IT-related discipline   178
7.4 IS/IT context dimension: IS/IT-related trust   180
7.5 IS/IT context dimension: IS/IT-related support   181
7.6 IS/IT context dimension: IS/IT-related structural factors   184
8.1 IS/IT targets   193
8.2 Managerial processes for IS/IT strategic development   200
8.3 Characterizing the final outcome of ISSD, i.e. a move towards higher levels of IS/IT-related organizational maturity and learning   215
9.1 The current turn in the managerial paradigm   223

BOX

3.1 Autopoietic systems   57

Acknowledgements

Acknowledgements go to the following people, whose support in various ways has been decisive for the successful completion of this project. To my partners and colleagues from EUROSIS, Mr João Noronha, Mr Felix Guzman, Ms. Manuela Andrade, Mr Abdul Sacoor and Mr Samir Salé for their friendship and support; to Mr Rui Fernandes, ex-CEO of Telecomunicações de Moçambique, for the opportunity to test some academic ideas on real-world situations; to my academic supervisors at the London School of Economics, Prof. Ian Angell and Dr Lucas Introna (now at the University of Lancaster), for their dedication; to Dr Tony Cornford and Prof. Chrisanthi Avgerou, also from the LSE's Information Systems Department, for the healthy criticism and guidance; to Prof. Georg von Krogh from the University of St Gallen in Switzerland for being a very supportive external examiner; to Prof. Xavier Pintado, Prof. Fernando Adão da Fonseca and Prof. Borges de Assunção, from Universidade Católica Portuguesa in Lisbon, for their personal and institutional support in the PhD programme which has led to this book. Also many thanks to Sandra Luisa for the continued support at various points in our lives.

The reasonable man adapts himself to the world; the unreasonable one persists in trying to adapt the world to himself. Therefore all progress depends on the unreasonable man.

(G.B. Shaw, 1925:238)

1. Introduction

INFORMATION SYSTEMS AND ORGANIZATION

Information Systems and Information Technology (IS/IT) are becoming ever more infused, absorbed, integrated, appropriated and diffused into or by organizations, creating a host of contradictory impacts. IS/IT are responsible for delayering and relayering of organizational structures, for deskilling and upskilling of personnel, for more autocratic and more participative management styles, for breaking down and for erecting organizational boundaries. In a nutshell, the information age or the knowledge era with all its confusing promises, expectations, myths and consequences is here to stay and presents a new wave of challenge to people, society and organizations.

At the same time, more than ever before, we live in a world of organizations. From the growth of the internet to the mounting complexity of world politics; from the increasing use of air travel to the renewed struggle against world poverty; from the busy construction of a United Europe to the world race on the vaccine for AIDS and other plagues, all we see around us are organizations emerging, forming, changing and dying at an impressive speed. In an increasingly complex world, the endeavour for the survival of the human species has be organized and managed. But how to organize and how to manage appropriately and effectively in the new age? What drives the so called 'new economy'? How to make sense of the new mix – IS/IT and the organization?

This book is about information systems and information technology (IS/IT) in the context of organizations and their management. It is a multi-disciplinary approach which characterizes many of the so called 'new' disciplines in both the hard physical sciences and the soft social sciences. In our case, information systems and information technology fall under both types of sciences with the IT (information technology) part being very close to software engineering and computer science and the IS (information systems) section finding itself associated, by and large, with management and organization sciences. In this book we propose to contribute towards a better understanding of the concept of organization and of organizational behaviour in general, within the information systems discipline.

SOME DEFINITIONS

For purposes of establishing an initial platform of dialogue between us and the readers, we will use a set of definitions of the discipline of information systems which has been put forward for discussion by the UK Academy for Information Systems (UKAIS, 1997:5). These definitions were formulated by the Board of the Academy, with the help of the Committee of IS Professors and Heads of Department.

Definition

Information systems are the means by which organizations and people, utilizing information technologies, gather, process, store, use and disseminate information.

Domain of study

The study of information systems and their development is a multidisciplinary subject and addresses the range of strategic, managerial and operational activities involved in gathering, processing, storing, distributing and use of information, and its associated technologies, in society and organisations.

If we accept the premise that information systems is a multidiscipline we must be very clear about the concepts of multidisciplinarity or inter-disciplinarity. If we look around we will find examples of other emerging multidisciplines, and maybe these will help us understand the nature of the IS discipline. Let us take International Relations, which is formed by a variety of established disciplines, including Political Science, Law, Economics, Sociology and perhaps a few others.

Is there such a thing as *the* International Relations professional? Perhaps not, or not yet. People who take courses in International Relations can go into a variety of careers such as the diplomatic service, national politics, journal-ism, public relations or marketing. The choice of career will depend, among other things, on the previous academic and/or professional experience of the candidate. Before the International Relations qualifications existed, these careers were filled by graduates from the more established disciplines. How-ever, a new socio-economic global environment has created a need for a more interdisciplinary approach. So, what the new qualification will do is to enable old problems to be seen in a new light. Hence, International Relations is not yet a discipline but it is recognized as something increasingly relevant in today's world to help deal with today's international issues.

Like International Relations, IS is also an emerging discipline, whose need is clearly felt by practitioners and academics, but which still does not have a 'distinct entity' in terms of other academic disciplines. It is in the nature of any emerging discipline not to have a distinct identity. The issues related to, and the consequences of, the integration of IT in organizations and society are only now beginning to be felt. So it is very early days for a fully-fledged identity of the IS discipline to emerge. It is complicated to start talking of 'IS professionals' as opposed to 'IT professionals' as it gives an indication that the former will eventually replace the latter. Will that be the case? We doubt it. Coming back to the example of International Relations, it would be the same as saying that the new International Relations graduates will eventually replace Political Science graduates in international affairs.

IS brings a new dimension to various older and more established disciplines, such as Computer Science, Management, Organization Science, Psychology and Sociology, among others. It will probably not replace any of them but it will definitely give science a contribution that no other discipline or interdiscipline can give. The type of contribution that IS can give with its interdisciplinary approach, for example, to Computer Science, is in finding new ways of making the technology more accessible to people and organizations. Such an objective for IS might be derived from and validated by the following statement by Michael Dertouzos, Head of MIT's Laboratory for Computer Science: 'Some people maintain that increased complexity is an inevitable consequence of the times and that the role of computers is to manage complexity. Nonsense (...) the purpose of technology is to make new artefacts fulfil the needs of humans, not to make their lives more complicated' (1997, p. 297).

Having said this, we believe that although IS is not likely to replace any of the more established disciplines, it must work hard and efficiently towards establishing its own intellectual domain. All of the above disciplines, which together make up the interdiscipline of IS, have also been concerned, for a long time, with the same interface areas that today IS claims to represent (e.g. the human–computer, the organization–computer or the society–computer interfaces). One needs only to look at the better known academic journals from those disciplines and search for research articles on topics that we would easily identify as IS topics. Hence, independently, various academic disciplines are tackling research issues which are typically IS issues. Some do it better than others but what IS as an autonomous discipline is striving for is to show that it can do it better and more competently.

The UKAIS definition above claims that 'Information systems are the means by which organizations and people, utilizing information technologies, gather, process, store, use and disseminate information', but does not explain what it means by *means*. Hence we have to go further and get into the actual constitution of the entity called *information system*. Let us take three complementary definitions.

According to Land (1985:215, our emphasis) an information system is:

> a social system which has *embedded* in it information technology (...) it is not possible to design a robust, effective information system incorporating significant amounts of the technology without treating it as a social system.

From the point of view of Symons (1991:186/187, emphases added) an information system is:

> a complex social object which results from the *embedding* of computer systems into an organization (...) where it is *not* possible to separate the technical from the social factors given the variety of human judgements and actions, influenced by cultural values, political interests and participants' particular definitions of their situations intervening in the implementation of such a system.

And finally, Checkland and Holwell's (1998:110) view is that:

> any and every *information system* can always be thought about as entailing a pair of systems, one a system which is served (the people taking the action), the other a system which does the serving [i.e. the processing of selected data (capta) relevant to people undertaking purposeful action].

From these definitions, two key points stand out:

1. talking about an information system implies talking about two different types of entities: one of a social nature (i.e. the system which is served) and the other of a technological nature (i.e. system which does the serving).
2. the process of integration (i.e. embedding) between the two entities is a fundamental issue in the problematic of the information systems discipline.

The definitions above are also useful in bringing out the problem of the distinction (or the non-distinction) between IS and IT. IS/IT (information system/information technology) is the new social object which results from the integration of technological artefacts which are brought in from the external environment with the data, the information, the procedures and the processes generated within the organization. However, as Symons points out, the separation between the two is difficult and sometimes impossible, and when talking about information systems or about *an* information system sometimes one is focusing on the social object and other times on the technological artefacts. The distinction is far from being clear-cut and for that reason the dual acronym *IS/IT* is often used in the literature. The same happens throughout this book.

THE SPREAD OF INFORMATION TECHNOLOGIES AND THE RISE OF KNOWLEDGE AS THE KEY FACTOR OF WEALTH CREATION

Ever since the 1960s increasing volumes of data have been reduced to text and stored in computer memories. Data which before existed only in paper form or which was not even worth recording on paper given the static nature of this medium in terms of data manipulation, now can be retrieved, combined, re-combined, condensed or transmitted with the greatest of ease. It is this IS/IT-supported capability which now has achieved maturity and critical mass in organizations, thus bringing the issue of information technologies in organizations to a new level of debate. Some say that now it is no longer a question of managing data or even managing information, but it is a question of managing knowledge.

While agreeing that IS/IT do support or enable the development of organizational knowledge it is important not to fall into the temptation of treating data and information as being the same as knowledge. This happened, to a certain extent, in the 1980s and 1990s with the 'knowledge base' euphoria. In line with the advances in artificial intelligence, a 'knowledge base' (as opposed to a 'data base') was proposed as a technological artefact where significant parts of human knowledge would be stored and eventually replaced by dynamic electronic memories supported by powerful storage and retrieval software engines. Although this line of research continues with enthusiasm in some sectors of software engineering, its contribution towards the topic of knowledge in organizations has been marginal. However, the knowledge-base fad has been replaced by other fads such as data-warehousing, customer relationship management (CRM), workflow or document management, often marketed by vendors under the banner of 'knowledge management systems'.

Much of the confusion in the field stems from the meaning attributed to the three foundational concepts – data, information and knowledge. Data are usually taken as being semantic representations of reality by means of symbols (words, numbers, etc). Information, on the other hand, is often thought of as being the result of a combination of data, thus giving it meaning. Finally, knowledge, is often understood to be a kind of major store of information, which can be recorded indiscriminately in people's minds or on computer disks. According to this viewpoint, data, information and knowledge are different manifestations of the same objective phenomena, only organized into different levels of complexity. And this is the source of the confusion.

From the three concepts, the only one that can be considered as reasonably 'objective' is data. Information cannot be an objective concept; for there to be meaning there must be some form of human cognitive intervention and if there is human intervention, information must be subjective. The processes of interpretation of data and attribution of meaning that we call information must be carried out against some form of personal and pre-existing cognitive backdrop. This backdrop or personal context is what we understand as being knowledge. Individual knowledge is something subjective, partly explicit and mostly tacit, hence not amenable to being recorded, stored or retrieved electronically no matter what technological means are used.

This clarification of concepts is important because the spread of IS/IT in organizations impinges on another area of academic endeavour where individual and organizational knowledge also play key roles. The organization's collective stock of knowledge is rated by most business strategists as being the key differentiating factor between firms in terms of their competitive potential in the so called *new economy*. The new economy is a new model of production and work relations founded upon the social, political and technological macro-trends which characterize the third industrial revolution, also known as the information age, the knowledge society or the globalization era. In the *new economy* only a small percentage of the value of companies (as small as 15 per cent) can be traced to tangible assets on a balance sheet. The rest is derived from such intangibles as work-force skills, culture, speed, flexibility, technologies, brands and so forth. IS/IT are crucial for measuring and managing these assets.

In the world of business strategy, there is a general recognition that the positioning of companies in the competitive market is not enough to maintain sustainable advantage. The knowledge economy environment for both manufacturing and service organizations requires new capabilities for competitive success. The ability of a company to mobilize and exploit its invisible or intangible assets has become far more decisive than investing and managing physical, tangible assets. Intangible assets enable organizations to develop customer relationships, retain the loyalty of existing customers, serve new segments more effectively and efficiently, introduce innovative products and services, produce customized products with high quality, low cost and short lead times, mobilize employee skills and motivation for continuous improvements in process capabilities.

Thus, the knowledge economy is creating organizations built on a set of operating assumptions which are quite different from those of the past. Some of these assumptions are as follows (Kaplan and Norton, 1996):

- Cross-Functions – Integrated business processes that cut across traditional business functions.
- Links to Customers and Suppliers – IT enables the integration of supply, production and delivery processes.

- Customer Segmentation – Customized products and services with high quality, low cost and short lead times.
- Innovation – Product life cycles continue to shrink.
- Knowledge Workers – The divide between the intellectual elite (managers and engineers) and the manual labour force is disappearing.
- Global Scale – digital networks allow multinational companies to do all of the above on a global scale.

In the industrial economy of the past when capitalists spoke of wealth, they spoke of the property of natural resources, factory plants or industrial machinery. In the knowledge economy of the present when capitalists speak of wealth they are speaking of control over knowledge and knowledge resources. As an example, Bill Gates, one of the richest men in the world, owns mostly knowledge.

PARADIGM CHANGES

Much of this book centres on changes in various paradigms: IS/IT paradigms, scientific paradigms, organizational paradigms, strategic thinking paradigms and others. According to Kuhn (1970), the most fundamental set of assumptions adopted by a professional community which allows its members to share similar perceptions and engage in commonly shared practices is called a paradigm. Thus, we might say that the information systems paradigm is reflected in the definitions, the literature and the practices accepted and shared by the various communities who research, teach, work with and comment on information systems. Within a paradigm, it may be possible to find tendencies which are central and dominate, and tendencies which are marginal and which are trying to establish themselves. This is the case with information systems, where the information technologies (hardware, software and communication technologies) are the dominant part of the paradigm and the organizational-oriented tendencies are still at the margins.

The interest in the area broadly known as information systems started with a strong technological leaning, still the dominant part of the discipline's paradigm and covering areas such as systems analysis, systems specification, database management, software development, systems integration, software implementation or software auditing. In the last 20 years, a minority trend of the paradigm, focused on the organizational and managerial issues which are amongst the consequences of the spread of IS/IT in organizations, has been emerging. Such issues are manifold. They cover changes in work practices, work structures and professional training; impacts on organizational power and institutional politics; consequences at the strategic level and on organizational forms; strong impacts on organizational infrastructure and so on. However, although this minority trend has been steadily gaining ground, the problems associated with the development and implementation of IS/IT are still very apparent and create a major source of dissatisfaction in organizations.

The dominant discourse in IS/IT has been pitched at the micro-level where each IT application is analysed in isolation, not only in what concerns its development (either in-house or as a customized off-the-shelf package) but also regarding its implementation. It is customary to find implementation programmes (often called *change management* programmes) which deal exclusively with that application, ignoring others as well as organizational units which are not at the centre of the implementation in question but which could, and most certainly would, be affected by it.

This state of affairs has been the cause of many medium and long term failures of IS/IT implementation programmes, from the point of view of the customer. From the point of view of the implementer, usually a short-term view, the implementation programme is successfully completed when all the deliverables have been delivered OTIB (on time in budget). However, in view of the fact that the implementation programme has ignored a host of important organizational variables, as soon as the implementer leaves the problems start. The most frequently quoted examples of this are the ERP (Enterprise Resource Planning) software implementations which have caused and are still causing countless problems to organizations. The reasons behind the problems are never technological (in the sense that the software does what it is supposed to do), but always organizational. In spite of the intensive training programmes (sometimes included in the change management effort), many organizations still have great difficulty in actually changing the old manual processes in order to take the full benefits of the investments made in the software application.

In fairness to implementers of IT applications it must be said that often the implementation programmes are trimmed out to the barest of essentials in response to demands from the customer for keeping costs as low as possible. And this is precisely one of the key issues which this book is intended to tackle. But who is responsible for the commissioning of IS/IT implementation projects and, therefore, ultimately responsible for cutting down on (organizational) implementation costs? Top and senior managers are responsible.

Although they do not often appear as ultimately responsible for the poor performance of new investments in IS/IT given the various protection layers of hierarchical decision making and of institutional politics (including blaming the implementer), top and senior managers are responsible. In part, they are pressured by a need to show positive business results which, at least in the short term, can be achieved by shrinking implementation costs. But, as all experienced managers know, in the medium to long term we end up paying for (or benefiting from) the decisions taken in the short term. And in addition to this managerial myopia, many top and senior managers suffer from an acute lack of awareness regarding the power and depth of organizational issues.

When you open up a book on information systems implementation/management the issue of organization is only touched upon, usually to describe organizational forms, structures and processes. Likewise, when looking at a book on organization, information systems rarely appear as a topic and when they do, the debate is centered on the impact of IT on a variety of macro-organizational issues. Following the trend of deep fragmentation between the sciences in general, the topics of organization and information systems are treated as independent and almost divorced from each other. As a result, IS/IT development, IS/IT implementation and IS/IT management issues are presented as quite separate from strategic analysis, organizational development or change management topics. This places severe limitations not only on the development of the discipline but also on the solution to the practical problems that information systems specialists find when confronted with real-world organizations.

On the other hand, over the years, organization scientists and practising managers have become increasingly aware that the tools, techniques and advice found in textbooks and manuals intended to guide the activities of organizing and managing have always been somewhat *off target*. This becomes evident when, as a teacher of management and organization, one of the most frequent comments to be heard, especially from students with some work experience, is 'ok, it sounds fine in theory but it's hard to see how it all applies in practice'.

Such has been the situation until recently, when a new compromise between theory and practice – a major paradigm change – seems to be finally on the horizon. The compromise, which is receiving increasing amounts of attention from the organization science and management communities, rests upon the so called 'new science'.

New science is making us more aware that our yearning for freedom and simplicity is one we share with all life. In many examples, scientists now describe how order and form are created not by complex controls but by the presence of a few guiding formulas or principles repeating back on themselves through the exercise of individual freedom. The survival and growth of systems that range in size from large ecosystems down to the smallest microbial colonies are sustained by a few key principles that express the system's overall identity combined with high levels of autonomy for individuals within that system (Wheatley, 1999: 13).

Based on notions such as complexity (as opposed to reductionism), self-organization and self-steering (as opposed to determinism), chaos and unpredictability (as opposed to command and control) or sensemaking and understanding (as opposed to rationalizing and predicting), the 'new science' offers new ways for bridging the gap between theory and practice. Bundled under the banner of the Complexity paradigm (Waldrop, 1992), the new tenets make total sense as far as the activities of organization and management are concerned and contain the seeds for the legitimation of a *new order* that many organization scientists and practising managers had long been waiting for.

Constructs such as organization, organizational knowledge, organizational climates or contexts are all informed by one or more epistemologies. Epistemologies, in turn, influence the methodologies which are used in researching and theorizing about such constructs. A methodology influenced by a positivist epistemology will treat organizations as objective entities with given features which can be freely researched by an independent observer. A methodology informed by an interpretivist epistemology will recognize that organizations cannot be researched as wholly objective phenomena and that, in fact, organizations are the result of joint action of their members in their effort to make sense of the reality among and around them. For example, Ghoshal and Moran (1996) defend the position that organizations are much more than economic instruments that mirror the market or respond to market forces. Instead, they argue that 'organizations' real contribution to economic progress is in their unique ability to create their own distinct contexts' (p. 63), and that such contexts are what enables companies to 'actually defy the relentless gale of market forces' (ibid.).

In viewing organizations as a result of the action of the people within them, with their vast reserves of knowledge and aspirations, Ghoshal and Moran are supporting an interpretivist stance in managerial thought. Such a stance, also part of a paradigm change, is placed in a middle ground between two opposing schools of strategic management: the strategic planning orthodoxy and the emergence or incrementalist heterodoxy. Joyce and Woods (1998) call this intellectual posture the *new modernist* school of strategy, an approach which blends the unreserved optimism and wishful thinking of rational planning (modernist thinking) with the systematic scepticism of the postmodern management thinkers about most forms of planned change.

This new managerial epistemology is characterized by the abandoning of strict reductionist and positivist methods and the adoption of a more tolerant perspective towards ambiguity and everlasting change. It is a fundamentally action-oriented perspective which goes back to basics regarding the business of management, thus returning the figure of the manager together with leadership and managerial action to centre-stage of the theorizing about strategy and organization. In a way, it is a return to the pioneering ideas of thinkers such as Mary Parker Follet (1924), Chester Barnard (1938), Peter Drucker (1955), Philip Selznick (1957), Burns and Stalker (1961) or Charles Handy (1978), reinforced by contemporary academic management authors such as Argyris and Schon (1978; 1996), Ghoshal and Bartlett (1993; 1994), von Krogh and Roos (1995), Nonaka and Takeuchi (1995) or Von Krogh, Nonaka and Ichijo (2000).

Thus, one of the key arguments in this book is that the current technology-oriented paradigm, upon which the information systems discipline has been founded, is changing. The new paradigm, supported by the new scientific order announced by the Complexity archi-paradigm, will help the discipline to build an holistic, all-encompassing and action-oriented framework for the achievement of its final aim: the integration of information technologies and the social structures of organization. Complexity and new approaches to organization theory also support a revival of managerial action as the key focus of attention for the strategic development of organizations. In this book we aim at applying such managerial thinking to IS/IT strategic development, including issues such as IS/IT alignment, IS/IT corporate governance and IS/IT-related consulting, education and training.

SUMMING UP THE PURPOSES OF THE BOOK

This book is the result of a series of intellectual challenges related to academic, managerial and consulting activities in the areas of business information, information technology, strategy, organizational development and change management, which have presented themselves to the author over the years. Such challenges, which make up the purposes of this book, may be expressed as follows:

1. Arguing that there is a need to show that the knowledge imperative in business and organizational development can only be attained if organization and information systems are treated as one integrated topic and not as two separate ones.
2. Understanding and explaining that the approach to organizational (knowledge) development depends upon one's intellectual stance on human knowledge and cognition and these, in turn, depend on the stance in relation to scientific methodology.
3. Attempting to introduce Complexity as a new scientific epistemology and Complexity-influenced approaches to cognition and social systems which point to behaviour and action as the bases for intervention in both organization and information systems.

4. Aiming to relate the economic imperative of knowledge creation to action-based managerial models dealing with context formation, organizational change and IS/IT strategic alignment/development.
5. Exploring the concept of IS/IT-related organizational contexts and identifying the dimensions of such contexts as the shapers of IS/IT strategic alignment.
6. Suggesting the notion of *IS/IT strategic development* (incorporating IS/IT alignment) as a contribution towards the opening-up of new avenues in the management of IS/IT and of new forms of intervention regarding the organizational integration of information systems.
7. Doing all of the above trying never to lose sight of the needs of practitioners, meaning not only IS/IT managers, top and first-line managers but also other stakeholders involved in IS/IT corporate governance.

Although the book is not intended as 'light' reading for managers, it does take, as a starting point, the needs of managers, both in terms of understanding and of acting upon the phenomena of organization and information systems. Thus, an important objective in this book is to contribute towards new ways of perceiving, understanding and handling IS/IT-related organizational phenomena, as close as possible to the world of practice.

In terms of audience, the intention of this book is also to provide the people who are in a position to bring about change (i.e. academics with a pragmatic bent, applied researchers, postgraduate students and high-impact managers) with an epistemological/theoretical background which will help them to break away from the status quo. The status quo is the climate of positivist, rationalist and reductionist thinking imported from the hard sciences which has led academics and practitioners to believe that quantitative management tools, engineering-inspired organizing methods and mechanistic change programmes were the 'right way' to manage, to organize and to make information systems more effective.

THE RESEARCH METHOD

Our research method emphasizes multidisciplinary theory-building, based on what Itami and Numagami (1992) call 'logical compound synthesis'. This method is presented as an alternative to the three more conventional research methodologies – mathematical model analysis, statistical data analysis and in-depth case analysis – and derives its plausibility from 'the robust coherence among its components and from the logical connections among its conceptual constructs' (ibid, p. 133). Logical compound synthesis gets its inspiration from the chemical sciences, where researchers synthesize various materials into a compound which is new to the world. In this book we have also selected various theoretical concepts and empirical findings as material and have synthesized them into a plausible logical story. The theoretical concepts and empirical findings come from the research literature on management, organization science and information systems, and the synthesis is a new organizational approach to information systems development, implementation and management.

In an applied field of knowledge such as information systems, the research methodology must always strike a balance between the inductive and the deductive methods of theory building. Being firmly anchored in the management sciences, the information systems discipline must be mindful of the views put forward by well-known management researchers, such as Alfred Chandler. That author argues that theory development in management should be carried out 'from the point of view of the busy men responsible for the destiny of the enterprise, rather than being [just] deducted from the disciplinary premises of social scientists' (quoted in Ghoshal and Bartlett, 1993:25). The resulting method, also applicable to this book, may be described as something close to speculative reasoning, in the way that has been suggested by Lundberg (1984):

> speculative reasoning which is carefully done and which probes the pragmatic dimension of a major, increasingly crucial phenomenon, has utility for it begins to inform and guide practice and to stimulate enquiry (quoted in Stickland, 1998: 28).

In the main, the book rests upon conceptual and empirical research carried out as part of a PhD programme at the London School of Economics (Magalhães, 1999) and as such is firmly anchored in the existing published literature in the various fields investigated. To this academic research some new ideas have been added, especially from the new literature on Complexity. Being a body of knowledge which is barely emerging, some of these ideas may still have to be validated in terms of the traditional processes of scientific accreditation.

ROAD MAP OF THE BOOK

A brief history of the new organizational approach is presented in Chapter Two, as an introduction to the increasing complexity of the integration between IS/IT and the organization. In this context, IT can be regarded as the new organizational technology. In Chapter Three, Complexity is introduced as the starting point for many changes to come in the fields of economics, management and organization theory. This chapter opens up the way for

Chapters Four and Five, where the new approaches to organization, management and strategy are discussed, with an emphasis on knowledge and action-oriented approaches. Chapter Six is about the evolution of the various perspectives on IS/IT development and implementation, ending with the perspective developed in this book: organizational holism. Chapter Seven contains a conceptual discussion about a new perspective on *IS/IT* strategic alignment, based on the managerial action–organizational context duality. Chapter Eight comprises a practical reflection on IS/IT strategic development and Chapter Nine wraps up the book with some conclusions.

For a graphic representation of the book's road map, please see Figure 1.1.

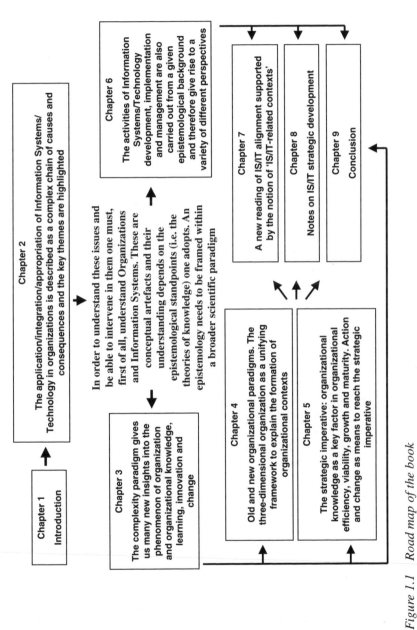

Figure 1.1   Road map of the book

2. Causes and consequences of information technology

> Information technology is no infrastructure issue to decide upon and then lay aside in order to attend to business. Information technology is what we make business with (...) and it is on this [electronic] market that we must compete, by experimenting with new technology, new ways of organizing, moving quickly, like nomads.
>
> (Dahlbom, 2000:226)

INTRODUCTION

In this chapter we start the discussion about the process of integration (i.e. embedding) of technological artefacts into the social structures and processes of the organization. As the discussion will show, the mutual impacts and the level of amalgamation is such that the bundle known as information systems and technologies (IS/IT) can quite adequately be labelled as *organizational technologies*. Such a label (used interchangeably in the plural or in the singular) is intended not only as a means of demonstrating the merger which has already been reached between the technological artefacts and the social fabric of the organization but also as a way of marking the difference between these technologies and the production technologies of a different era.

The history of the Industrial Revolution is founded upon the replacement of human labour by the steam engine first and by other types of engines and machines later. The history of the Information Revolution, which is in the process of being written, is also about major changes in the way people work and do business but such changes are of a very different nature. Industrial technologies changed factories, industrial plants and the means of production in general. Information technologies, while also changing the means of production, for example through robotics applications, have the capabilities to change the whole organization which is behind the factory or the industrial plant.

Information technology can be seen in two complementary ways. On the one hand, IT can be seen as material artefacts, arranged in various configurations of hardware and software as well as the applications of such configurations (services for capturing, manipulating and exchanging data). On the other hand, IT can also be seen as the human activities that design and use those artefacts which, in turn, are part of the social structures of an organization (interacting individuals and groups going about their daily routines). When these two 'realities' (i.e. the technological and the human) come together, the process of integration of IS/IT and the organization starts through a dialectical interplay of co-produced 'reality' (Orlikowski, 1992; Walsham, 1993; De Sanctis and Poole, 1994).

While it is true that 'technology not only constrains what the firm can do technically, but frames and drives the way people think' (Itami and Numagami, 1992:131) there are, however, some important differences between the impact of industrial technologies and of information technologies in organizations. Regarding the types of technologies, one tends to think of industrial technologies as being more endogenous to the firm than information technologies because the former are often grown within the company through its R&D and market intelligence efforts while the later are developed outside by hardware and software vendors and are imported into the company in a piecemeal fashion. By piecemeal we mean that, given the cost advantages and the quality of the market offerings, most companies prefer to buy ready-made software applications as and when they are needed, rather than growing their own. This form of acquisition may (and often does) create platforms with technological inconsistencies and incompatibilities which may be regarded as something rather exogenous to the firm.

However, the fact of the matter is that, in spite of a somewhat haphazard development of many technological platforms, the degree of endogeneity achieved by information technologies in organizations is much greater than that ever achieved by industrial technologies. Even though software applications are mostly developed outside the organization, due to their internal features they have become so intimately linked to the organization's internal and external routines and processes that they have caused dramatic changes to the structure of not one single firm but of whole industrial sectors. The new changes have to do with how information is represented, with how information is communicated, with the increase in the speed of communications and with the pace of business and social change in general. The so-called new economy is the end result of all such changes.

In this chapter we attempt to draw a brief sketch of the organizational approach to IS/IT. We start off on a note of scepticism on the research efforts carried out in academia regarding the search for specific cause-and-effect relationships regarding the adoption of IS/IT by organizations. From there, we move on to a general discussion on the key impacts of IS/IT on organizations, to focus on four themes which we consider as fundamental for an understanding of the organizational approach to IS/IT and which will be developed throughout this book. The themes are: organizational knowledge as a competitive market pressure, the new strategic alignment needs for IS/IT, the emergence of the newest functional area in large companies, i.e. the IS/IT sub-organization, and its new integration needs, and finally we discuss the lack of an organizational orientation in much of current mainstream IS/IT literature and the need to reverse such a trend. To conclude the chapter, a number of propositions are put forward, thus establishing the link with the remainder of the book.

THE INCONCLUSIVE SEARCH FOR CAUSE-AND-EFFECT IN IS/IT

The discussion about the causes and consequences of IS/IT in organizations is central on the study of information systems and has been the object of many a research study. A significant amount of the academic research material produced on this topic, especially in the early days of the discipline, tended to be of a positivist nature in the sense that research projects were designed with a view to linking specific causes to specific effects, in the search for elusive independent variables. However, the true complexity of the problem has rapidly become apparent and most researchers now agree that it is not feasible to conceive of linear chains of causality between the adoption of IS/IT and their impacts on the organization.

In one of the earliest reviews of the literature on the impact of computers on organizations, Attewell and Rule (1984) wrote:

> What puzzles us is that people remain so willing to speak and write as though the overall effects of computing technologies were a foregone conclusion, as though they could be determined a priori (...) We argue the opposite: that evidence on these subjects is actually fragmentary and very mixed, and that a priori arguments are particularly inappropriate in light of the range and variety of variables at work in these situations (p. 1184) (...) We suspect that the transformations in organizational life through computing are so multifarious as to encompass the most disparate cause-effect relationships (p. 1190).

In other words, it is not possible to disentangle the many causes and many effects of the successive decisions to implement IS/IT artefacts, which feed on each other along the temporal dimension. For this reason some writers avoid using the expression 'impact' in view of its deterministic connotations, in terms of cause and effect. Our use of the word is in its broadest possible sense, to mean the consequences, the influences or the changes brought about by the adoption of IS/IT in organizations.

A type of report which became popular in the IS/IT literature of the 1980s was the techo-optimist paper dedicated to forecasting the future in terms of changes in organizational structures, managerial processes, communications or working methods. Huber (1990), for example, put forward a general theory of the 'effects of advanced information technologies on organizational design, intelligence and decision making', where the overall conclusion is that improvements in intelligence development and decision making will be made possible by the availability of more accurate, comprehensive, timely and available organizational intelligence. This conclusion and many others in the same vein is drawn on the assumption that organizational intelligence will increase or improve because technology makes it possible. However, the assumption that the presence of advanced information technologies will lead to better intelligence development and better decision making and hence to improved performance is just too simplistic.

Over the years, the research on the impact of IS/IT on various aspects of organizational life has remained quite inconclusive. Daniel Robey, one of the most persistent researchers in this area, wrote in a review of research into the relationship between organizational structures and IT published as early as 1977:

> structure does not primarily depend on any internal technologies for information processing, but rather on the nature of the task environment. Under stable conditions computers tend to reinforce centralization. Under dynamic conditions, computers reinforce decentralization. Earlier positions are difficult to support because they are locked into the idea that computers *cause* changes. The present review points to the value of looking beyond computers to more theoretically grounded causal variables in the organization's task environment (p. 974).

In 1981, the same author wrote:

> we have found several different organizational structures compatible with computer information systems. These cases seem to fuel arguments *against* technological determinism. Newer organizational forms such as the matrix and other dual authority arrangements seem as equally receptive to computer technology as the more traditional bureaucracies. Our studies indicate little uniformity in the way that information systems mesh with formal organizational structure (p. 686).

And, 18 years after his first review, the situation still had not changed. In 1995, Robey writes

> Indeed, some of the tightest studies in terms of research design, measurement and statistical analysis have produced the most direct evidence of inconsistent, paradoxical and ironical [organizational] consequences of technology (…) [It is] suggested that researchers relax the usual deterministic causal assumptions involving technology and social systems and assume that technology's consequences are 'emergent'. That is, effects are not entirely distinct from causes and technology and organizations may mutually affect each other (p. 58).

These findings are consistent with many other articles and books on the same topic (see, for example, Gutek et al., 1984; Strassman, 1985; Eccles, 1991; Kelly, 1994; Petrozzo, 1995; Landauer, 1995).

THE WEB OF CAUSES AND CONSEQUENCES OF ORGANIZATION AND TECHNOLOGY

Having made the point that the traditional scientific method approach cannot be applied to a linear search of causality regarding the impacts of IS/IT in organizations, it is important to give the reader an overview of the complexity of the problem. As Figure 2.1 shows, the issue of the organizational integration of IS/IT can be seen as an intricate web of many causes and many consequences where some links between some causes and some consequences may be stronger than others but where there are no exclusive one-to-one relationships. The web is made up of a number of interrelated factors or phenomena which sometimes act as the cause and other times act as the consequence of the integration of IT artefacts into organizations. For example, *compression of competitive time* is related to *hypercompetition*, but so is *competitive market pressure*, *convergence of info-com* or the *breaking up of conventional business boundaries*.

Although all the causes are related to all the consequences, an author can address more of his attention to one or more of the factors presented in the figure. This is the case in point, where the factors shown in italics represent this book's foci of attention.

We start unweaving the web with *the automation of tasks and processes*, one of the earliest steps taken on the road towards the knowledge society. The topic crept into the management literature as early as 1958 with Leavitt and Whistler's rather futuristic account of *Management in the 1980s*. But it was not until the eighties proper that the impact of the application of IT on the workplace started to be reported both as a general management priority (Forester, 1980; Large, 1984) and an academic management concern (Child, 1984). The topics covered ranged from ergonomics and usability, job design, deskilling and upskilling, employment and careers to industrial relations implications, organizational design and the role of users.

Related to the spreading of IT application to *automate tasks and processes*, there is the interesting phenomenon of the increasing *textualization of information* in the workplace. Such phenomenon, tied to the representational qualities of IT, was the object of a major study by Shoshana Zuboff (1988) published in the book *In the Age of the Smart Machine*. The following quotation taken from a later paper by the same author summarizes accurately the gist of her groundbreaking ideas on the transformation of work (Zuboff, 1995:15, italics added):

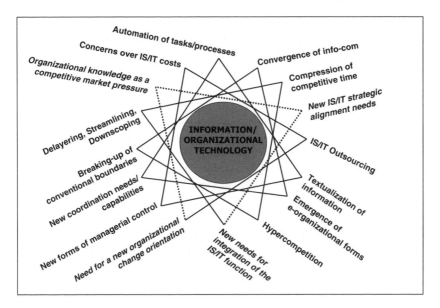

Figure 2.1 *The web of causes and consequences of information/*
organizational technology

This century's long trend towards the abstraction of work has been dramatically accelerated since the early 1980s by the adoption of information technologies. These new technologies were widely regarded as simply the next phase of *automation*. The logic of their development and deployment hardly varied from the ancient impetus towards labour substitution. But we have learned that these technologies are different, that the intelligence at their core provokes a discontinuity in the history of technological development. This is because even when information technologies are applied to automate, they simultaneously set into motion an entirely unique set of reflexive processes, translating newly automated activities into data and information for wide-ranging display. Information technologies symbolically render processes, objects, behaviours and events so that they can be seen, known and shared in a new way. In other words, these technologies codify and illuminate interior detail, creating transparency where there was opacity, an explicit public text where there was once fragmentation, privacy and intuition. The organization, its internal processes and exchange relationships, becomes visible in a wholly new way, whether that pertains to thousands of newly codified variables in the production process or the global flow of cash tracked on an hourly basis. The word I coined to capture this unique capacity of information technology is *informate*.

What is interesting and challenging about Zuboff's work is not the new technology per se but the innovative and even contradictory ends to which it can be put by different managers in different contexts. In some contexts, the technology may have an 'automate' effect, i.e. it turns manual tasks which were previously interesting into dull, repetitive and unmotivating tasks; but in other contexts, the technology has an 'informate' effect, meaning that the manual tasks become more challenging and interesting due to the richer information environment provided by the technology. This highlights clearly the *uncertainty* about the path which certain IT-related developments may take.

Also related to the *automation of tasks and processes*, there is the issue of *concerns over IS/IT costs* which have not stopped escalating since the early days of computing. Nolan (1979) has suggested that the growth of computing goes through periods of *slack* and *control* and that these are due to market forces outside the organization and managerial forces inside the organization. Slack and control or *expansion* and *control* (Huff, Munro and Martin, 1988) are useful notions to explain that the introduction of a new type of technology triggers the need for the organization to learn and to expand, both in terms of knowledge and skills and in terms of computing resources. But after such periods of slack or expansion there is usually a need on the part of management to contain the expenditure and a period of tighter control of the development of computing is then initiated. The balance between these two types of forces continues to be one of the characteristics of IS/IT organizational integration.

Following such reasoning, Nolan (1979) has postulated that IS/IT evolution in organizations follows six sequential stages: Initiation, Contagion, Control, Integration, Data Administration and Maturity. Furthermore, that author adds, due to the forces of slack and control, such evolution follows two S-shaped learning curves: the first starting with very low levels of learning at the Initiation stage, followed by rapid growth through Contagion, levelling off at the Control and Integration Stages; the second curve starts at the levelling off of the previous curve, has slow growth at first and then more rapid growth through the Data Administration stage, levelling off again at the Maturity stage. The idea of modelling IS organizational growth through development stages has played an important role in the understanding of information systems phenomena (Huff, Munro and Martin, 1988; Galliers, 1991; Choo and Clement, 1994).

The increasing *textualization of information* in organizations has had another very important consequence, i.e. the rise of *new forms of managerial control*. With the rapid advances in database management and in data storage technologies, information about everything happening in the organization has been stored in powerful data-warehousing systems. A wide variety of decision support systems has also been developed to combine and extract information in such a way that traditional management accounting has been totally redefined. Such systems have a direct impact on the way that the competencies and performance of employees can be monitored and improved

by performing very fine cross-referencing of multiple variables and identifying relationships which were not possible to establish before. One example is
the EIS (Executive Information Systems) designed to support the Balanced
Scorecards Methodology (Olve et al., 1999).

The Balanced Scorecards Methodology (BSC) is also a consequence of a
development in strategic management thinking which highlights the company's intangible assets as the main source of competitive differentiation (Teece,
2000). Intangible assets encompass items such as the relationships between
customers and suppliers, the routines and procedures embedded in business
processes, the organizational culture and the skills and competencies of organizational members. Such assets are part of the organization's intellectual
capital, a distinction which Skandia, a Swedish insurance company, helped to
promote when it published, in 1994, a ground-breaking report about its
intellectual capital. The report entitled *Vizualizing Intellectual Capital*
(Edvinsson and Malone, 1997) was meant as an appendix to the company's
annual accounts, the idea being that in addition to its financial capital report,
the company should also report about its investments in its intellectual capital, certainly the part of the company's capital with greater potential for the
creation of value in the long term.

As part of these developments, Skandia put forward an innovative management control model named *Navigator*. The model contains four levels of
indicators (roughly the same as those found in the BSC Methodology): financial data, customer data, business process data and data about development
and innovation. The methodology transforms strategic business objectives
into departmental objectives going all the way down to individual level
objectives and turning them into quantitative and qualitative indicators. These
and the accompanying decision support system, allow Skandia's management
to *navigate* the company on the basis of *the past* (by means of its historical
financial records), through *the present* (by using its customer and business
process indicators) and towards *the future*, through the manipulation of its
development and innovation indicators.

The *Navigator* and the BSC Methodology are extremely important developments in the integration of IS/IT into the strategic management of
organizations. These new tools come about in response to the dramatic effect
of *compression of competitive time* which, in turn, is brought about by communication technologies and especially by the internet. What is meant is that
the life expectancy of competitive strategies based on customer and business
process indicators has become so short that future-oriented indicators (i.e.
development and innovation) are rapidly becoming the most important in
terms of management control. As Pascale et al. (2000:72) note 'the future is
the means to alter behaviour', meaning that in order to achieve what we want
in the present we have to use the future as the means.

The internet is at the core of a new economic space, in the continuous movement towards a world economy based less and less on physical assets and increasingly dependent on knowledge and information. In what concerns the impact of the Net in business, Dertouzos (1997) suggests that half of all the businesses conducted in the industrial world will be affected by this huge information market, generically known as e-commerce or e-business. The rise of this new way of conducting business transactions means, in the first place, an extension of the company's value chain brought about by the reduction and/or replacement of its distribution processes; in the second place, it also means a major change in the value of the services offered to the customer, by means of the incorporation of 'informational' value into such services. The competitiveness of companies in the e-commerce world depends, to a large degree, on their capacity to produce or reproduce information.

Product evolution is extremely rapid in the internet marketplace. For example, Netscape was only established in February 1993 but by June 1996 the third full upgrade of the Navigator software had already launched (Kenney, 2001). This is in line with what D'Aveni (1994) has termed *hypercompetition* and which is defined as

> a condition of rapidly escalating competition based on price-quality positioning, competition to create new know-how and establish first-mover advantage, competition to protect or invade established product or geographic markets, and competition based on deep pockets of alliances (p. 2).

From the point of view of *hypercompetition*, the question of applying IS/IT to business processes in order to achieve greater speed (and better timing) seems crucial. So, what are the implications of D'Aveni's views on *hypercompetition* for IS/IT development, use and management? In order to address this question, it is useful to also think about IS/IT as sets of new skills and capabilities which, according to Curley and Pyburn (1982), organizations have to learn. These authors make the distinction between type A and type B learning. Type A is the kind of learning which ensues from intensive training given to, for example, operators of a new manufacturing tool (industrial technologies). Type B is the kind of learning required for what those authors call the 'intellectual technologies', such as the computer. They characterize type B learning as being 'ongoing' and 'adaptive' as opposed to the intensive training which is better adapted to the industrial technologies.

From the above explanation, it may be concluded that the question of *hypercompetition* and of the timing advantages that D'Aveni (1994) discusses cannot be solved purely by the acquisition or application of IS/IT artefacts. These take time in terms of both individual and organizational learning. Conceivably, IS/IT take even longer than other organizational resources for appropriate skills and competencies to be developed. Therefore, IS/IT skills and competencies must be dealt with as an issue of strategic and organizational development with its own foundations, tools and techniques. This is one of the aims of the present book.

The issue of IS/IT skills and competencies is also related to a 'hot' information systems topic: *outsourcing*. For a number reasons, a growing number of companies have opted for outsourcing, that is, the contracting out of not just the development but also the implementation, the maintenance and even the management of their information systems and technologies. The key reasons are the escalating costs and the poor quality of internal development and management of IS/IT applications. However, the issues faced by the management of outsourcing are manifold and one of the most complicated problems is the question of the loss of internal IS/IT-related knowledge in the company. Being an area so closely interwoven into the company's processes, routines and even into personal relationships, it is difficult to conceive a situation of total separation between IS/IT and the rest of the organization in a move towards total outsourcing of IS/IT. According to Dertouzos (1997:210) 'outsourcing IT would be almost like outsourcing all the firm's employees'. However, IS/IT outsourcing is a reality and the answers to the problems seem be to be found in a selective mix of outsourcing and insourcing as well as in the turning of the outsourcing agreements into carefully planned and managed strategic partnerships (McFarlan and Nolan, 1995; Lacity and Hirscheim, 1995).

The issue of *hypercompetition*, like all the others in our web, is both a cause and a consequence. As such, it is linked to several other factors but one of them, a technological dimension, deserves a special mention as one major driving force of the knowledge economy: the *convergence of info-com*. The growing convergence between information and communication (info-com) technologies has changed the business environment dramatically, as correctly predicted by Keen (1988:279): 'telecommunication is a whole new arena where business imagination combined with understanding of just a few aspects of the technology opens up entirely new ways of thinking about customers, markets, productivity, coordination, service, competition, products and organization'. Thus, the *breaking up of conventional boundaries*, *delayering, streamlining and downscoping, new coordination needs and capabilities* and the *emergence of new organizational forms* are all consequences of the *convergence of info-com*.

The first industries to be affected by such impacts were those directly related to information and communication (Chakravarthy, 1997), that is, information providers (media, publishing), information processors (computer and office equipment services), communication providers (broadcasting, telephony, cable) and communication support (telecom equipment and consumer electronics). But now it was not only in these industries that the effects of the *convergence of info-com* is felt. In all types of industries, organizational frontiers are being redefined, electronic market places are being set up, buying and selling strategies are being revised and organizational structures are being reshaped, all due to the electronic interfaces which now link virtually every organization with suppliers on one side (Business to Business or 'B2B') and with customers on the other side (Business to Consumer or 'B2C').

The *convergence of info-com* together with the internal organizational changes brought about by the spread of hardware and software technologies gave rise to an explosion of literature, especially from Harvard and the MIT in the US. The following are just some of the topics addressed by such literature: changes in internal and external business frontiers (McFarlan, 1984; Cash and Konsysnski, 1985; Clemons, 1993), the role of networking in sustaining competitive advantage (Bradley, 1993), changes in organizational structures and managerial processes (Applegate, Cash and Mills, 1988), the growing interdependence of organizational functions (Rockart and Short, 1989), computers as coordination technology (Malone and Rockard, 1993), reengineering and process redesign (Davenport and Short, 1990; Hall et al., 1993; Hammer and Champy, 1994), managing by wire (Haeckel and Nolan, 1993), changes in individual, group and managerial work practices (Sproull and Kiesler, 1991) and the emergence of new organizational forms (Applegate, 1994; Semler, 1994).

Much of this literature is descriptive, reporting on well-known cases of success at the time (McKesson Drug Co, Frito-Lay, Phillips 66, American Airlines, SABRE and others) and attempting to draw conclusions generalizable to other companies. However, as events have proven since the writing of these cases, there are no general laws which can guide the integration of IS/IT since IS/IT are just one type of variable among many which may influence the success or failure of such integration. As a result, the acceptance of such literature born and bread in the US among European organizations has not been at all clear-cut (Ciborra, 1994).

Thus far we have discussed the general topics associated with the integration of IS/IT in organizations. For the remainder of the chapter we will be focusing on four themes which we have elected as central for an explanation of the organizational approach to IS/IT. They are also the topics to be developed further throughout this book.

THE KEY THEMES

1. Organizational Knowledge as a Competitive Market Pressure

As suggested in Chapter 1, the global spread of information technologies in the last 30 years has facilitated the establishment of knowledge (individual and organizational) as the driving force of the economy. Thus, in the early 21st century, we can safely talk of *organizational knowledge as a competitive market pressure* as a major cause/consequence of the organizational integration of IS/IT. The knowledge outcomes of the integration of IS/IT can be considered as the third stage of a cycle of IS/IT organizational growth, which starts and ends with competitive market pressures (Figure 2.2).

An organization's positioning on the competitive market determines, to a certain extent, the level of investment of that organization in IS/IT. For example, it is not possible for a bank nowadays to invest significantly less than all the other competing banks and still stay in business. Porter and Millar (1985) have introduced an analytical tool called the *IT intensity matrix* in order to discuss the positioning of a company or industrial sector in relation to two factors: (1) the amount of information processing required throughout the company's value chain and (2) the amount of information content of the company's products or services. On both counts the level of IT intensity tends to increase. In other words, the pervasive and ever increasing penetration of IT artefacts in organizations means that both in terms of the value chain and in terms of the content of the product itself the intensity of IS/IT is always mounting.

The two factors featured in the IT intensity matrix and which highlight the degree of strategic relevance of IS/IT for a particular company's business can be amalgamated into one dimension – *IS/IT Infusion* (Sullivan, 1985). Such a dimension has been the object of a variety of frameworks designed to increase the strategic impact of IS/IT, namely, the critical success factors methodology (Rockard, 1979), the customer resource life cycle framework (Ives and Learmonth, 1984) and the strategic option generator model (Wiseman, 1988). In reality, what all such frameworks intend to do is to plan the expected achievements of the investments of IS/IT in terms of efficacy, efficiency and, sometimes, effectiveness.

By efficacy, one tries to answer the question 'do the means work well?'. By efficiency, one addresses the issue of the use of resources and attempts to answer the question 'is the minimum possible level of resources being used?'. Finally, the effectiveness dimension addresses the question of the contribution of the proposed IS/IT investment to the long-term aims of the organization (Checkland and Holwell, 1998). In a way, effectiveness encapsulates the

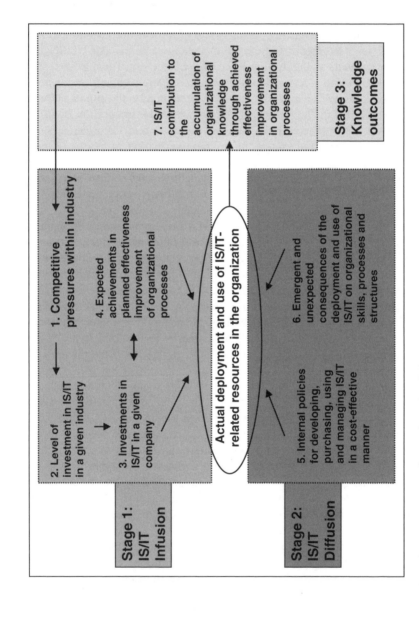

Figure 2.2   The organizational growth cycle of IS/IT

other two questions because, being a strategic dimension, it can only be achieved once efficacy and efficiency are assured.

While the concept of *Infusion* addresses the problems of strategic relevance and competitive positioning, the concept of *Diffusion* (Sullivan, 1985) is proposed as a measure for the level of deployment, internal use and management of the investments made in IS/IT within the organization. In other words, while the needs imposed by strategic positioning may lead companies in the same sector to carry out similar levels of investment in IT (i.e. similar levels of infusion), the deployment, use and management of those investments within the companies almost certainly is different.

While infusion depends largely upon market forces, diffusion depends mainly upon the effectiveness of the organization's IS/IT corporate governance processes. However, given the pressures from the competitive market, the trend for both infusion and diffusion is a continually upward movement. And, as rightly predicted by Sullivan (1985), as organizations approach a stage of high infusion and high diffusion, 'processing and data, which had been viewed as central, begin to look peripheral and [organizational] communication, which had been peripheral, begins to look central' (ibid., p. 9).

Thus, enabled by IS/IT, human networking and organizational communication have become key ingredients in the overall improvement of the effectiveness of organizational processes which, in turn, provides a major contribution to the creation and accumulation of knowledge in the organization. This becomes even clearer when supported by Nonaka and Takeuchi's (1995:59) definition of organizational knowledge creation, i.e.:

> a processes [that] takes place within an expanding 'community of interaction' which crosses intra- and inter-organizational levels and boundaries [and which] 'organizationally' amplifies the knowledge created by individuals and crystallizes it as part of the knowledge network of the organization.

Organizational knowledge is credited nowadays as the key variable in sustainable competitive growth. And as more knowledge is created and accumulated within and across organizations with the contribution of IS/IT, causing organizational processes to be ever more effective, the demands from the market for more infusion and more diffusion of IS/IT continue to increase. No organization can afford to be left behind, so the cycle goes on.

2. New IS/IT Strategic Alignment Needs

As mentioned above, the convergence of info-com together with the internal organizational changes brought about by the spread of hardware and software technologies gave rise to an explosion of interest in the strategic impact of IS/IT. One of the issues widely discussed under this topic has been *IS/IT stra-*

tegic alignment. The notion of IS/IT strategic alignment was introduced in the literature through the study *Management in the Nineties* (Scott Morton, 1991) carried out by researchers at the MIT and which produced the framework known as SAM (Strategic Alignment Model). For the contributors to this study, the overall effectiveness of IS/IT implementation was attributed to the quality of the alignment achieved between the strategies for IS/IT and the organization's strategies.

Alignment of IS/IT with corporate strategy simply ensures that organizations are getting the greatest return for their investment in IS/IT. Investment in IS/IT cannot be justified on their own merit because it is impossible to isolate the IS/IT component from the larger set of corporate resources needed to reach strategic goals. IS/IT do not stand alone. To be successful, a business software application requires training programmes for users, the reorganization of horizontal processes, the reviewing of incentive programmes and IS/IT-related leadership. However, each of these ingredients comes from different parts of the company. But because firms are usually organized around disciplines the problem is left for the IS/IT departments while other managers attempt to align their own functional areas with the organization's strategy. The result is financial executives do not understand critical issues such as the customer value proposition or development strategies, marketing experts are oblivious of the needs of HR strategic competencies and few managers understand the real issues of *IS/IT strategic alignment*.

The implementation of IS/IT strategies, in turn, causes the development of the IS/IT infrastructure which embraces the human resources allocated to the IS/IT function, the communication network which supports the main management control functions, all shared systems and applications, the larger systems applications dedicated to the routine transactions of the firm and the strategic applications aimed at gaining competitive advantage. The ultimate aim of *IS/IT strategic alignment*, therefore, is to maintain the IS/IT infrastructure permanently in tune with the organization's strategy. However, placing the IS/IT infrastructure in the organization's strategic agenda is not a simple task. The technology is complex and difficult to understand. Technical jargon and the propensity of IS/IT professionals to bandy it about create a communications gap. Much of IT's infrastructure is difficult to justify because it cannot be linked to specific applications or projects. IS/IT have a high rate of obsolescence, creating legacies that limit flexibility. And finally IS/IT are expensive, and that creates pressure on those outside IS/IT to understand their costs and benefits.

As a result, more than a decade after we might say that the initial aims of the MIT's SAM have failed. IS/IT infrastructures are not aligned with the organization's strategy, at least not with the synchrony and control which the

IS/IT literature of the 1980s and 1990s from Harvard and the MIT made us believe was possible to achieve:

> IT strategic plans have been around for many years and their link with the business strategy should have brought, however indirectly, some form of alignment. Often they have not, so there must have been a problem all along related to the difficulty or impossibility of alignment (Ciborra et al., 2000:27).

Ciborra et al. (2000) believe that the situation is not one of control in the management of IS/IT but one of *technology drift* and they ask: 'what if our powers to bring to life sophisticated and evolving infrastructures must be associated with the acceptance of the idea that we are bound to lose control?' (p. 39). And to conclude, these authors point out that by now the 'classic' scholars of IS/IT alignment must have come to accept that the concept originally put forward is no longer tenable in view of its non-dynamic and deterministic foundations. However, before moving on to an updated and perhaps slightly less mechanistic version of SAM, they rightly stress that we should reflect about its theoretical premises and work on new approaches with radically different fundamentals. In other words, the whole notion of IS/IT strategic alignment should be re-assessed and *new IS/IT strategic alignment needs* should be identified.

3. New Needs for Integration of the IS/IT Function

What is the IS/IT function and how is it changing? The information technology/systems function comprises the following four major operational areas (Sprague and McNurlin, 1998):

- Computer operations: running and maintaining computers and networks
- Systems development: developing, maintaining and updating systems
- Architecture development: providing a framework of policies and standards both for information technologies and for information contents
- Business information requirements: helping users to articulate their needs in terms of the systems architecture.

As Figure 2.3 suggests, these traditional functions of IS/IT departments are undergoing major changes, due to a variety of factors which can be divided into two major categories: (1) changes from within the organization, where a combination of more user-friendly technologies and users more knowledgeable about IT can, in some ways, replace the work of traditional IS specialists; (2) changes from outside the organization, where all kinds of new computer services are being offered, making it more cost-effective for many companies

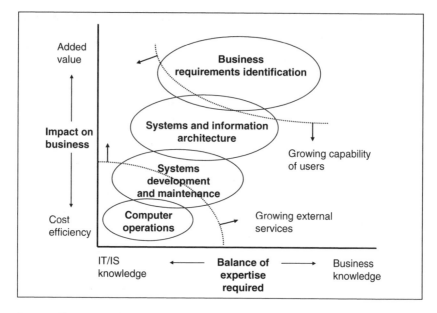

Source: Sprague and McNurlin (1998).

Figure 2.3   Major IS/IT management activities and trends for the future

to outsource rather than insource various types of IT services. All such changes are creating a need for new types of relationships in the organization, in other words a new context, which comprises the new technologies and the accompanying new *modus operandi*.

The following passage from Sprague and McNurlin (1998:59) is illustrative of and summarizes accurately the transformations taking place:

> We used to do it *to* them – meaning, IS/IT required end users to obey strict rules for getting changes made to the system, submitting job requests, and so on. Next, we did it *for* them – meaning, IS moved to taking a service orientation. Now, we do it *with* them, which reflects partnering. And we are moving toward teaching them how to do it themselves.

In fact, the issue of the IS/IT function is no longer restricted to the role of the IS/IT director and her department. Many of the traditional roles of the IS/IT department are being transferred to or shared with top management, line departments and end-users (Sullivan, 1985; Elam et al., 1988; Henderson, 1990; Zmud, 1988; Rockart, Earl and Ross, 1996; Ross, Beath and Goodhue, 1996; Sprague and McNurlin, 1998). In Table 2.1, a summary of some of the articles published in reputable journals about the 'transformation', 'impera-tives', 'emergence' and 'key issues' of the IS/IT function is presented.

From an aggregation of the trends summarized in Table 2.1, the following can be said to be a representative list of emerging trends in the IS/IT function:

1. Building and managing the IT infrastructure, i.e. developing a coherent blueprint for a technology platform responsive to present and future business needs.
2. Building and maintaining partnerships between IT specialists and IS/IT users.
3. Achieving high performance and rapid technical progress by the IS/IT organization.
4. Managing the organization's IS/IT sourcing strategy and identifying new technological solutions.
5. Centralized top sight of the IS/IT function and the need for personal involvement and commitment from top management.
6. Decentralized implementation of IS/IT through a federal-type IS/IT or-ganization.
7. IS/IT staff acting more as business consultants and less as technicians.
8. Improving IS/IT strategic planning, i.e. integrating IS/IT planning efforts with business objectives.
9. Developing IS/IT human resources and creating a strong IS/IT workforce.

Thus, we may conclude that there are *new needs for integration of the IS/IT function* and the rest of the organization, as one of the ongoing causes/consequences of the infusion/diffusion of organizational technology. Further-more, we believe that such needs are not being meet as adequately and promptly as they should. Keen (1991:214) made the following observation regarding IS/IT professionals:

> There is nothing about IT that makes in any more difficult to manage than finance, marketing, production or human resources. The real problem seems to be the history of relationships or lack of relationships in most organizations: the growth of the data processing and telecommunications professions as a technical elite isolated from the wider business.

Although this remark was made 12 years ago, we believe that the assimila-tion of the IS/IT function by the organization is still far from being accomplished.

In support of this assumption, Grindley (1992:57) has identified the *culture gap* between IS/IT professionals and their business colleagues as being a 'key factor in limiting the successful utilization of IT'. Interestingly, in the survey which served as the basis for Grindley's article, 52 per cent of the respond-

Table 2.1   Emerging trends in the organization and management of the IS function

Ross, Beath & Goodhue (1996) – The three key IS/IT-related business assets	Rockart, Earl & Ross (1996) The eight imperatives for the IS/IT organization	Cross, Earl & Sampler (1997) The seven transformations of the IS/IT function at BP	Feeny & Willcocks (1998) The nine core capabilities of the emergent IS/IT function	Brancheau, Janz & Wetherbe (1996) – The top ten key issues in IS management (ranked)
A reusable technical base (the IT platform) ❶	Building and managing the IT infrastructure ❶	From business to industry IT standards ❶	Creating a coherent blueprint for a technology platform responsive to business needs (present and future) ❶	1. Building a responsive IT infrastructure ❶
	Delivery and implementation of new systems ❸	From systems provider to infrastructure planner ❶	Rapidly achieving technical progress to one means or another ❸	2. Facilitating and managing business process redesign ❼
	Building up high performance ❸	From craftsmen to project managers ❷	Envisioning the business processes which the technology makes possible ❼	3. Developing and managing distributed systems
A solid partnership between IS/IT specialists and the users ❷	Two-way strategic alignment ❽	From systems analysts to business consultants ❼	Integrating IS/IT efforts with business purpose ❽	4. Developing and implementing an information architecture

A strong IT workforce ❾	Effective relationships with line management ❷		Getting the business constructively engaged in IS/IT issues ❷	5. Planning and managing communication networks
	Designing and managing the federal IS/IT organization ❻	From decentralized bias to centralized top sight ❺	Managing the IS/IT sourcing strategy which meets the interests of the business ❹	6. Improving the effectiveness of software development
	Reskilling the IS/IT organization ❾	From large functions to lean teams ❾	Ensuring the success of existing contracts for IS/IT services ❹	7. Making effective use of data resources
	Managing vendor partnerships ❹	From monopoly supplier to mixed sourcing ❹	Protecting the business's contractual position, current and future ❹	8. Recruiting and developing IS human resources ❾
			Identifying the potential added value of IS/IT service suppliers ❹	9. Aligning the IS organization with the enterprise ❺
				10. Improving IS strategic planning ❽

Note: The numbers in circles in some of the cells are an attempt at grouping the trends presented in the five articles. The definition of each trend or issue varies from author to author, thus it is not possible to establish an exact matching of trends.

ents said that, in their estimation, it would take four years to solve such a *culture gap*. However, that did not seem to have been the case. In Charles Wang's (1994) book *Techno Vision*, the *disconnect* between IS/IT and business management was still a very prominent issue; in an article by Ward and Peppard (1996:38) these authors acknowledge that the IS/IT organization 'does not have a harmonious relationship with the rest of the business', and in a chapter published in 1997, Markus and Benjamin agree that IS/IT specialists run into 'difficult credibility crunches' (ibid., p. 135) when trying to convince clients to collaborate on issues of IT infrastructure.

For an idea of the type of relationship that still exists among the key actors involved we reproduce in Table 2.2 below a list of typical situations (adapted from Ward and Peppard, 1996:57).

Table 2.2   Typical climate surrounding the IS/IT function in large organizations

---

- There is a climate of elitism due to education and technical mysticism and usually a separate location for IT specialists, surrounded by security systems. There is also a reputation of IT specialists being overpaid, always having to work overtime.
- As regards power struggles within the organization, there is rivalry amongst 'clients' competing for IT resources. IT steering committees are known not to work and budget constraints are used to threaten both users and IT departments.
- Functional thinking still prevails among IT specialists. Their major concerns are grounded on the issues involved in managing the delivery of IT systems and technical activities involved.
- IT specialists are known for being concerned with the 'trees' and losing sight of the 'forest', by means of their preoccupation with tight financial control, budgeting and charging out. Internal controls of the IT department, on the other hand, are 'secret' in terms of how time and money is spent.
- IT specialists are slaves to methodology. Reports about everything filled with technical jargon seems to be their speciality. There is no acceptance of ambiguity and 'paralysis by analysis' is a common occurrence.
- There is a feeling that in the cost–benefit ratios for IT specialists there is a heavy leaning towards the cost side. They earn large salaries, always seem to be away on training courses and the IS/IT disastrous projects keep on happening.
- The IT function mindset seems to be 'We are here to serve the business but we do what we think they want, in a way we want to do it. Our systems are too good for you ignorant users!'

---

4. Need for a New Organizational Change Orientation

Returning for a moment to the issue of *IS/IT strategic alignment* we would like to express the view (to be expanded later) that, like IS/IT organizational integration, alignment is not something that just happens in a given point in time, but is something which is built up or *constituted* with the passing of time. The notion of *constitution* is not new in management literature. Constitution is used in this literature to signify a formation process of climates or contexts (Normann, 1985; Ashforth, 1985; Ghoshal and Bartlett, 1994, 1998) by means of structuration (Giddens, 1984) and sensemaking (Weick, 1995).

Although all such literature exists and is well known by people in many areas of business strategy and organizational behaviour, it never seems to find its way into the information systems discipline. For example, Earl (1996) has put forward an IS/IT strategic alignment model (to be discussed in some detail in Chapter Seven) where the notion of an *IS/IT constitution process* is advanced as one of four processes leading to the fit of organizational strategy with IS/IT strategies. Strangely and in spite of being totally relevant, the literature on organizational context or climate formation is never mentioned in Earl's (1996) work.

Checkland and Holwell (1998) claim that organizational behaviour is one of the four streams which makes up the knowledge base of the information systems discipline (the other streams being information systems development, information technology and systems theory). This, however, does not prevent these authors from feeling that 'the current wisdom of IS/IT is based upon a rather poverty-stricken view of what an organization is' (ibid., p. 60). Furthermore, they point out rather incisively that the relative ignorance in the field about the diversity of concepts of organization and, therefore, about the existence of alternative approaches to IS/IT development, implementation and management based on alternative views of organization, is one of the reasons why the information systems discipline is in a state of widespread confusion.

Walton (1988), criticizes traditional approaches to IS/IT implementation for focusing selectively on either the content, the context or the process of such implementation. That author recommends an 'extended implementation' (ibid., p. 8) approach which should treat the materialization of IT content as a process that occurs over time (before, during and after systems development) and in a context (strategic, organizational and political). Swanson (1988) also touches upon the organizational angle of IS/IT implementation by emphasizing that:

> Systems are not typically isolated even when originally conceived as such; rather, they tend to congregate within organizations, often as families. The realization of

any one system, therefore, is likely to be intimately related to the realization of others. Problems and solutions associated with one system naturally spill over to others. Thus, the realization of one system informs the realization of another (p. 37).

In his search for an answer to the lack of much of the research effort into information systems development, Land (1992; Land et al., 1983, 1983a, 1989) has touched upon the issue of organizational climate as a key factor. In articulating a set of guidelines for the management of change needed in information systems implementation, Land states: 'for effective transfer of technology into the workplace it is essential that those who will be affected by the change share values and visions' (Land, 1992: 149). Although that author has made several recommendations regarding the need to pay more attention to the issues of organizational climates and organizational change for the successful implementation of IS/IT, such topics still do not rank with any significance among the favourite research topics in the information systems discipline.

One of the tenets of the Complexity paradigm is holism. The construct of 'organization' is also an aggregate construct. In the words of Herbert Simon (1997:230) 'some phenomena are more conveniently described in terms of organizations and parts of organizations than in terms of the individual human beings who inhabit those parts'. The notion of organizational *constitution*, also known as *climate* or *context*, is one of those phenomena, which is better described in terms of wholes and parts of wholes rather than in terms of individual behaviour. Schneider (1990:386) states that 'the utility of the climate construct is that it explicitly assumes that there will be numerous routines and rewards requiring assessment, because it is the perception of multiple routines and rewards that is assumed to communicate the meaning of what is important in a setting'. Furthermore, that author emphasizes that it is misleading to talk of organizational climate as being one omnibus concept applicable to the whole organization. Each organization creates a number of different types of climates and one way of thinking about these climates is to consider either the kind of behavioural outcome that the climate would lead to (e.g. leadership climate or climate for conflict resolution) or the organizational unit of analysis of interest (e.g. the climate for after-sales service or the information systems climate).

Thus, it would be reasonable to assume that an IS/IT-related climate or sub-culture exists in organizations and that, as a constitutive phenomenon, IS/IT strategic alignment would depend upon such a climate or sub-culture. Some information systems authors have dealt with this topic: Kraemer et al. (1989) talk about the organization's *state of computing*, Orlikowski (1992) develops the notion of *technological frames*, Ciborra and Lanzara (1994) have created the notion of *IS/IT formative context*, and Boynton, Zmud and Jacobs (1994) have proposed the *IT management climate* as a factor contributing towards the absorption of IS/IT into the organization. This topic is related to the broader issue of organizational culture and its role in IS/IT implementation and management which has been touched upon by a small group of information systems authors (El Sawy, 1985; Morieux and Sutherland, 1988; Robey and Azevedo, 1994; Willcocks, 1994; Andreu and Ciborra, 1994; Avison and Myers, 1995; Ciborra; Pattriota and Erlicher, 1996).

CONCLUSION

As the main conclusions from the discussion in this chapter, we put forward the following working propositions:

1. The impacts of IS/IT on organizations cannot be pinned down to linear relations of cause and effect but have to be thought of as complex, weblike or ecological networks of causal relations. Such impacts can be described as a series of identifiable and overlapping factors, emerging as the consequences of the growth and development of IS/IT in society and in all types of organizations. Given the depth and the scope of the changes brought about by such growth and development, IS/IT can adequately be described as 'organizational technology', that is, technology that is totally enmeshed in the social fabric of the organization.

2. In our discussion about the web of causes and consequences of organizational technology we have identified organizational knowledge as a competitive market pressure, and have suggested a cycle of market growth whereby knowledge creation enabled by IS/IT will bring about more infusion and more diffusion of IT artefacts. However, in order to strengthen such an argument we need to know more about the nature of the construct *organizational knowledge* as well as about the strategic relevance of this construct.

3. Regarding the new *strategic alignment* needs for IS/IT, we suggest that this topic may usefully be approached by means of the notions of organizational climate or context formation by turning to the relevant literature from the field of organization behaviour. In step with this academic tradition, we argue that organizational climates or contexts are intimately related to organizational values and to the quality of organizational relationships. We further suggest that IS/IT strategic alignment, i.e. the adequate fit between the organization's strategy and the IS/IT strategies, is achieved not through a micro-planning of the variables involved, but through favourable IS/IT-related climates or contexts.

4. The emergence of a variety of changes to the IS/IT sub-organization or function and the need for its integration with the rest of the organization

are part of the broader issue of IS/IT-related contexts. Functions are related to formal and informal roles, skills and competencies and in an increasingly interdisciplinary world, all these issues have to be approached from a cross-functional perspective. In the case of the emerging IS/IT function in organizations it is necessary to tackle not only the problem of the cross-functional roles, skills and competencies but also the issue of the cross-functional values and inter-group relationships.

We believe that the recent writings on Complexity may shed some important light on all these issues, through their mounting impact on the organizational sciences. Hence, in the following chapter we introduce the theme of Complexity, in the belief that it will bring powerful new intellectual/scientific support to the arguments we have started to develop in this chapter.

3. Complexity and the new epistemological foundations of organization

> We need an organization theory because some phenomena are more conveniently described in terms of organizations and parts of organizations than in terms of the individual human beings who inhabit those parts (...) Employing a more aggregate level of discourse is not a declaration of philosophical anti-reductionism, but simply a recognition that most natural systems do have hierarchical structure, and that it is often possible to say a great deal about aggregate components without specifying the details of activity within these components.
>
> (Herbert Simon, 1997:230)

INTRODUCTION

In the last few decades, events have proven there has been a systematic mismatch between economic or organizational phenomena and the models, methods or systems designed to understand and handle such phenomena. Some examples. For the last 15 years or so the Word Bank has worked in Africa in accordance with a macroeconomic model and a set of policies aimed at diminishing poverty in that continent, through privatizations and the establishment of a free-market economy. However, evidence shows that instead of going down poverty is clearly on the increase. The systematic failures of computer-based information systems are another good example of the mismatch: at the Olympic Games in Atlanta, IBM and other major hardware and software vendors boasted of having conceived and designed a set of information systems to support the games heralded as the best ever. However, when the games began it soon became clear that although the technological artefacts might be first-class, the information content had countless problems and the whole campaign was nothing but a source of embarrassment for the companies involved. More recently, when the world is trying to come out of the 11 September 2001 crisis and more than ever the financial markets need to be confident that there are good accounting methods and systems to safeguard share owners from fraud related to companies' financial results, major scandals such of those Enron and Worldcom erupt and reveal how fragile the whole financial establishment really is.

These examples serve to show that something crucial is missing or perhaps plainly wrong with some of the fundamentals of the 'sciences' of economics, management and organization. One of the most lucid contemporary thinkers in this regard is Ikujiro Nonaka (1988, 1994). He and Takeuchi (1995) have persuasively argued against the 'scientification' of management and strategy. These authors explains that by virtue of an obsessive Cartesian and dualist mindset, Western authors have insisted on treating the most fundamental resource that companies have – knowledge or intelligence – as an objective entity. Thousands of person/hours of research work have been carried out and volume upon volume of research results have been published in trying to quantify, measure and predict organizational knowledge over the last 50 years. However, the outcome is very meagre and the reason for the lack of success is that the epistemological foundations of the problem were not appropriate. Organizational knowledge and therefore organizations are holistic and complex issues which cannot be researched or theorized through positivist or reductionist models associated with the traditional 'scientific method', the hallmark of what is becoming known as 'old science'.

There is, however, a 'new science' on the way, inspired by a new breed of theories in many scientific fields which have been made possible (once again) by the astonishing advances in the computing power of hardware and software technology. This has enabled the creation of models and simulations which would have been unthinkable only 20 years ago. Chaos theory, fractal geometry and non-linear dynamics are some of the theories which have jointly shown that many of the assumptions behind the predications, quantification and validation of the 'old science' are no longer not tenable.

Most natural systems exhibit non-linear behaviour (as opposed to cause-and-effect behaviour) which varies in degree of non-linearity, depending upon the changes in their oscillations, cycles, periods and rhythms. Some systems can absorb and assimilate change in some conditions while the same change can produce very different results under other conditions. The net result of the Complexity movement – the envelope designation for all such new theories – has been a decentring of determinism; certainty, coherence and order, which have been the tenets of modern science (Young, 1991).

Thus, in the 'new science' practising managers and organization scientists have found many answers to hitherto intractable issues. Notions such as self-organization and self-steering (as opposed to deterministic motion), chaos and unpredictability (as opposed to command and control) or sensemaking and understanding (as opposed to rationalizing and predicting) all make a great deal of sense in the real world of organizing and managing. As Guedes (1999) puts it, just as the Newtonian revolution unified heaven and earth, the Maxwellian revolution unified electricity and magnetism, the Einsteinian revolution unified mass and energy, the Complexity revolution is unifying science and everyday life. Seen from a different but converging angle, Complexity is a 'broad-based enquiry into the common properties of all living things – beehives and bond traders, ant colonies and enterprises, ecologies and economies, you and me' (Pascale et al., 2000:5).

In this chapter we start looking at the foundations of an new approach to organizations inspired by the latest writings on Complexity, which we regard as essential for an understanding of one of the core concerns of information systems as a discipline: organizational integration. Such foundations are epistemological and methodological in nature. By epistemological we mean the understanding of the 'origin, nature and validity of knowledge' (von Krogh and Roos, 1995:7). In the case of organizations, epistemology is concerned with the theories of knowledge behind organizational knowledge (and learning). By methodological we mean 'both the ways of attaining and the ways of interpreting knowledge' (ibid., p. 7). Hence, methodology encompasses epistemology but goes further for the reason that it aims at making sense of the knowledge that is being analysed. However, the two concepts are deeply intertwined and sometimes they are used interchangeably.

The epistemological and methodological questions will be approached mainly from the perspective of two interrelated theories, one from the cognitive sciences – enacted cognition – and the other from biology – autopoiesis. These theories are interrelated because, in explaining the evolution of living organisms, autopoiesis supports enacted cognition which aims to shed light on how human beings get to know the world and how knowledge is formed. The literature on autopoiesis and enacted cognition is already very extensive so a detailed explanation of this important new body of knowledge will not be attempted here (Mingers, 1995, provides an account of the scientific state of play of autopoiesis and of its many ramifications). In this chapter, only the major features and concepts from enacted cognition and autopoietic systems will be highlighted, our objective being to move from the domains of cognition and biology to the domain of social theory. The approaches from sociology and socio-cybernetics which we will bring into the discussion are also aligned with many of the key notions of Complexity.

COMPLEXITY

The paradigm of Complexity is the foundation of the second metamorphosis of science (Guedes, 1999). With the first metamorphosis of science, also known as the Enlightenment, the mission of the human knowledge advancement project has been to take the process away from the hands of the gods, chance, nature or fate and place it in the hands of scientists and politicians. Since the days of Newton, the mission has been to formulate hypotheses with which to predict outcomes, to falsify or validate theoretical predictions, to replicate and re-replicate findings until a logical coherent theory which subsumed the behaviour of all systems for all time was reached. But the findings of the Complexity programme changes irreversibly the mission of science. Instead of a quest for universal laws promising prediction, uniformity and stability, the findings of Complexity place variation, change, surprise and unpredictability at the centre of the human knowledge mission (Young, 1991).

Complexity is a property of description of an object; it is not a property of the object. Complexity proposes models of systems in which elements and constitutive parts interact dynamically and in sufficiently intricate ways so that results can never be accurately predicted; systems in which so many variables are simultaneously acting and interacting that its global behaviour can only be interpreted as an emerging consequence of the contextual sum of the myriad of behaviours contained in it (Casti, 1997 quoted in Guedes, 1999). Complex systems are non-linear and holistic, meaning that not only is it impossible to establish definitive cause-and-effect relationships of the variables acting and interacting in them but also that the level of analysis of the system should be of the joint behaviour of the large number of elements comprising it, not of individual parts separately. An example of a non-linear and holistic complex system is a crowd in a soccer match. It is pointless to try and dissect the behaviour of such a crowd into single cause-and-effect relationships; understanding is only made possible if the phenomenon is analysed as a whole.

Reductionism and fragmentation were at the heart of the method of the 'old science'. In order to be analysed and explained, firstly, phenomena should be reduced to their simplest level, then hypotheses should be formulated and rigorously tested and, finally, general and verifiable laws should be arrived at. Over the years such a scientific method has been applied to all the sciences, including organization and management and the results have been less than satisfactory. Reductionism and fragmentation have de-contextualized the phenomena that researchers and practitioners have been trying to understand and instead of producing explanations they have produced more confusion. How can an organization be understood by studying each of its components in isolation? Pasting together what we know about the strategy, the structure and the systems of a company will not tell us anything about the behaviour of the company as a whole.

One of the starting points of the debate on Complexity is the distinction between conservative and dissipative systems (Nicolis and Prigogine, 1989). In the light of the former, the universe was viewed as a system in which, despite the continuous interchange among its different parts, a primordial element existed which remained untouched by change. This was the situation regarding the physical sciences until the 19th century, when it became apparent that a contradiction existed between the physical and the biological sciences. In the former, energy conservation was regarded as the source of order while irreversibility and dissipation were interpreted as degradation. In the later, consumption or dissipation of energy was associated with evolution and increasing complexity. Nowadays many physical systems are regarded as having similar characteristics to biological ones, in so far as they are also dissipative systems.

Dissipative systems, also known as far-from-equilibrium, can be explained as all systems where dissipation of energy in the transfer of heat or in friction does not imply loss or degradation but instead implies the maintenance of structure and often the emergence of a new order or new patterns of behaviour. Such a definition lies at the foundation of chaos theory, which claims that order and organization can happen in a spontaneous manner, out of disorder and chaos and through processes of self-organization. Related to this is the interesting notion of edge of chaos and the suggestion is that life can only exist in the equilibrium between the forces of order and the forces of chaos and that complex systems are those that can survive by reaching such equilibrium. The edge of chaos is a fourth type of behaviour or state of dynamic systems as discovered by Wolfram through his experiments with cellular automata (Lewin, 1993).

Dynamic systems are represented by equations which contain parameters intrinsic to the system and which translate the influence of environmental variables, such as temperature, pressure, force fields, availability of resources, governmental policies, etc. When the parameters are altered the system may shift from one dynamic state to another dynamic state, with different characteristics. Such a shift is also known as a bifurcation. Dynamic systems were known to have three types of behaviour: (1) fixed point, where structures exist but information cannot be transmitted; (2) periodic forms, which show periodic motion but cannot change (an example is crystal growth); (3) chaotic forms, where information moves so freely that its structure cannot be maintained. The fourth is an intermediate type of state, sitting between chaotic and periodic types of behaviours, where information is both stable enough to support a message structure and loose enough to transmit messages (Trisoglio, 1995). This is the only dynamic state capable of supporting complex systems and, therefore, life. And because it is an in-between state between chaos and stagnation, life can be said to exist at the edge of chaos.

Pascale et al. (2000) provide some excellent examples from the natural world about the concepts we have just outlined. One of the most striking is the war against fire ants in the US. In spite of a $172 million campaign to eliminate these ants, not only have they not disappeared but they have multiplied phenomenally. In about 50 years they have spread from a single location in Miami, where they are thought to have arrived from South America, to 11 states in the US covering an area of more than 260 million acres. The pesticides which have been sprayed by bombers for more than 16 years and covering more than 130 millions acres of ground has caused the ants and their ecosystem to react to being pushed into chaos with amazing and unexpected consequences. When the ecosystem is normal and undisturbed, there is only one queen per colony, but faced with the threat of extinction the ants changed their instinctual behaviour and colonies were found housing as many as 300 queens in some cases! Scientists also found that under the pesticide attack, colonies merged and the density of ants inside them increased exponentially. Instead of the normal distribution of 40 mounds per acre, 400 mounds were found in the same space, bringing the density to something like 22.6 million ants per acre!

In this very brief effort to characterize the Complexity paradigm, the last field of study we would like to touch upon before moving on to the areas of cognition and knowledge, is the field of fractals and fractal geometry. Fractal geometry is at the heart of Complexity and it came into being as a response to modern science's lack of adequate measurement tools for a universe which is not linear but fragmented and irregular. The tools provided by classical geometry – Euclidean – do not allow us to measure with any degree of accuracy many natural forms and events around us. For example, clouds cannot be measured as if they were spheres, mountains cannot be measured as if they were cones and maritime shores cannot be measured as if they were straight lines. Also, Euclidean geometry could not cope with the strange patterns of behaviour of turns, twists and skips exhibited in phase-space by systems at the edge of chaos (strange attractors). The fractal dimension, postulated by Mandelbrott, is an estimate of the efficiency with which a given system occupies the space available to it (Young, 1991). A very ragged coastline, for example, does not saturate the entire three dimensions of space available to it nor is it restricted to two dimensions. Thus, applying the fractal dimension to such a coastline (by means of a grid where each square is calculated individually), enables a new type of measurement which falls somewhere between the second and third dimensions.

The implications of fractal geometry are immense and extend to all fields of knowledge from the physical to the social sciences. One of the properties of fractal phenomena is self-similarity of the pattern on all scales. For example, looking at a cauliflower at various amplification scales, the shapes of the plant exhibit remarkably regular patterns on all scales. The same happens to the ragged coastline example above and to many others in nature. If we bring in the self-organization property of complex systems which we have mentioned above in connection with dissipative systems and if we consider that many systems in the natural world are dissipative, we might think of fractals as being the past tense or the evidence of self-organizing systems in the evolution of life and the universe (Zimmerman and Hurst, 1993). Another interesting implication is the realization that if a fractal is, by definition, an estimate then it may be legitimate to speak of 'fractal causality' (Young, 1991) instead of 'absolute causality' when analysing and theorizing about phenomena, be they physical or social. Hence, the acceptance or rejection of hypotheses in accordance with traditional positivist research methods is called into question by fractal geometry.

As regards the application of Complexity to economics, management and organization, there has been a great deal of interest, especially amongst the financial community, after the non-linear, unpredictable and chaotic characteristics of events such as the stock market crash of 1987 or the economic consequences of the Twin Towers' tragedy of 11 September 2001 which led to the minor crash of 2002. It is not within the scope of this work to review this already extensive body of literature. However, drawing upon the more general texts, and mindful of the difficulty inherent to the drawing of simple conclusions about an entire field of study, we believe the following summary adapted from Trisoglio (1995) is fairly representative of the emerging literature (Zimmerman and Hurst, 1993; von Krogh and Roos, 1995; Guedes, 1999; Wheatley, 1999; Pascale et al., 2000; Lewin and Regine, 2000; Stacey, 2001):

- Economics theory and much of management theory is based on reductionist, linear and equilibrium-centred models of the world.
- Although they may be simple, such models are seriously misleading as descriptions of a reality that is non-linear.
- Non-linear and chaotic systems show creation of order and disorder as well as pattern and regularity, but they are also unpredictable and prone to sudden change.
- In a state of equilibrium living systems become less responsive to change and are faced with extinction; hence they tend to exist at the edge of chaos where experimentation is possible and new solutions are more likely to be found.
- Living systems include human systems, economies and organizations, the essence of which is life, intelligence and evolution.
- Life, intelligence and evolution are non-linear, self-organized, emerging complex systems in constant transformation at the edge of chaos.
- Hence, Complexity rather than Reductionism is a more appropriate theoretical paradigm for the study of economics, management and organization.

Adopting the Complexity paradigm as a new foundation of a theory of organization means having to go to the root of the problem and ask questions such as 'if intelligent behaviour is a prerequisite for the existence of organizations, where does intelligent behaviour come from?', or 'are organizations the result of the sum total of the intelligent behaviour of the people within them or can organizations develop a collective form of intelligent behaviour different from the individual form?', or still 'what are the basic rules that might influence the development of intelligent behaviour in organizations, either individually or collectively?' And here we are entering the realm of cognition and cognitive science, a federation of disciplines comprising neuroscience, artificial intelligence, cognitive psychology, linguistics and epistemology.

COGNITION AND KNOWLEDGE

Cognition and knowledge (individual or collective) are related issues given that the key task of cognitive science is try to answer questions such as 'what are the mechanisms which enable us to perceive the world?', 'how do we know what we know?' or 'what is knowledge?' There are a number of classifications or taxonomies of the major scientific currents in the cognitive sciences (Varela et al., 1991; Varela, 1992; Von Eckardt, 1993; Freeman, 1999; Buckley, 2001) but which might, reasonably, be summed up into three major groups: materialism, cognitivism/ connectionism and pragmatism/enaction. The materialists, the group closest to the physical sciences, view the mind as physical flows of matter, energy or information which have their sources in the world. They focus their attention on atoms and chemicals made of atoms as the physical vehicles for the performance of brains and bodies and as the means to modify and control behaviour. Their interest is not in individuals and how they perceive reality but in the bodily mechanisms which they believe to be connected to perception and behaviour. An example of this school of thought is Pavlovian psychology in maintaining that all behaviour is described by hierarchies of reflexes (Freeman, 1999).

Although the materialists have achieved remarkable success in the use of chemicals and surgical operations to treat behavioural dysfunctions and in changing all manner of emotional states, there are problems with this school of thought when it is applied to the variety of forms of human cognition. For example, it fails to account for phenomena such as the way in which attention selects stimuli before they appear or the selective perception of figures embedded in very complex backgrounds or the range of Gestalt phenomena we have alluded to earlier on. So, in a way, materialism can be said to represent a trend which is still pre-cognitive science. The hallmark of the cognitive sciences is really cognitivism or the information-processing school of thought, of which connectionism is a sub-field. Hence, we will devote more time to the discussion of this school of thought, as well as to the reaction to it, in the form of pragmatism/enaction theories.

THE COGNITIVIST/CONNECTIONIST HYPOTHESES

The cognitivists argue that the mind is not made of matter or energy but of representations of the real world, through symbols and images. This school of thought is rooted in Plato's idealist philosophy, which maintained that the world of ideas existed apart from the world of matter which was made up of a set of ideal patterns. It was only through the human intellect that people could have access and comprehend the ideal shapes by contemplating only the shadows of reality. This intellectual posture was later developed by Descartes with the notion that matter exists not only apart from the mind but also that matter exists because of the mind.

What does it mean to say that cognition can be defined as information processing? Computation or information processing are operations carried out on symbols, that is, on elements which represent aspects of the real world. On the basis of this, the cognitivist hypothesis is that intelligent behaviour presupposes the ability to represent the world as containing certain features and characteristics. Hence, for the cognitivists the only criteria for effectiveness of the cognitive systems can be described in the following question: is the world appropriately described in terms of symbolic codes which are physically realized in the brain (or in a machine)? From this, it follows that for the cognitivists, the key problem to be solved is how to correlate the ascription of representational states with the physical changes that the person undergoes in performing actions. In other words, it must be demonstrated not only that representational states are physically possible but also that they cause behaviour.

The problem with the cognitivist hypothesis is that because computation is fundamentally symbolic, it is also semantic, that is, symbols have semantic values. So immediately there is a limitation or a restriction on the computational capability, which is the restriction inherent in such semantic values. This means that we can only compute those aspects of reality which we can describe semantically. Another problem is that the computer can only act on the physical form of the symbols it computes, but is has no access to their semantic value. People, however, can ascribe different meanings to the same symbol with no difficulty. In a computer program the syntax of the symbolic code contains or encodes its semantics. In the case of human language, it is not possible to state that all semantic distinctions can be encoded syntactically. To sum up, the cognivist hypothesis 'postulates a distinct, irreducible symbolic level in the explanation of cognition' (Varela et al., 1991:41).

Connectionism is a departure from cognitivism but in some respects it shares the same hypotheses as the computational metaphor of the mind. Connectionism appears as a reaction against two 'practical' (as opposed to epistemological) deficiencies of cognitivism: (1) symbolic information processing is based on rules applied sequentially and creates difficulties when a large number of operations have to be performed simultaneously; (2) symbolic processing is localized and the loss or malfunction of any part of the symbolic content or of the rules set can cause the breakdown of the whole system. In response to these shortcomings, the connectionists have been exploring, for a number of years, the potential of sequential processing and of distributed operations, within the computational framework. The approach differs from cognitivism, essentially, with regard to its basic unit of analysis. Hence, the focus is no longer abstract representations of reality but the basic nerve cell – the neuron – which when appropriately assembled and connected exhibits interesting global properties.

The connectionist approach starts from a learning rule (Hebb's rule) which suggests that learning could be based on changes in brain activity at the level of neurons, i.e. if two neurons tend to be active together their connection is strengthened, if not, their connection tends to diminish. Hence, the system's connectivity becomes tied to the history of transformations at the behaviour level. Neuron networks have been a field of active research in many areas, including management science, where special attention has been paid to statistical analysis aimed at the drawing of conclusions about the probabilities of systems arriving at convergent states. Such states of global coherence are emergent and they are the result of the dynamic interconnections of rules and symbols at the local level. In this approach each component operates only in its local environment, so there is not a one-to-one correspondence between the external agent and the resulting global states.

In the connectionist approach, the computation of symbols are replaced by numerical operations, that is, a single symbolic computation would be performed as a result of a large number of numerical operations which govern a network of simple units. In such a system the meaningful items are the complex patterns of activity generated by the network and not the symbols, as in the cognitivist approach. However, in reality the two approaches are complementary: in the cognitivist, the symbols come into the brain, so to speak, in a top-down manner; in the connectivist, symbols emerge from the creation of global states in the brain. In other words, 'symbols are higher-level descriptions of properties that are ultimately embedded in an underlying distributed system' (Varela et al., 1991:101). So, if human perception is still a representation of the world in the connectionist approach, the problem of the ascription of meaning to the symbols, which have been discussed above, remains. This time the problem becomes 'how to ascribe meaning to emergent global states?'

So, what other problems are there with the cognitivist/connectionist hypothesis? The idea of representing features of the real world, as an aid to cognition and without making any epistemological or ontological assumptions, has nothing wrong with it. For example, to speak of a map as being a representation of the terrain without considering how maps acquire meaning or to think of a sentence as representing a set of conditions without making further assumptions about the rules of language is perfectly acceptable. The problem is when, on the basis of such assumptions or ideas, one starts to generalize to construct theories about how perception, language and cognition must work. The theory upon which representationism is based makes the following assumptions: (1) the world is made up of pre-established information; (2) our cognition of the world is based on representations we have made of its features; (3) we act on the basis of our interpretation of such representations (Varela et al., 1991).

Hence, we rely on external sources of information in order to know and, on the basis of such knowledge, we act. In other words, this is the input-output mechanism which defines the computational view of cognition, input in the form of information, output in the form of behaviour. However, with the self-organizing and emergent properties which the brain has been proven to have (Damasio, 1994; Freeman, 1999) how do we specify inputs and outputs in any meaningful way? 'It makes no sense to speak of brains as though they manufacture thoughts the way factories make cars. The difference is that brains use *processes that change themselves* – and this means we cannot separate such processes from the products they produce. In particular, brains make memories which change the ways we will subsequently think' (Minsky quoted by Varela et al., 1991:139).

If we cannot rely on the relationships between externally generated information and corresponding behavioural outcomes in order to understand cognition, what can we rely on? According to Varela et al. (1991), we have to rely on the characteristic of operational closure of systems which, interestingly, seems to be one of the key characteristics of the functioning of the brain. *A system is operationally closed when the results of its processes are those processes themselves.* Operational closure is a way of specifying classes of processes which in their operation 'turn back upon themselves to form autonomous networks' (p. 139). Such networks belong to a class of systems (Boulding, 1956) which are defined by internal mechanisms of self-organization and not by external mechanisms of control. Hence, operationally closed systems cannot work on representations of the external world but they have to work on *enactions*, that is, on domains of distinctions which are 'inseparable from the structure embodied by the cognitive system' (Varela et al., 1991:140).

PRAGMATISM, ENACTION OR EMBODIED COGNITION

The third major scientific current in the cognitive sciences has its earliest roots in the philosophy of Aristotle and his doctrine of active perception. According to this doctrine, the organism learns about the world and realizes its potential by its actions in the world. Likewise, pragmatists view the mind as dynamic structures that are a result from actions into the world. 'Actions of the body exit by the motor systems, changing the world and changing the relations of the self to the world' (Freeman, 1999:36). This is very far from the postulates of materialists and cognitivists who claimed that action is ultimately determined by a stimulus that drives organisms from the outside. So, what can pragmatists bring to the discussion in order to show that we, as organisms, are not driven from the outside, but that we drive ourselves? Pragmatists and enactionists bring in a powerful argument from the Complexity paradigm – self-organization – and argue that 'the self organizes itself' (Freeman, 1999:40).

Varela et al. (1991) start their exposition on enaction or embodied cognition with a remarkable subtitle: *Recovering Common Sense* (p. 147). Because the issue of common sense is also so germane to management and organization, we cannot resist the temptation of quoting a passage about the need to recover common sense:

> Consider, for example, a mobile robot that is supposed to drive a car within a city. One can single out in this 'driving space' discrete items, such as wheels and windows, red lights and other cars. But unlike the world of chess playing, movement among objects is not a space that can be said to end neatly at some point. Should the robot pay attention to pedestrians or not? Should it take weather conditions into account? Or the country in which the city is located and its unique driving customs? Such a list of questions could go on forever. The driving world does not end at some point; it has the structure of ever-receding levels of detail that blend into a non-specific background. Indeed, successfully directed movement such as driving depends upon acquired motor skills and the continuous use of common sense or background know-how.

For Varela et al. (1991) cognition cannot be understood without common sense. And by common sense they mean our bodily and social history, the mutual co-specification between the knower and the known, or the subject and the object. They use the *enactment* to mean interpretation or the act of *bringing forth meaning from a background of understanding*. They hold a non-objectivist view of knowledge, which they claim to be the result of an ongoing interpretation that emerges from our ability to understand and which enables us to make sense of our world. The notion of the embodiment of cognition has been strongly influenced by the philosophy of European thinkers such as Heidegger, Merleau-Ponty and Foucault who, since the beginning of the 20th century have challenged one of the most entrenched positions of our scientific heritage, i.e. the rationalists' view of world as independent from the knower. Adding to these philosophical influences, Varela et al. (1991) provide evidence from a variety of studies ranging from linguistics to psychoanalysis to prove their argument, i.e. that cognition is enacted.

Varela et al. (1991) provide the following seemingly tautological formulation of the assumptions that have to be made in order to explain the central question of what is enaction or the enactive approach to cognition. They state that:

(1) perception consists in perceptually guided action and
(2) cognitive structures emerge from the recurrent sensorimotor patterns that enable action to be perceptually guided (p. 173).

Let us start with the first statement. What does action guided by perception mean? Let us answer the question by using an example provided by the studies of Held and Hein on perceptual guidance of action using kittens raised in the dark (cited in Varela et al., 1991). A first group of animals was allowed to move around freely but each of them was harnessed to a little carriage with a basket. The kittens in the second group were not allowed to move freely by themselves but they were allowed to accompany the movements made by the kittens in the other group by sitting immobilized in the baskets that the others were carrying. When the animals were released and after a few weeks of recovery and treatment, the ones from the first group behaved normally, that is, they were able to move around in the same environment where the experiment was conducted without bumping into objects. The second group, however, was totally unable to move around effectively. Such an experiment is used to support the claim that 'objects are not seen by visual extraction of features but rather by the visual guidance of action' (Varela et al. 1991:175).

Another example comes from the studies in the perception of colour vision by Maturana and Varela (1980). These authors conclude that colours are neither 'out there', independent of our perception and cognitive capabilities, nor are they 'in here', independent of our surrounding biological and cultural world. Instead, research shows that colour categories are experiential, but are also part of our shared biological and cultural worlds. As it was shown above in the experiment with the kittens, colour perception too is not about recovery either of a pre-given outer world (out there) or of a pre-given inner world (in here), but it is about *embodied action*. By the expression *embodied* the authors wish to emphasize two points: (1) that cognition depends upon the kinds of experience associated with the body with its sensorimotor capacities and (2) that such capacities are themselves embedded in a broader biological and cultural context. The term *action*, on the other hand, is meant to emphasize the fact that perception and, therefore, cognition cannot be divorced from doing something. In other words, perception and action must evolve together.

The second part of the working definition of enacted cognition above refers to 'cognitive structures' emerging from 'recurrent sensorimotor patterns'. What are cognitive structures and how do they relate to the recurrent sensorimotor patterns which, in turn, are tied to the embodied action we have just been discussing? This point links up with the work carried out in developmental psychology by Jean Piaget. Piaget inaugurated a field of research known as genetic epistemology which aims at explaining the development of the child from a basic sensorimotor form of intelligence to the capabilities of abstract reasoning in adulthood. At the early stages of development, the child's cognitive ability is limited by the child's own movements. The simplest act of cognition can only be understood in terms of the child's activity. As cognitive development unfolds, the child begins to form cognitive structures which emerge from recurrent patterns of sensorimotor activity. The process of formation of cognitive structures can be thought of as a process of categorization by which each unique experience is 'transformed into the more limited set of learned, meaningful categories to which humans and other organisms respond' (Varela et al., 1991:176).

The last example we have selected in order to support the assumptions behind the enacted cognition hypothesis comes from studies in robotics and artificial intelligence (AI) carried out by Brooks at the MIT (cited in Varela et al., 1991). The report is about an experiment which entailed the building of completely autonomous mobile robots which would be seen by humans as being intelligent beings in their own right. The project is interesting because it takes a radically different approach to conventional projects in AI, that is, instead of the usual decomposition of a system by function, in this project the system is decomposed by activity-producing sub-systems. In the project, activity-producing sub-systems or layers were the building blocks of the artefacts to be built. Each layer represented an independent activity pattern of interactions with the world and connected sensing to action. Each layer had the capacity to decide when to act, independently from the other layers. The rationale behind the architecture of such an artefact is truly distributed and moreover, it was built with no clear distinction between a central coordinating sub-system, a perception sub-system and an action sub-system. The outcome of the experiment was that some compatibility in the activity of the various layers was achieved by means of self-organization and that 'out of the local chaos of their interactions there emerged, in the eye of an observer, a coherent pattern of behaviour' (Brooks, quoted in Varela et al., 1991:211).

The key conclusions that Varela and colleagues draw from this example is that the enactive approach to cognition is emerging from the efforts to discover a better way of describing and of modelling intelligence (as in the case of the

AI field). They say that enaction is 'no mere philosophical preference but the result of forces internal to research in cognitive science, even in the case of those hard-nosed engineers who desire to build truly intelligent and useful machines' (Varela et al., 1991:212). The same conclusion has been reached by hundreds of researchers and authors in all fields of science and technology writing about holism, emergence, self-organization and non-linearity, as briefly described in the discussion above about the Complexity paradigm.

We have come to the end of this brief review of the main schools of thought of human cognition, with the emphasis on the pragmatist, enactionist or embodied cognition approach. To conclude, we offer in Table 3.1 below a synthetic overview of the current evolution of ideas within this field.

Table 3.1   Evolution of views in the cognitive sciences

According to the Cognitivist/ Connectionist epistemology, knowledge is:	**According to the Pragmatism or Embodied Cognition epistemology, knowledge is:**
Task-specific	Creative
Problem-solving	Problem definition
Abstract, symbolic	History, body-bound
Universal	Context sensitive
Centralized	Distributed
Sequential, hierarchical	Parallel
World pre-given	World brought forth
Representation	Effective action
Implemented by design	Implemented by evolutionary strategy
Abstract	Embodied

Source: Varela (1992).

AUTOPOIESIS THEORY

The Enacted Cognition/Pragmatist propositions are supported by a variety of theories coming from various corners of the scientific spectrum. The quotations below are two examples, both stressing the fact that human cognition has a biological basis:

> Man knows and his capacity to know depends on his biological integrity; furthermore, he knows what he knows. As a basic psychological and, hence, biological function cognition guides his handling of the universe and knowledge gives certainty to his acts (Maturana and Varela, 1980:5).

Neural populations sustain the chaotic dynamics of intentionality, because the dynamics provides the biological basis for the flexibility, creativity and meaning of human behaviour (Freeman, 1999: 48).

Although aimed at the same objective (i.e. understanding and explaining human knowledge), each of the above statements has a different focus and comes from a different background. In the case of Maturana and Varela, their focus is on the definition and evolution of living organisms. In the case of Freeman, his focus is the workings of the brain and on the relationship between brain activity and behaviour. In view of the fact that our ultimate purpose is to be able to understand and apply a theory (or theories) to the development of social (and organizational) knowledge, the route of the evolution of living organisms, which ultimately leads to social evolution, seems the most appropriate. For this reason, we have opted for Maturana and Varela's autopoiesis, a theory which not only supports the enacted cognition epistemology, but also contributes in a very relevant fashion to the social theory which underpins the new organizational paradigms discussed in the chapters to follow.

Autopoiesis is a Greek word, which means 'self-production'. An autopoietic system, therefore, is characterized as one that contains within its own boundaries the mechanisms and processes that enable it to produce and reproduce itself. The system's operations specify their own boundaries in the process of self-production. Maturana and Varela (1980; 1987/1992) talk about 'autopoietic machines' in order to differentiate them from 'allopoietic machines', which are systems not capable of self-production. Those authors define the autopoietic system as follows:

> A Network of processes of production (transformation and destruction) that produces the components which: (i) through their interactions and transformations continuously regenerate and realize the network of processes (relations) that produced them; and (ii) constitute it (the machine) as a concrete unity in the space in which they (the components) exist by specifying the topological domain of its realization as such a network (ibid., 1980:79).

Autopoietic systems produce the components and processes which realize them as unities whereas in allopoietic systems the product of their operation is different from themselves. The distinction between autopoietic and allopoietic is the basic distinction between living and non-living systems. The *autopoietic network* then, is the crucial differentiating factor of the autopoietic system from any other kind of unity, for example a man-made machine such as a motor car:

> In a man-made machine in the physical space, there is an organization given in terms of a concatenation of processes, yet these processes are not processes of production of the components, which specify the car as unity, since the compo-

nents of a car are produced by other processes which are independent of the organization of the car and its operation (ibid., 1980:79).

Maturana and Varela talk about 'unities'. What do they mean by this? A *unity* is anything that is distinguished by an observer, that is, a whole that is distinguished from the background (Mingers, 1995).

Another key concept is that of *the observer*. 'Everything said is said by an observer' (Maturana and Varela, 1980:8). This is one of the most often quoted sentence by these authors, perhaps indicating the relevance of the concept. What Maturana and Varela are trying to emphasize is that it is very easy to forget how subjective all observations and all judgements are. Linked to the notion of the observer, there is the closely associated notion of *distinction*, which is the ability to tell that something is different from the background. The relationship between the observer and the ability to make distinctions is better understood in Maturana and Varela's (1980:8) own words:

> For the observer an entity is an entity when he can describe it (…) the observer can describe an entity only if there is at least one other entity from which he can distinguish it and with which he can observe it to interact or relate. This second entity that serves as a reference for the description can be an entity, but the ultimate reference for any description is the observer himself.

The biological cell is the paradigmatic example of an autopoietic system as it possesses all the features that define a first-order autopoietic system, that is, it is autonomous, it is operationally closed, it is self-referential, it has its own organization and its own structure and it is capable of structural coupling with its environment. As organisms evolve and become more complex, other forms of autopoiesis arise, namely second-order and third-order autopoiesis where the same basic characteristics or criteria apply, but of higher orders of complexity.

In Box 3.1 the reader will find a brief summary of the basic categories and characteristics of autopoiesis theory, starting with the bottom rung: first-order autopoietic systems.

BOX 3.1   AUTOPOIETIC SYSTEMS

First-order Autopoietic Systems

Organization and structure. The distinction between organization and structure is crucial for understanding the nature of first-order autopoietic systems. By 'organization' it is meant the necessary relations (or network of relations) which define the system, hence the invariant part of the system. By 'structure' it is meant the actual relations between the components which integrate the system; these can vary provided that they satisfy the constraints placed by the 'organization'.

Organizational closure. Autopoietic systems do not need inputs from the environment in order to be characterized. This is one of the major breakthroughs of this theory which places it diametrically opposed to hitherto mainstream thinking in open systems theory. According to Varela (1984:26):

> the study of biological systems forces us to consider a complementary mode of description [to the input-output type description], which is based on the fact that some systems exhibit, intuitively speaking, an internal determination of self-assertion. For such autonomous systems, the main guideline for their characterization is not a set of inputs, but the nature of their internal coherence, which arises out of their interconnectedness. Hence the term operational closure (...)

Autonomy. By autonomy it is meant that a living system is capable of specifying its own laws for its own functioning, independent of its environment. Autonomous systems subordinate all changes to the maintenance of their own organization and do not depend on pre-established or designed relations (couplings) with their environments whereas non-autonomous systems (i.e. non-living or mechanistic) do, through input/output mechanisms.

Self-reference. The self-referential feature refers to the fact that in their organizational closure, all living organisms make constant use of past knowledge or past experience in order to continue their self-production. Maturana and Varela (1980:25) explain this feature as follows:

> The closed nature of the functional organization of the nervous system is a consequence of the self-referring domain of interactions of the living organization; every change of state of the organism must bring forth another change of state and so on, recursively, always maintaining its basic circularity. Anatomically and functionally the nervous system is organized to maintain constant certain relations between the receptor and effector surfaces of the organism.

Structural coupling. Changes in autopoietic systems are induced by independent events (signals) and do not depend on inputs or outputs, in the sense used by traditional systems theory.

However, systems are not isolated from their environments and they may be stimulated or disturbed by events, which are known as 'perturbations'. But such perturbations remain always external to the system and are not in any way allowed to become internal components of it. The environment creates perturbations that can lead to changes in the structure of the system, in accordance with its self-defined organizing rules, but it does not determine, direct or control such changes. Such changes in structure are known in autopoietic terminology as structural couplings.

Structural couplings follow the rule of self-reference and when a history of recurrent interactions between two or more systems is established, such couplings become stable and they may lead to the development of second-order autopoietic systems. In fact, when a system is subject to repeated perturbations and a structural coupling is established, this may be seen as being equivalent to an input (Mingers, 1995).

Let us now look at the ontogeny of autopoietic systems.

Second and Third-order Autopoietic Systems

As organisms evolve and in some cases develop nervous systems, the possibilities for the organism to exhibit behaviour are expanded dramatically. The nervous system emerges in the history of living beings as a network of a special type of cell (neurons), which is embedded in the organism in such a way as to couple points in the sensory surfaces with points in the motor surfaces. It participates in the operation of a metacellular organism as a mechanism that maintains its structural changes within certain limits (for example, changes in the heartbeat following an upsurge in the flow of adrenaline). Multi-celled organisms are networks of first-order autopoietic systems, which are structurally coupled, operationally closed and which develop their own internal organization (identity) and structure. They exhibit, therefore, all the properties of first-order autopoietic systems (Maturana and Varela, 1987/1992).

Thus the presence of a nervous system allows behaviour to become observable, which, in turn, makes interaction between living beings possible. Such interactions, which can also be called social phenomena, are at the basis of a higher level of autopoietic activity. 'We call social phenomena those phenomena that arise in the spontaneous constitution of third-order couplings and social systems the third-order unities that are thus constituted'

(Maturana and Varela, 1987/1992:193). Third-order autopoiesis is especially relevant as it forms the basis of language and languaging – the essence of any social system. Social systems are of course not exclusive to the human species. They are to be found in all species endowed with a nervous system and vary in sophistication in close relationship with the species' nervous system complexity. However, what all species have in common is an internal phenomenology which is unique to that species and which causes uniform patterns of behaviour to appear among the members of that particular third-order unity. Such behaviour patterns usually require reciprocal coordination among the group and it is this coordinated behaviour triggered among the members of a social unity which Maturana and Varela (1987/1992) call *communication*.

Among social insects, for example, the mechanism of structural coupling and of coordination of behaviour takes place through the interchange of chemical substances, called trophallaxis. Trophallaxis, then, is communication for social insects. It is worth noting here that in autopoiesis theory, communication is not defined, as is the tradition, as exchange of information, but instead it means *doing* something. Communication has to imply action; in this case, coordinating action.

Communication can be innate or acquired. Innate communicative behaviour depends on structures that arise in the development of the organism independent of its particular history of social interactions, whereas acquired communicative behaviour does depend on such a history of social interactions. Learned communicative behaviour constitutes a *linguistic domain*. Human beings are not the only animals who are capable of generating linguistic domains in their social life. Many other species are capable of developing linguistic domains, that is, learned communicative behaviour. There are many well-known examples of highly developed communicative behaviours such as that of primates or dolphins. In the words of Maturana and Varela (1987/1992), 'linguistic domains arise as cultural drift in a social system with no pre-established design. The process is one of behavioural transformation contingent on conservation of the social system through the behaviour of its components' (p. 209). A linguistic domain, however, is not to be confused with language.

The domain of language is uniquely human, first of all because it coordinates all social action. Language works for human beings in the same way as trophallaxis does for social insects:

'social unity is based on "linguallaxis" (a linguistic trophallaxis): a linguistic domain constituted as a domain of ontogenic coordinations of actions' (Maturana and Varela, 1992:212). Secondly, language is unique to the human species because it is closely related to the notions of consciousness and reflection. To operate in language means to be able to make linguistic distinctions of linguistic distinctions. In other words, it means to be conscious that a word (for example PROFIT) carries a linguistic distinction (for example the contrary of LOSS) and to reflect such awareness back in action. Language enables those who operate in it to (1) develop and maintain 'an ongoing descriptive recursion, which we call the *I*' (op. cit. p. 231), i.e. consciousness, and (2) 'describe themselves and their circumstances' (op. cit. p. 210), i.e. reflection.

Thirdly, language is uniquely human because it generates meaning. Language does not exist as isolated items of behaviour, but must be seen as an ongoing process of *languaging*. 'To an observer, linguistic coordinations of actions appear as distinctions, linguistic distinctions. They describe objects in the environment of those who operate in a linguistic domain. Thus when an observer operates in a linguistic domain, he operates in a domain of descriptions' (Maturana and Varela, 1987/1992:211). The notion of observer and observing is crucial in autopoiesis. An autopoietic process can never be observed from the inside and it must always depend on one (or more) observers for its description. So, languaging arises when two (or more) observers engage in an exchange of linguistic distinctions, which, in turn, gives rise to *meaning* being created and re-created. And 'meaning becomes part of our domain of conservation of adaptation' (op. cit. p. 211), as members of the human species.

SELF-REFERENTIAL SOCIAL SYSTEMS

In this section, we enter the realm of social systems, the realm where organizations are to be found and where the rest of this book is to be staged. So far, we have seen that human beings evolve within a framework which can be described as autopoietic, i.e. a framework which follows all the key characteristics of first-, second- and third-order autopoiesis. And we have also seen that language and languaging are the glue that holds social groups together and that language itself can be considered to be autopoietic. However, autopoiesis theory was not conceived as a social theory and not all of its tenets hold when the analysis changes to the social realm.

Luhmann (1986; 1995) has partially solved the problem by saying that it is not the social groups which are autopoietic but communication and meaning are. Therefore, social systems are systems of meaning produced autopoietically, that is, produced by the social group itself. Following the original work of Maturana and Varela, Luhmann has also developed a three-level classification of autopoietic systems: living systems, psychic systems and social systems. The first level pertains to the functioning of cells and metacellular organisms. Individual human beings belong to the second level and groups of individuals are placed on the third level. The first level uses life as its mode of reproduction while the second and third levels use meaning, which is produced and reproduced over time, also as a mode of reproduction.

Meaning is produced primarily by individuals through the use of language. But in interacting with other individuals in the social system, individual minds assimilate to each other and create transcendent social entities. Meaning is assimilated in many ways, through educational, religious and military institutions as well as through our intense desire to understand others and be understood. In other words, social groups develop their own systems of meaning and, because social systems are also third-order autopoietic systems, their systems of meaning become autonomous, operationally closed and self-referential. Social groups acquire their own knowledge and, in this sense, individuals are no longer part of the social autopoietic system, according to Luhman; instead, individuals become observers placed in the system's environment: 'social systems are not comprised of persons and actions but of communications' (quoted in Mingers, 1995:145).

The exclusion of the individual from the definition of the social system as well as other aspects of Luhmann's applications of autopoiesis to social theory have been pointed out as problematic as regards the creation of a theory of an ontologically autopoietic society (Mingers, 1995; 2001). For example, how can *self-production* be applied, literally and not just metaphorically, to social groups? Social groups do not produce themselves nor do they have clearly established boundaries, as is the case with biological organisms. Hence, the application of enactive cognition and autopoiesis to social systems must be carried out within the boundaries acceptable to social theory. One of the fields of social theory where there has been active work with such purpose is the field of socio-cybernetics.

Socio-cybernetics consists of the 'applications of first- and second-order cybernetics to the social sciences and their further development within the social sciences' (Geyer and Van der Zouwen, 2001:1). The distinction between first- and second-order cybernetics was created in the early 1970s by von Foerster and can be summarized as the former being the cybernetics of *observed systems* and latter being the cybernetics of *observing systems*. In second-order cybernetics the observer is explicitly included in the system to be studied in an attempt to avoid the Cartesian divorce between subject and object. In second-order cybernetics it is said that reality is co-produced by the subject and the object, an intellectual position defended by the pragmatist or enactionist school of thought discussed above.

Mingers (2001) argues that although autopoiesis cannot be transferred as a whole to social theory, there is one key principle of autopoiesis which can – the principle of organization closure. Such argument is based on the assumption that throughout the entire hierarchy of systems, as proposed by Boulding (1956), all the systems' levels exhibit characteristics of organizational closure. As we have seen above, for autopoiesis the main guideline for the characterization of living, autonomous systems is not a set of inputs and outputs, but the nature of their internal coherence, which arise out of their interconnectedness (Varela, 1984). In turn, organizational closure 'requires some form of self-reference, whether material, linguistic or social, rather than the more specific process of self-production' (Mingers, 2001:111). Thus, it is suggested that organizational closure and self-referentiality are criteria which unequivocally define social systems.

There are many simple examples of organizational closure and self-referentiality in everyday life. Conversations are one case in point. In order to maintain its internal coherence, a conversation between two persons has to be self-referential, meaning that it must be anchored on statements already made and for the conversation to remain meaningful it must build on past knowledge. Our own perception of events around us is also self-referential. An example comes from Gestalt theory in psychology and concerns the phenomenon of apparent movement. When the light in one place is turned off and the light in another place is immediately turned on, we experience the perception of light movement. This illusion is the basis of the apparent movement of neon advertising signs. The observer does not see two lights going on or off and he or she immediately infers that something is moving. The immediate perception, on the basis of past knowledge, is one of movement and it is only by careful analysis that the observer realizes that there was no physical movement (Hill, 1997).

In Table 3.2 below it is explained how social systems evolve from the level of the individual to the level of society, consistently maintaining the attributes of organizational closure and self-referentiality. Starting from the non-social individual, we have seen from the discussion above on enacted cognition that knowledge of the world is formed through the establishment of enduring relationships between the movement of the body and the changes in the neuronal activity of the brain. In the words of Varela (1992:260) 'to know is to evaluate through our living, in a creative circularity'.

Table 3.2 Evolutionary levels of self-referential (social) systems

Level	Type of component	Structural relations	Mode of organizational closure or self-referentiality	Emergent properties
Society/Organization	Societal communication	Interaction generates society and society structures interaction	Closed communication domains	Closed networks of communication bound by structural rules reproduced through social interaction
Social networks	Recurrent interaction within groups	Structural coupling to a behavioural domain in terms of meaning, legitimation and power	Conversations	Enduring social or cultural practices
The social individual	Direct interaction between people	Expectation of other's behaviour in terms of meaning, emotion and behaviour	Double contingency	Creation of interpersonal bonds
The embodied individual	Body, action and nervous system	Neuronal and bodily relations	Enactive or embodied cognition	Self-awareness. Learning

Source: Modified from Mingers (2001).

The next stage is the stage where the first interpersonal bonds are created. In order for the non-social individual to become a social individual the first and crucial ingredient is communication, the most fundamental social category. As defined by Luhmann, communication is 'the reciprocal interaction between two individuals' (Mingers, 2001:116). Whereas actions may not be inherently social, communication is always social and for action to be classified as social there must be communication involved. Furthermore, communication generates understanding, meaning, emotions and behaviour, the bases for the formation of bonds between people. 'Double contingency' is the basic mechanism behind the creation of such bonds.

'Double contingency' is an expression coined by Luhmann (Mingers, 2001:117) to explain the situation that everybody faces in interpersonal interactions of not knowing what the other person knows or thinks. Given that knowledge is personal and self-referential, when we speak or when we listen our interpretation of what we said or of what we heard is always subjective and we are permanently engaged in an ongoing effort to 'guess' what the other person's expectations are. Thus, double contingency can be summed up in the following sentence: 'I will do what (I think) you expect of me if you do what (you think) I expect of you'. Still according to Luhmann, it is the resolution of this daily conundrum that leads to the establishment of an emergent order of regular patterns of behaviour known as social structure.

To recap: two self-referential systems (i.e. two persons) will establish a communicational interaction based only on what they can observe of the other and also on the influence that they think their actions will have. The outcome of initial interactions is necessarily uncertainty but with recurrency it becomes more and more stable and predictable, through the generations of shared expectations in both parts of the dyad. 'For Luhmann, social structure is precisely the structure of expectations that develop in response to the double contingency of interaction' (Mingers, 2001:118). When a social structure begins to develop we enter the third level in the development of social systems – the level of social networks.

The explanation regarding the level of social networks and its evolution to the level above – society/organization – rely also on the social theory developed by Anthony Giddens. Giddens (1984) makes an important contribution to an understanding of how social systems are formed and how reality is socially constructed. For that author, the evolution of society is radically different from the evolution of living organisms in that society is a human production. Giddens' central proposition – structuration theory – provides a conceptual basis for explaining how social systems are formed through communication, with new meanings and new words being generated through a continuous process of narrative making by social actors. He states:

analysing the structuration of social systems means studying the modes in which such systems, grounded in the knowledgeable activities of situated actors who draw upon rules and resources in the diversity of action contexts, are produced and reproduced in interaction (ibid., p. 25).

For Giddens social action is analysed by distinguishing *system*, that is, the observable patterns of events and behaviour from *structure* which comprise the unobservable rules and resources used to generate the system. Structuration is the process of producing and reproducing social structures (i.e. reality) through the daily activity of social actors. When interacting, people draw on unobservable resources which can be of three types – signification, domination and legitimation. Signification resources are used in order to allow the formation of meaning during an interaction. Domination resources are deployed in order to bring power into the interaction and to influence its outcome. Legitimation resources are brought into play in order to bring in authority, to command and to sanction. All three elements of structure are present in communication in a totally intertwined manner.

One form of communication is a *conversation* which can take place between two or more persons. When conversations happen and become recurrent among the same group of people, a social network, a group or a micro-community is formed. Conversations allow the structuration process to evolve and, once the structure of the network is formed, conversations become organizationally closed and self-referential. Metaphorically speaking, conversations have embedded in them the genetic code of the social network, through the three elements of structure – signification, domination and legitimation. All groups with their internal dynamics, their roles and their values develop through conversations. Hence, for a newcomer to become part of a group – a behavioural domain – he or she has to learn, through participation, the group's genetic code and his or her role in it. And in this way, the social individual becomes structurally coupled to the social network.

> Each social system is constituted as a network of co-ordinates of actions or behaviours that its components realize through their interactions in mutual acceptance (Maturana, 1988:67) As a particular social system is realized and conserved through the participation of its members in the network of conversations that constitute it, [such network] specifies the characteristics and properties that its members must have (ibid., p. 69).

Membership is very important in human social systems. To become a member means accepting the unwritten rules of the group and also being accepted by the group, but the decisions about acceptance and rejection are emotional rather than rational. Maturana (1988) argues that emotions are *the* ingredient, which makes social phenomena possible, through mutual acceptance (love, in his terminology). Without mutual acceptance cooperation and social action are not possible.

> A social system is a closed system that includes as its members all those organisms that operate under the emotion of mutual acceptance in the realization of the network of co-ordinations of actions that realize it. Due to this, the boundaries of social systems are emotional ones (Maturana, 1988:69).

Thus, social boundaries, social norms, and the emerging social practices transcend the individual and remain even after the individuals have departed. Particular members may join or leave but the social organization carries on. This is true of small groups, such as families, micro-communities or sub-cultures in the workplace but it is also true of larger groups such as clubs, associations, firms, armies or nations. The transcendental or extra-subjective properties of social organization are the same at both the level of social networks and of society/organization.

The difference between the two is that at the level of social networks the physical presence of the network's members is frequent and enduring while at the level of society/organization, the great majority of the members of the many networks that make up the society or organization are not physically present. At the society/organization level, people have an indirect presence and are represented through institutions. Institutions are the so-called systems that regulate society, such as the justice system, the education system or the social security system and which contain many of the social norms, values and practices which have their origin in social interaction. In a business firm, an example of institution are the policies and procedures that regulate the organizational command and control functions.

At the society/organization level, societal communication is the key component. The various institutional systems and sub-systems which make up this level become closed domains of communication, meaning that they become autonomous and independent, while maintaining strong links of interdependence since they rely on each other's existence to perform many societal functions. Interaction between sub-systems is quite well defined in social organizations. For example, in a business firm, environmental communications give rise to strategic marketing communications which, in turn, trigger further communications in the product development, budgeting and production sub-systems. All such communication activity arises from interaction which, in turn, shapes the rules and resources which enhance and/or constrain further communication activity. Hence, in epistemological terms, we have, throughout all levels of social systems, the same self-referential, closed loop. This conceptual loop is founded upon Gidden's notion of structuration (the structure being produced and reproduced by the system) and Luhmann's view of society as a network of communication that continually regenerates itself (Mingers, 2001).

CONCLUSION

As regards its impact on organizational theories, Complexity represents the third wave of intellectual approaches which point towards holism rather than reductionism as a more useful paradigm for organizational analysis. The first wave was the Gestalt movement founded by a German psychologist, Wertheimer, in the early 20th century. According to this movement, psychology should not be studied by breaking up consciousness into units such as sensations, images and ideas, but instead consciousness should be studied as it appears, i.e. as a whole. Gestalt psychology was not particularly influential as far as mainstream organization theory is concerned but the same is not true of the second wave of holistic approaches – general systems theory.

General systems theory emphasizes the need to build models supported by pure mathematics which would attempt to organize highly general relationships into a coherent system, a system which might not have necessarily any connection with the real world. The idea was to study all thinkable relationships abstracted from any concrete body of empirical knowledge and it grew out of the need to overcome the increase of 'specialized deafness' (Boulding, 1956:199) which has plagued a scientific community which can only understand the language of its own discipline. Although the open systems approach was quite influential in management and organization theory, it did not leave an equally strong impression among the wider scientific community. One reason for this may have been the inexistence at the time (from the 1950s to the 1970s) of computing power capable of handling the non-linear equations needed to model the complex interactions of multiple variables (Guedes, 1999). However, 15 years later such a shortcoming was overcome and powerful non-linear mathematics re-opened the way to the study of holistic or complex systems.

The biologist and philosopher Francisco Varela (1984:31) confirms that there are signs which show that such a third wave of intellectual approaches is gaining ground:

> I firmly believe that there is a major change or a trend of change in our contemporary sensibilities and scientific epistemology in the sense that we are becoming more and more interested in an epistemology which is not concerned with the *world-as-picture*, but with *laying down of a world*, where a unit and its world co-arise by mutual specification.

There are indications of similar changing trends among all scientific communities, including management and the organization sciences (Boje et al., 1996). The information systems discipline should, likewise, be aware of such developments and be open to the adoption of an organizational discourse informed by the theories and approaches behind the Complexity paradigm.

In this book, we must emphasize once again that our key objective is to contribute towards new ways of perceiving and handling the phenomenon of IS/IT organizational integration through an *action-oriented* perspective on the organizational implementation of information systems. One of our contributions would be in the mapping out of an alternative route to achieving better results in IS/IT implementation, i.e. a route not focused on systems planning, systems development and rigid structures for systems management but a route emphasizing the holistic properties of the merger between IS/IT and the organization. In the new route, IS/IT-related contexts, managerial action and competency-based management assume the leading role, while the issues related to the technical implementation of IS/IT are given a supporting role.

4. Organizational paradigms: old and new

> The intellectual disease of analysing data to the exclusion of the situation may be called *data fixation*. Its principal symptom is a certain obsessiveness with arithmetic (…) I must confess that I regard the invention of statistical pseudo-quantities like the coefficient of correlation as one of the minor intellectual disasters of our time; it has provided legions of students and investigators with opportunities to substitute arithmetic for thought on a grand scale.
>
> (K. Boulding, 1958, *Administrative Science Quarterly*, **3** (1):16)

INTRODUCTION

The *learning organization* has been one of the most attractive ideas that has been put to managers in the last few years, but what does it mean? And most importantly, how is it achieved? Can an organization learn? What does organizational knowledge mean? We submit that the *learning organization* will only become a viable proposition when managers come to the realization such an organization stands on the opposite side to the *machine organization* (Morgan, 1997). Machine organizations are those we see around us every day and which are still being created today, based on the century-old command-and-control management paradigm. It is not possible to create learning organizations out of machine organizations simply because the assumptions behind the latter are radically different from the assumptions that would be needed to create the former.

Morgan (1997) in his *Images of Organization* has suggested two metaphors which together explain what the learning organization is. They are the organization as *flux and transformation* and the organization as a *living culture*. We believe that these two metaphors contain a more realistic picture of the day-to-day workings of organizations and stand in opposition to the machine-like image inspired and supported by mainstream approaches such as decision-making theory or the open systems model. As all managers know, organizations acquire a life of their own and are only partially controllable through traditional management systems. Acquiring a life of their own means that somehow organizations learn and change all the time, both through managerial choice and decision making and through bottom-up emergent action. But, at the same time, organizations are averse to change because of their dominant cultural paradigm, that is, the inertia associated with 'the way we do things around here'. So, are we faced by dichotomous and perhaps irreconcilable views of the same phenomenon?

Based on the discussion about Complexity, cognition and self-referential social systems in the last chapter, we argue that the *flux and transformation* and the organization as a *living culture* metaphors have similar epistemological groundings and can usefully be presented as one single proposition. In other words, the same foundations that underpin the view that organizations develop collective cognitive mechanisms which have come to be known as organizational culture also underpins the notion that organizations are in a permanent state of change through languaging, emergence and self-organization.

The chapter is structured as follows. First, we aim at making sense of the field of organizational thinking by contrasting the paradigm which is behind the *machine* metaphor with the paradigm which is behind the *organizational learning* desiderata. Thus, the chapter opens up with a discussion about the Old Paradigm founded upon the Newtonian ideals of determinism and equilibrium, i.e. von Bertalanffy's (1950) open systems model and Herbert Simon's (1945; 1977) decision-making theory, two of the best known emblems of such a paradigm. Then, it moves on to the New Paradigm where the discussion is centred on a non-positivist view, greatly influenced by the tenets of Complexity and characterized by a series of dichomous features of organization, i.e. the permanence of language, conversations, values and organizational cultures versus the transience of learning, knowledge creation, flux and transformation.

In the final part of the chapter, we put forward a three-dimensional model of organization which is an attempt to synthesize many of the views outlined under the New Paradigm. Inspired on the notion of self-referential social systems discussed in the last chapter, the model also features three autonomous but interlinked dimensions: the level of theory or cultural knowledge, the level of group dynamics or micro-communities of knowledge and the level of dyadic activity or interpersonal behaviour. The model is intended as a general frame of reference for thinking about the formation of contexts in organizations and as a lead into Chapter Five where the related topics of *organizational knowledge*, *action* and *change* will be discussed in more detail.

THE OLD PARADIGM: DETERMINISM AND EQUILIBRIUM

The Newtonian scientific paradigm was based upon the basic conviction that the world is simple, ordered and governed by fundamental laws (Prigogine and Stengers, 1985). This mindset evolved into the *machine age* and has been very influential among management and organization theorists since the publication of Max Weber's (1947) *The Theory of Social and Economic Organizations*, written in German in the 1920s. This seminal work is the best and still valid example of the alignment of the managerial worldview with the Newtonian deterministic perspective of the universe. Weber's ideal organizational form, bureaucracy, was intended as the organization's optimal response to the ordered and mechanistic nature of the outside world.

Sociological systems theory has also been enormously influential in helping to convert managers and organization theorists to the ideals of order and predictability as regards organizations and their environments. At the roots of sociological systems thinking one finds Emile Durkheim (1938) and the notion that social systems are made up of many mutually dependent elements (i.e. individuals) functioning in ways that contributed to the maintenance of the whole (i.e. society). This systemic view of society has been transferred to the concept of organization and among its many features two have been particularly influential: (1) the idea that all social systems tend towards stability and equilibrium and (2) the notion that organizations are open systems.

The idea that all social systems tend towards stability and equilibrium was developed by Talcott Parsons (1952) with the notion of a self-regulating society. Parson's argument was that in any social system some of its parts contribute towards the maintenance of the whole (i.e. the functional parts) whereas others detract from the integration and effectiveness of the whole (i.e. the dysfunctional parts). So, it was postulated that in order for a system to continue to exist, and therefore for it to be always in equilibrium, four functional imperatives should be adequately fulfilled (Parsons and Smelser, 1956):

- Adaptation – relationships have to be established between the system and its external environment.
- Goal Attainment – goals must be defined and resources must be identified and managed in order to achieve the goals.
- Integration – the system must have the means to coordinate its activities.
- Latency – organizational actors must be motivated to act in ways which are appropriate for the three remaining requisites to be achieved with minimum tension.

The first letters of each of these functional imperatives were composed into a mnemonic – AGIL – which became well known in sociology as well as in management textbooks. Like all social systems, organizations should meet the four requisites of AGIL in order to survive. And so, organizations were structured in such a way that each of the four imperatives and their functional requirements were dealt with in terms of managerial activity. In this manner, the maintenance of equilibrium within the boundaries of the organization should be possible. Together with von Bertalanffy's (1950) open systems theory, Parsons equilibrium-function model became major cornerstones of modern organization theory.

THE OLD PARADIGM: OPEN SYSTEMS THEORY

Von Bertalanffy (1950) believed that biological phenomena needed more advanced research models than those available from the physical sciences and committed himself to presenting a new theory which would offer to the scientific community a more contextualizable approach supported by a theoretical body of systematic constructs. Von Bertalanffy's major breakthrough in the biological sciences was the suggestion that living organisms could not be studied in accordance with the laws of classical thermodynamics but that, instead, they should be modelled as *open systems*. In other words, organisms should not be seen as static systems closed to the outside world and formed by stable components, but should be conceived as open systems with matter and energy flowing in and out, in a state of quasi-equilibrium.

Open systems theory was adapted to organizations by Katz and Kahn (1966) in *The Social Psychology of Organizations*. According to this well-known textbook, there are nine characteristics which define organizations as open systems. They are as follows:

1. Importation of energy from the external environment.
2. Transformation of the input in the system.
3. Exportation of the output to the environment.
4. Outputs furnish new sources of energy for the inputs so that the cycle can continue.
5. Negative entropy is generated by acquiring more energy from the environment than is spent.
6. Information about the environment is gathered selectively through a coding process, so that corrective action can be taken.
7. Homeostasis – a steady state is achieved by the system in spite of the continuous inflow and outflow of energy.
8. Differentiation – the system tends towards greater specialization of functions and elaboration of structures.
9. Equifinality – the system is capable of reaching the same final state from different initial conditions and in different ways.

According to this theoretical model, organizations import energy from the external environment, transform the inputs inside the system and export the output back to the environment. Outputs furnish new sources of energy for the inputs so that the cycle can continue. If organizations acquire more energy from the environment than is spent then negative entropy will be generated, and this must be avoided as there must be permanent equilibrium between the organization and the environment. Thus, the task of management is to be on the alert in order to take corrective action and restore such equilibrium or, in other words, to guarantee the organization's homeostasis – a steady state is achieved by the system in spite of the continuous inflow and outflow of energy.

The open systems perspective in management theory has been reinforced by influential authors, such as Thompson (1967) or Galbraith (1973). Thompson (1967) emphasized technologies and the unique ability to operate successfully a given technology as being at the root of the concept of organization. The central assumption, according to this viewpoint, is that the task of managers is to seek to achieve technical rationality, i.e. producing optimally with the technologies at their disposal. But, in doing so, managers are always being confronted with uncertain or uncontrollable environmental elements which, in turn, create a first line of managerial responsibilities: setting up organizational mechanisms to reduce the influence of unstable environmental conditions. Thus, according to Thompson, the final aim is to maintain equilibrium between the organization and its environment.

Galbraith (1973) takes a similar line of argument, in saying that organizations can be conceived as information-processing networks and that the organization's structure should be set in accordance with two basic variables: existing environmental uncertainty and information needed for decision making. Like Thompson, Galbraith uses the open systems model and the fundamental interplay between the system and its environment to reinforce a rationalistic and deterministic conception of organization.

THE OLD PARADIGM: THE INFORMATION PROCESSING METAPHOR

Simon (1945; 1977) and March and Simon (1958) have put forward a theory of problem solving and decision making based on the assumption that human cognitive capabilities are inherently very limited. Given that human decision makers have to operate within conditions of 'bounded rationality', the decision-making processes have to be clearly identified, so that for each decision all the variables are accounted for and the information that has to be processed by the decision maker can be reduced to a minimum. In order to achieve this, Simon and colleagues have developed a model of organizational decision making based on the inner workings of a computer, whereby human beings act as information-processing systems which extract meaning structures from information inputs and store such structures as knowledge for later use in decision making.

The information-processing view has been the major influence in development of the behavioural theory of the firm, especially through the work of Cyert and March (1963). According to this theory, organizations are treated as objective entities, rather than as concepts, endowed with a capability for cognition through some type of collective mind. Organizations are, therefore, seen as capable of containing representations of the environment in which they operate, very much in the same fashion that the human brain is said to contain representations of the outside (objective) world. Following this line of reasoning to its logical conclusion, it can easily be accepted that organizations are capable of learning, with adaptations to the environment as the main evidence of such learning – 'organisations exhibit (as do other social institutions) adaptive behaviour over time' (1963:123).

Cyert and March have postulated a learning cycle between the environment and the firm which would operate roughly in the following fashion. External sources of disturbances which cannot be controlled by the organization create shocks for the organization. There exist decision variables inside the organization which are manipulated by decision rules. Each combination of external shocks and decision variables changes the state of the organization, thus each organizational state is determined by the previous state, the corresponding external shocks and the decision rules which were used. Any decision rule that has led to a preferred state becomes more likely to be used in the future, in other words, organizational learning takes place.

The information-processing view of the organization has maintained its influence throughout the 1980s and 1990s. Hedberg (1981:6) states: 'There are many similarities between human brains and organisations in their roles of information processing systems', and Huber (1991:89), in a major review of the field of organizational learning, defends that 'an entity [a human, a group or an organization] learns if, through its processing of information, the range of its potential behaviours is changed'.

Besides the strong cognitivist bias, the other important trend of this view of organizational learning is the stimulus-response paradigm borrowed from classical learning theory in behaviourist psychology. Just as individuals learn from a combination of stimuli and responses, likewise organizations learn by selecting from the environment stimuli to respond to and by assembling appropriate responses within the organization and sending them back to the environment (Weick, 1991).

A VERDICT ABOUT THE OLD PARADIGM

From what we have seen so far, the Old Paradigm of organizational thinking in the Western world has been strongly marked by a deterministic perspective about the internal and external workings of the organization, a belief that organizations always tend towards internal equilibrium in order to match changes in the environment and a view of organizations as brains or computers which process content information regardless of context information. Most of the time such tendencies have been put forward under the framework of the open system model of the organization and jointly they have established the intellectual paradigm which has governed organization science over the last 50 years.

However, in spite of such domination there have been many authors who have tried to draw attention to the misuse of open system theory in organization science research. In a remarkable article whose intention was to 'invent the future for organization theory' Pondy and Mitroff (1979:4) explain how a model which is not amenable to positivist research designs is often forced into reductionist formats, thus losing many of the features of open systems such as, for example, self-organization (i.e. the property of equifinality). In this article, Pondy and Mitroff argue that 'we have seriously misunderstood the nature of open systems and have confused them with natural or control systems' (ibid., p. 22).

The major achievement of Pondy and Mitroff's paper has been to show the huge gap that exists between theoretical development about organizations and the reality of organizational life. They claim that 'organization theories seem to have forgotten that they are dealing with human organizations, not merely disembodied structures in which individuals play either the role of in-place metering devices (...) or the role of passive carriers of cultural values and skills' (ibid., p. 17). These authors conclude that the models we use to study organizations should take into account the capacity that people have for self-awareness, for the use of language and for learning from their experience. Unfortunately, the article did not have much impact on the Old Paradigm and the future for organization theory has been somewhat delayed.

The information-processing view of organizations has also been challenged by many authors and from many points of view. One of the more outspoken has been Boland (1987). Boland centres his criticism around the notion of information and on the way that the computer metaphor has created a mindset in organizational and managerial parlance about information. Such a mindset is embodied in various *fantasies of information* and especially in the fantasy that *information is structured data*. This fantasy originates in the Simonian notion that it is possible to create information simply by manipulating data and decision premises, and that when structured in certain ways data acquires meaning. The next logical step along this line of thinking is to start using the expressions 'structured data' and 'meaning' interchangeably. In other words, it is the same as saying that meaning can be established independently of the receiver of the data and, therefore, independently of the use of language. According to Boland, such fantasy is pernicious 'because it undermines the possibility for taking the problem of language seriously' (ibid., p. 370).

A good example of the Old Paradigm is a well-known paper by Walsh and Ungson (1991) in which the authors set out to develop a more coherent and integrated theory on the topic of organizational memory. They define organizational memory as 'stored information from an organization's history that can be brought to bear on present decisions' (p. 61). According to this theory, the information is stored as a consequence of the implementation of decisions, by means of individual recollections and through shared interpretations. As regards the retrieval of information, the organizational memory works along the following lines: 'information about a past decision stimulus and response can be consciously retrieved, but only by an individual or a collection of individuals (with or without the aid of information technology)' (p. 70).

The following conclusions, representative of many of the tenets of the Old Paradigm, can also be drawn about Walsh and Ungson's (1991) paper:

1. It is assumed that somewhere in the organization there is a brain or a nervous system which will make action come about in response to a stimulus from the environment and that each important response will be stored in an illusive individual/collective memory.
2. Organizations are portrayed as disembodied structures in which individuals are reduced to stimulus-response mechanisms (i.e. in-place metering devices) taking in information from the environment, finding the best response (from a storage of past responses) and sending information back to the environment.
3. It is assumed that the organization will function as an information-processing and storage system where information (i.e. structured data) about the past somehow will stay unchanged as it goes in and comes out of the organization's memory system.
4. Information and its storage are treated as objective activities carried out virtually without human intervention, i.e. by individuals who are carriers of meaning-forming capabilities, skills and cultural values.

Walsh and Ungson's work is typical of a great many papers published on the topic of organizational knowledge and learning in authoritative journals such as *Academy of Management Review, Organization Science, Journal of Management Studies* or *Administrative Science Quarterly* (see Magalhães, 1998, for a review). Although the Old Paradigm is by no means over because resistance to change from the management and organization science establishment is fierce (Boje et al., 1996), there are many signs that a New Paradigm is gaining ground. Let us see how and why.

THE NEW PARADIGM: KNOWLEDGE CREATION AS OPPOSED TO INFORMATION PROCESSING

Ikujiro Nonaka (1988) is among the latest wave of writers to show the severe limitations of the information-processing metaphor on the grounds that it fails to take into account the capacity of human beings and of organizations to create and to deal with meaning:

> As long as one maintains the viewpoint that there is a limit in the human ability to process information, the inevitable conclusion leads to the paradigm that the efficiency of systematic information processing is achieved by hierarchy, division of labour and operating procedures. The paradigm of information processing is a view of the world which evolves around the axis of syntactic information (…) The importance of semantic information was never recognized in organizational and strategic theories until the rise of the theory of organizational culture (p. 71).

The point that the author is trying to make is that people in organizations are not just processors of information but that, above all, they should be considered as creators of knowledge. It is argued that although the literature keeps referring to the importance of knowledge and learning in the post-industrial society very few studies have been carried out on the specific issue of how knowledge is created within or between business organizations. The main reason for this failure is the Cartesian dualism between subject and object or mind and body which is still very prevalent in Western thinking. To talk about knowledge in Western organizations is to talk about the explicit and objective aspects of knowledge while the tacit and subjective dimensions are almost completely neglected. This one-sided view has some major limitations: firstly, the preoccupation with explicit and quantifiable information has made managers ignore the creation of new visions or value systems; secondly, the emphasis on top-down strategy implementation has neglected a wealth of knowledge which exists at lower levels in the organization.

Nonaka and Takeuchi (1995) set off to create a new theoretical framework for the creation of organizational knowledge. They put forward a model where the various elements of knowledge creation are identified and interrelated in a dynamic whole which incorporates three basic dimensions: epistemological, ontological and temporal. The epistemological dimension, perhaps the major breakthrough of this theory, draws on the dichotomy between tacit and explicit knowledge, a theme scholarly developed by Michael

Polanyi (1973). Tacit knowledge is personal and context-specific; it is also hard or sometimes impossible to articulate in language. Examples of tacit knowledge are playing the piano or riding a bicycle. It is not easy to explain what you actually do when undertaking these activities, although they can be taught or explained by means of analogy or metaphors. Explicit knowledge refers to knowledge which is codifiable and transmittable in formal language. The key distinguishing features between these two types of knowledge are shown in Table 4.1.

Table 4.1   Differences between the notions of tacit and explicit knowledge

Tacit knowledge	Explicit knowledge
Knowledge of experience (body)	Knowledge of rationality (mind)
Simultaneous knowledge (here and now)	Sequential knowledge (there and then)
Analogue knowledge (practice)	Digital knowledge (theory)

The theory's key proposal is that the interactive processes of knowledge conversion, between tacit and explicit knowledge, lies at the heart of knowledge creation (Nonaka, 1994; Hedlund, 1994; Nonaka and Takeuchi, 1995). There are four possible modes of knowledge conversion, at the epistemological level: from tacit to tacit (socialization); from tacit to explicit (externalization); from explicit to tacit (internalization); and from explicit to explicit (combination). The ontological dimension considers four different levels of knowledge creation: individual, group, organization and inter-organization.

As regards the temporal dimension, it concerns two types of movement, respectively along the ontological and the epistemological axes. Along the ontological axis, the movement starts with the individual's tacit knowledge, is amplified through the four modes of knowledge conversion and is finally crystallized at higher ontological levels (organizational or inter-organizational). The movements between the modes of knowledge conversion are, in turn, characterized by four processes: dialogue, networking, learning by doing and field building.

The four modes and the four processes are intimately related. Externalization is triggered by dialogue or collective reflection. Combination is triggered by networking of newly created or of existing knowledge from different parts of the organization. Action or learning by doing is the key process in the facilitation of the internalization mode. Finally, socialization starts with the building of a field of interaction, which 'facilitates the sharing of members' experiences and mental models' (Nonaka and Takeuchi, 1995:71). Organizational knowledge creation, which is the result of the workings of this dynamic system, is defined as 'the process that organizationally amplifies the knowledge created by individuals and crystallizes it as part of the knowledge network of the organization' (Nonaka and Takeuchi, 1995:59).

Nonaka et al. (2001) explain further that the organizational knowledge systems can only function adequately in the presence of a set of enabling conditions or an enabling context, known as *Ba*. *Ba* is a Japanese word which denotes 'a context that harbours meaning' and 'not only a physical space but a specific time and space, including the space of interpersonal relations' (Nonaka et al., 2001:19). Knowledge created within individuals needs to be shared, recreated and amplified through interactions with others. *Ba* is the space where such interactions take place. Various levels of *ba* can be identified as, for example, a *cyber ba* if the interaction space is created through any virtual means of communication or a *dialoguing ba* in the case of face-to-face meetings. In an organization, the various types of *ba* overlap and are all connected to the overall enabling context or *basho* (greater *ba*).

THE NEW PARADIGM: ORGANIZATIONS AS LIVING CULTURES

Emergent behaviour and self-organization are two characteristics of adaptive complex systems which are particularly useful for understanding the extra-subjective, conceptual or cultural level of organization. Based on Bohm's (1980) duality of the implicate (enfolded) and the explicate (unfolded) orders of the universe, Morgan (1997) argues that in order to discover the 'secrets' of the organization, we have to understand the generative processes that link implicate and explicate orders. These generative processes are the basis for an understanding of emergent behaviour which traditional organizational theories have some difficulty in dealing with.

Bohm's ideas, based on the advances of theoretical physics from the first half of the 20th century, were a key contribution towards the Complexity paradigm which became popular only a few decades later. The following passage highlights the gist of Bohm's contribution:

> Modern physics states that actual streams are composed of atoms, which are in turn composed of 'elementary particles', such as electrons, protons, neutrons, etc. For a long time it was thought that these latter are the 'ultimate substance' of the whole of reality and that all flowing movements, such as those of streams, must reduce to forms abstracted from the motions through space of collections of interacting particles. However, it has been found that even the 'elementary particles' can be created, annihilated and transformed, and this indicates that not even

these can be ultimate substances, but rather that they too are relatively constant forms, abstracted from some deeper-level movement (1980:49).

Bohm's notion of a *deeper-level movement* is behind the formulation of all the major theories which form the Complexity paradigm, namely, chaos, fractals and dissipative systems. The best way to explain the essence of this simple notion is through the analogy of the whirlpool in the river, also created by Morgan. The whirlpool, i.e. the phenomenon under scrutiny, cannot be analysed divorced from its underlying generative mechanism, i.e. the river. The flow of water in the river is always changing and so is the form of the whirlpool, meaning that whatever analysis one undertakes of the whirlpool it will always depend upon the flow of the water. And if the flow stops, no more analysis of the whirlpool is possible. In organizations the situation is the same, i.e. whatever phenomenon one wishes to study will always be dependent upon a higher-level context which, in turn, has dynamic links with the event under scrutiny. The whirlpool in the river analogy and its intellectual backing are powerful tools for supporting the New Paradigm concept of organizations as *living cultures*.

The field of organizational culture has gained notoriety in the management literature over the last 20 years. In accordance with the best known school of thought in the field – the cognitive school – culture is defined as:

A system of knowledge, of standards for perceiving, believing, evaluating and acting. Culture is the form of things that people have in mind, their model for perceiving, relating and otherwise interpreting them. It consists of whatever it is one has to know or believe in order to operate in a manner acceptable to the members of one's society. As a product of human learning, culture consists of the ways in which people have organized their experience of the real world so as to give it structure as a phenomenal world of forms, that is their precepts and concepts (Allaire and Firsirotu, 1984:219).

There are two fields of study related to this conception of culture, the fields of organizational climate and of organizational learning. Climate is defined as 'an enduring and widely shared perception of the essential attributes and character of an organizational system. Its primary function is to cue and shape individual behaviour towards the modes of behaviour dictated by organizational demands' (Allaire and Firsirotu, 1984:219). In the field of organizational learning, organizations are seen as living entities capable of cognition and learning which, in turn, places organizational culture very close to organizational knowledge, in terms of themes of study.

Edgar Schein (1992), one of the leading contributors to the field of organizational culture, has put forward a model of organizational culture in three layers. The first layer – 'Artefacts' – refers to phenomena one can see, hear and feel in an organization. The key point made by Schein about this layer is that it is easy to observe but hard to decipher and that, therefore, it is dangerous to draw conclusions about culture just on the basis of such arte-facts. The second layer – 'Espoused Values' refers to corporate values (including business-mission values), which organizational members profess to but which are not necessarily the values 'in use' in the organization. Espoused values are strategies, goals, philosophies (espoused justifications) in the organization, which can become shared underlying assumptions 'if the action based on it continues to be successful' (1992:19). Basic underlying assumptions make up the third level in Schein's hierarchy and it is made up of unconscious, taken-for-granted beliefs, perceptions, thoughts and feelings, that is, ultimate sources of action according to Schein.

Although interesting, Schein's model lacks a generative or 'implicate order' component. In other words, the relationships between the three levels are not clear and neither is the process of evolution of the model as a whole. Fiol (1991) has taken up Schein's work and has given it a new reading in the light of the theory of semiotics. Semiotics is the study of how signs combine to convey meaning, using natural language in order to show how meaning is generated and conveyed in other systems of signification, such as behaviour. In her work, Fiol tries to explain how people make sense of particular organizational skills and how they use and transform such skills into action outcomes. Her generative model of culture is quite powerful as an explanatory framework for the linkages between behaviour and the larger social or organizational context (see Table 4.2). This is achieved by com-paring Schein's (1992) three layers of culture with the three levels of semiotic analysis: the level of words, the level of speech acts and the level of language.

The level of language can be equated to the level of deep underlying cultural assumptions; the level of speech acts is paired with Schein's interme-diate level of espoused values and, finally, the level of words, which can easily be recognized as being equivalent to the level of artefacts or observable behaviours. Just as in Schein's three levels of organizational culture, the three components of language include an underlying and unobservable set of rules and observable expressions in the form of words or behaviours.

The innovation in relation to Schein's model is the middle layer where Fiol introduces a mechanism for linking the other two levels – speech acts that contextualize words and serve as a link to the system of rules. 'None of the components can be understood without the others. Grammatical rules are the result of patterned speech acts over time, which, in turn, are the result of patterned word use over time' (ibid., p. 198). This has been an important advance in relation to Schein's layer of espoused values, explained as a set of 'strategies, goals and philosophies', but whose relationship to the other two layers is not clear.

Table 4.2 A comparative model of culture

Level	Definition	Generative mechanism	Purpose
Language/ Culture	Describes a general system of rules that governs meaning	Result of multiple converging speech acts/identities over time	General standard against which the meaning of discrete speech acts/identities are understood
Speech Acts/ Identities	Describes a contextual frame that links parts of the system to a whole	Result of patterned use of words or behaviours over time	Consensual incorporation and differentiation of new contextual understandings
Words/ Behaviours	Describes observable expressions/ behaviours that combine to form speech acts/ identities	Result of existing system of meaning and new contexts	Additions or substitutions to fit changing contexts

Source: Adapted from Fiol (1991).

Understanding the relationships between the three elements of semiotics theory can furnish us with new insights into the evolution of cultural knowledge in organizations. *Words* are the signs that combine to convey a form of meaning in natural language. *Grammatical rules* make up the system which governs the meaningful combinations of words, but without a strict one-to-one relationship between the words and the grammatical system. The content attributed to an expression depends on unobserved linkages between those two levels, which warrants a mid-level layer made up of *speech acts*. Speech acts imply contexts, which rest upon the general system of grammatical rules and which give precise meaning to individual words. And the whole system is in constant evolution, with the grammatical rules changing as a result of new meanings and with new words being introduced as a result of changing environmental contexts. In other words, the system has emergent properties.

In organizations, trying to understand culture by analysing the level of deep underlying assumptions would be the same as trying to understand a word only by looking at the general system of grammar. On the other hand, trying to understand culture by looking at behaviours would be misleading because behaviours can have many different interpretations. Hence, the level of *identities* or speech acts assumes a very special role in the linkage between those two levels. Fiol (1991) explains that the concept of *identity* serves as *a critical link between people's particular behavioural contexts and the underlying values that give them meaning.* Within the context of organizations, identity describes what people define in a consensual manner as being central, distinctive and enduring about their particular situation and the situation of others in their organization. In other words, the *identities* layer is the place where organizational roles are formed.

THE NEW PARADIGM: ORGANIZATIONS AS CLIMATES OR CONTEXTS

In line with Fiol, Falcione, Sussman and Herden (1987) writing about organizational climate also propose a socially constructed view of the organization. These authors defend the notion that communication is the 'constitutive force for all climates in an organization, no matter what the unit of analysis' (ibid., p. 203). They define climate as 'an intersubjective phenomenon that in its continuous structuring and restructuring affects individuals' actions and organizational outcomes' (ibid., p. 203). The construction of organizational climates starts off by the presence of various environmental conditions (internal and external) which are the sources of the messages or *cues* transmitted or communicated to organizational members, explicitly or implicitly. Such cues might be perceived consciously or might impinge on perceivers unconsciously or subliminally.

According to Falcione et al., the essence of organizational climate are the said cues or messages and metamessages, in so far as they reflect concrete organizational characteristics such as a degree of operational autonomy, type of organizational structure, use of rewards and the level of consideration, warmth or support between employees and management and among employees themselves. Climate formation proceeds from the individual level to the organizational level through stages of interaction within the organization. When individuals interact on a one-to-one basis, a localized *interpersonal* or *dyatic* climate is formed and when individuals interact in groups, localized *group* climates are formed. Likewise, at the organizational level, when the interaction occurs at *supra-group* level. Climate is described by these authors as the shared perceptions (of a dyad, group or organization) about molar (i.e.

enduring) factors representing the setting within which message sending and receiving processes occur and which affect such sending and receiving processes.

This description of organizations as sets of socially constructed organizational (communication) climates may become clearer when supplemented by Karl Weick's (1995) conceptualization of organization. Weick is well known for the introduction of sensemaking as the key cognitive mechanism for the social construction of reality. Sensemaking is about 'the enlargement of small cues'. It is about the 'search for contexts within which small details fit together and make sense'. It concerns 'a continuous alternation between particulars and explanations, with each cycle giving added form and substance to the other'. Finally, it is about 'building confidence as the particulars begin to cohere and as the explanations allow increasingly accurate deductions' (1995:133).

In the following definition of organization Weick highlights two layers of sensemaking which correspond to two layers of organizational activity: the intersubjective and the generic subjective:

> [Organizations are] social structures that combine to the generic subjectivity of interlocking routines, the intersubjectivity of mutually reinforcing interpretations, and the movement back and forth between these two forms by means of continuous communications. Tensions between the innovation of intersubjectivity and the control of generic subjectivity animate the movement and communication (1995:170).

The first level – intersubjective meaning – happens when at least two persons communicate their thoughts, feelings or intentions, moving the interaction from the 'I' state to the 'we' state. The intersubjective level is the level where 'social reality' begins to emerge. The next level is the generic subjectivity level, which corresponds to social systems where interacting human beings are no longer present as they have been replaced by roles or identities. 'Social structure implies a generic self, an interchangeable part – as filler of roles and follower of rules – but not concrete individualized selves' (Wiley, quoted in Weick, 1995:71).

Frequent interpersonal communication about work reinforces shared meanings (by 'mutually reinforcing interpretations'), making participants more mutually dependent and their activities more mutually predictable, thus increasing both intersubjectivity and generic subjectivity. According to Weick, organizations are adaptive social forms 'animated by movement and communication'. As intersubjective forms they create, preserve and implement the innovations that continually arise from personal interactions. As forms of generic subjectivity, they exert control over the energies generated by such innovations. Hence, there is a tension between the two forms of subjectivity inherent in the attempt to reconcile the innovation afforded by intersubjectivity with the control exerted by generic subjectivity.

At the top of the pyramid there is a third layer also mentioned in Weick's work: the extrasubjective level. This is a level of symbolic reality, which we might associate with culture or with the institutional realm. This third level can be taken to be the same as Schein's (1992) top level of the organization's culture of taken-for-granted beliefs, thoughts and feelings or Fiol's (1991) level of language. It is also reminiscent of the notion of *basho* or greater *ba* (Nonaka et al., 2001).

THE NEW PARADIGM: EMERGENCE, SELF-ORGANIZATION AND LANGUAGE

In Complexity, emergence and self-organization are explained as phenomena which follow a bottom-up, parallel-processing, distributed-control logic in which local interactions within populations of semi-autonomous entities are governed by a system of usually simple rules. When recursively applied to individual behaviours and interactions among the components of the system, unpredictable, global behavioural patterns may be observed under certain conditions. Local rules or principles embodied in the organization of the system generate global orders. In other words, simple systems generate complex patterns. As has been suggested by Nobel Prize winner Murray Gell-Mann, we are able to observe 'surface complexity arising out of deep simplicity' (Lewin, 1993:14).

The artificial intelligence literature has many examples based on computer simulations which have been used to demonstrate the notion of complex adaptive systems, where self-organization phenomena emerge from local neighbourhood interactions among individual components which have only localized knowledge of their own situation. The emphasis of these experiments is on the specification of generative rules for the individual parts of a system, which are then 'turned loose', and allowed to interact with one another. There is an interesting study by Craig Reynolds (Broekstra, 1998) which entails the simulation of the complex phenomenon of birds' flocking behaviour. Each of the computerized birds studied was subject to only a small number of rules, such as that each individual bird should try to match the speed and avoid bumping into its immediate neighbours as well as avoid bumping into other obstacles in its path. The outcome was that, over time, as the birds began to move according to these simple rules and through their self-organizing interactions, characteristic bird-flocking patterns start to emerge on the computer screen. It is argued that it is the recurring 'communicative' interactions among the birds that are the significant factor for dynamic order to emerge.

From this experiment an organizing system made up of three levels including the observer may be discerned. The first is the level of rules and individual behaviour; the second is the level of the interactive system of discrete birds, brought to life by recursively applying the rules to the local interactions; finally, there is the level of the observer describing, from a culturally embedded consensual language system, certain global emerging patterns in the complex system as a whole (Broekstra, 1998). We may assume that the birds themselves, focused on their local environment, have no notion of their global flocking behaviours. But in reflexive human systems such as in social organizations where the observers may themselves be participants in the operation of their 'social flocking', this level of cognition will in turn influence the other two levels either by changing the rules or the types of interactions in the system.

Broekstra's (1998) observation about the third organizing level, i.e. a level which is culturally embedded in a consensual language system, is very interesting as it allows us to establish a link with the role of language in human organizations. Von Krogh and Roos (1995:95) argue that 'the scale between socialized and individualized organizational knowledge is achieved by means of language'. Language is what allows all action to be coordinated in the organization, and such coordination is achieved by means of organizational members making distinctions about the organization, starting with the first and broadest distinction of them all, which is the concept of *organization* itself.

> The organization has no substance except for being a self-similar, autopoietic system of knowledge and distinctions. Rather it has its tradition from which new conversations can take place. It demands of its members to continue to language about it on all scales in order for it to survive or, in other words, continue its autopoiesis (von Krogh and Roos, 1995:98).

Linguistically, the organization has to be distinguished from its environment. The simple emergence of a new entity, in this case the organization, presupposes languaging. Organizational members feel part of the organization they are working for through language, and from this very broad distinction (i.e. that between the organization and its environment) myriads of finer distinctions can start to be made.

The recognition that each organization has its unique set of concepts and that the ability to analyse discourse and to manipulate language are essential components of management and organization development is a view shared by an increasing number of writers. Eccles and Nohria (1992) talk about the need to manage the 'language cycle', i.e. the notion that language also has a life cycle and that new words have to be introduced and old words must be discarded from the organization's vocabulary. Likewise, von Krogh and Roos

(1995a) argue that knowledge development in organizations comes about through the innovative use of old and new words and concepts, in other words, through a managerial effort towards language development. Boje (1995) puts forward the interesting notion that organizations can be theorized as simultaneous discourses, that is, as ongoing dialogues among various subcultures and van der Heijden (1996:274) defines organization as a 'community based on a system of interactions which exist in strategic conversation'.

A MODEL OF CONTEXT FORMATION IN ORGANIZATIONS

The three-dimensional model put forward in Figure 4.1 is intended as a kind of synthesis of the various trends of New Paradigm of Organization we have been discussing so far. At the same time, the model serves two purposes: firstly, it helps to explain our own understanding of the *learning organization* and its implications for management in general and for the management of IS/IT in particular; secondly, it contains our proposal for a descriptive model of formation of organizational contexts. Each dimension is subject to the same autopoietic characteristics of *operational closure* and *self-referentiality*

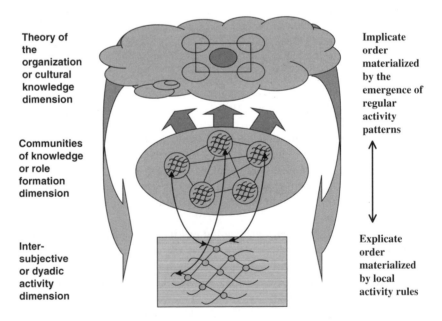

Theory of the organization or cultural knowledge dimension

Communities of knowledge or role formation dimension

Inter-subjective or dyadic activity dimension

Implicate order materialized by the emergence of regular activity patterns

Explicate order materialized by local activity rules

*Figure 4.1	The three-dimensional organization*

Table 4.3   The three-dimensional organization: concurring views from the literature

Organizational dimension	Concepts and authors
Theory of the organization or cultural knowledge dimension	Organizational Communication Climate (Falcione, Sussman and Herden, 1987). Culture (Fiol, 1991). Basic Underlying Assumptions (Schein, 1992). Extra-Subjective Level (Weick, 1995). *Ba* (Nonaka, Konno and Toyama, 2001)
Micro-communities of knowledge or role formation dimension	Group Communication Climate (Falcione, Sussman and Herden, 1987). Identities (Fiol, 1991). Generic Subjective Level (Weick, 1995). Communities of Practice (Lave and Wenger, 1991; Brown and Duguid, 1991). Micro-Communities of Knowledge (Von Krogh, Nonaka and Ichijo, 2000)
Inter-subjective or dyadic activity dimension	Dyadic Communication Climate (Falcione, Sussman and Herden, 1987). Behaviour (Fiol, 1991). Intersubjective Level (Weick, 1995). Models I and II of organizational action (Argyris and Schon, 1978, 1996)

and represents a level of sensemaking at which the organization can be analysed or diagnosed. Table 4.3 contains the corresponding support from the literature.

The model is inspired by the evolutionary logic of autopoiesis which explains the construction of social groups starting from their biological origins, by Mingers' (2001) hierarchy of self-referential social systems, by Fiol's (1991) three layers of culture and by Weick's (1995) levels of organizational analysis. It starts with intersubjective or interpersonal interactions, evolving to a group activity dimension and culminates in an all-embracing cultural knowledge dimension. Such evolution, however, is not linear nor unidirectional. The model is recursive with each layer constantly shaping and being shaped by the others.

As one progresses from the bottom to the top of the model, organizational phenomena become less concrete and more conceptual; in other words, in going from the *Inter-Subjective* or *Dyadic Activity Dimension* to the level of *Theory of the Organization* or *Cultural Knowledge Dimension* there is a progression from the tangible to the intangible or from an explicate order to an implicate order. Let us start by discussing these two dimensions first, leaving the third and intermediate dimension to last.

Inter-Subjective or Dyadic Activity Dimension

The Inter-Subjective or Dyadic Activity Dimension has as its key element the relationships between any two individuals in the organization. Each relationship is autopoietic, unique and recursive in the sense that it is *operationally closed* and *self-referential*, using reference points which are only common to the two individuals involved. Dyadic relationships are the foundations upon which the whole organizational edifice will be built because organizational knowledge is increasingly understood to be in the relationships between people and the qualities of those relationships (Lewin and Regine, 2000). Individuals engaging in conversation in the organization bring to bear not only tacit knowledge but also many of their own emotions, attitudes and personality traits, which exert a strong influence on the quality of the emerging relationships. Some of these attributes are strictly personal, such as the personality traits, but others are organizational in the sense that they are influenced by the *basho* or the cultural knowledge dimension. However, the *ba* or the organizational climate can operate at many levels of the organization, so it is legitimate to say that each relationship has its own interpersonal *ba*.

A theory which helps to understand the inter-subjective dimension of organization is the well-known theory of organizational learning put forward by Chris Argyris and Donald Schon (1978; 1996). A starting assumption of this theory is that learning in organizations is a paradox: on the one hand, organizations can only learn through individual members but, on the other hand, organizations create constraints that prevent their individual members from learning, by leading individuals into the creation of defence mechanisms. Defensive routines, in turn, are defined by the *theory of action*, which is held by each player in any organizational interaction. For these authors action means individual action and not group or collective action. It means that each individual manager operates from one of two theories of action: an espoused theory or a theory-in-use. Model I behaviour is a consequence of the espoused theory of action and Model II behaviour results from the theory-in-use type of action.

An espoused theory of action in non-technical terms means preaching one doctrine and acting in accordance with a very different doctrine. People in organizations are very often pressured into saying and doing not what they think is right, but what is right for the company. With time, this process becomes internalized, meaning that, on the surface, organizational members are unaware that they do not use the theories that they explicitly espouse and few are aware of the theories they actually use. However, through some deep emotional or psychological mechanism, individual organizational members find it necessary to justify for themselves the behaviours which they practise as opposed to the behaviours which they preach. This process of self-justification is the process of creation of defence mechanisms.

For Argyris and Schon knowledge structures are embedded structures in individuals in organizations, which can be described as systems of rules for action. In order to study these knowledge structures it is necessary to surface such rules. The rules themselves cannot be surfaced because they are hidden and unwritten, but we can easily detect the outcome of the application of such rules through action. Argyris' proposal is that by uncovering the theory of action which lies behind the behaviour of each manager, i.e. by discovering his or her theories-in-use, it is possible to change such theories, and if this process could be extended to all the managers then the organization would be much more effective. Although such a process which implies probing the minds of managers can be problematic because it tampers with people's innermost emotions, Argyris and Schon's theory provides a solid foundation for the analysis of interpersonal relationships in organizations, including power relationships.

Defensive routines are omnipresent in all corporate activities as part of the power struggles that influence and shape one-to-one interactions in organizations. The passage below shows the importance of a renewed view of power, in all social settings:

> Young or old, man or woman, rich or poor, a person is always located at 'nodal points' of specific communication circuits, however tiny these may be. Or better: one is always located at a post through which various kinds of messages pass. No one, not even the least privileged among us, is ever entirely powerless over the messages that traverse and position him at the post of sender, addressee of referent (Lyotard, 1984:15).

Let us take, as an example, the power held by a manager. In interacting with a normal subordinate, such power will take a particular form, but in interacting with a subordinate with whom this manager has a social relationship outside the workplace, the form or feeling of power will change radically. All dyadic relationships (inter-personal) are also power relationships. Power relations are not super-structural, that is, they are not in a position of exteriority with respect to other relationships, but are immanent in these relationships. It is through relationships that power becomes material. Furthermore, power is not essentially repressive. On the contrary, it plays a directly productive role and is multidirectional, operating from the top down but also from the bottom up. Resistance is integral to power and therefore action implies actions of the other, meaning that an act implies a counter act. Also, the existence of power relationships depends on a multiplicity of points of resistance which are present everywhere in the power network (Introna, 1997).

Theory of the Organization or Cultural Knowledge Dimension

In a crude comparison, the cultural knowledge dimension can be paralleled to the level of language in Fiol's (1991) model discussed above. Formal language is made up of a system of rules, some of which are embodied in formal grammatical structures. In the case of the organization's cultural knowledge system, although some rules also find material form in written procedures, most rules are unwritten and unspoken. For an observer, however, an organization's cultural knowledge system can be turned into an articulate and logical conceptual system. In other words, each observer of the organization forms his or her own explanation about what he or she believes to be *the theory*, i.e. a conceptual system of rules about that particular organization. Such a *theory* is then shared among the observers, the intensity of such sharing being dependent upon the degree of involvement of the observers with the day-to-day running of the organization.

The formation of the cultural knowledge dimension through the sharing of the individual theories or conceptual systems about that organization is better understood through the Japanese concept of *basho* (i.e. greater *ba*) which we have already referred to. *Basho* is 'the platform where [cultural] knowledge is created, shared and exploited, functioning as a medium for the resource concentration of the organization knowledge and of the individuals who own and create such knowledge' (Nonaka et al., 2001:19). To participate in a *ba* means 'to get involved and transcend one's own limited perspective or boundary' (ibid., p. 19). Thus, the concept of *ba* helps to understand the extra-subjective and self-transcending nature of the cultural level of organization, in the same way as described in Chapter Three for the society level of self-referential (social) systems.

In organizations there are many examples of self-transcendence, that is, the reaching out beyond one's own existence in order to create shared understandings, i.e. new collective knowledge. For example, in empathizing with colleagues and customers in the process of socialization, the boundaries between individuals are diminished; in the process of committing to the group and becoming part of the group, the individual transcends the boundaries of the self; in the process of internalizing knowledge, individuals enter the boundaries of the group or of the entire organization (Nonaka et al., 2001).

The organization's *theory* is not only made up of rules but it is also about resources which go beyond the subjectivity of each individual while governing the collective behaviour of all the individuals in the organization. As we have seen in Chapter Three, there are three types of totally enmeshed resources – domination, signification and legitimation. Domination resources account for the institutional power which affects the interactions between individuals. Signification resources entails the communication of meaning and provide the interpretative schemes that are essential for interpersonal activity to take place. Interpretative schemes are one type of consensual domain which social systems need to exist. Communication as a consensual domain means that the tokens we use in our language do not have meaning of themselves but depend upon the consensus or the interpretative schemes that people share in order to understand one another (Mingers, 1995).

Legitimation resources are the remaining type of cultural knowledge resources. These are especially interesting to organizations because their mode of influence in interpersonal activity is through orders, norms and control mechanisms. It is through legitimation resources that managerial choice plays a part in the formation of the organization's cultural knowledge dimension. Being a key variable in the structuring of organizations (Child, 1972) and in strategic decision making (Porter, 1991), managerial choice cannot be left out of any attempt to describe and model organizations and organizational action. Weick (1995:31) rightly points out that managers 'construct reality through authoritative acts'. This means that managers, in exerting their *choice* in terms of strategies, decisions, policies or procedures and in imposing such choice upon the organization, are co-determining the process of reality construction.

The point about managerial choice is that it is useful in understanding, for example, how very quick changes are possible in organizations whose cultures seem to be totally averse to change. The leitmotif of self-referential social systems inspired by Luhmann's (1995) social autopoiesis is persistence of the subject in the face of permanent change. So, it is appropriate to ask the question: how is rapid change possible in organizations where culture seems to have crystallized? Such change can be brought about by the intensive use of legitimation, but also of signification and domination resources. Change can be achieved through major shake-ups brought about, for example, by the arrival of a new CEO with a whole new managerial agenda to be implemented. In such cases cultural change is imposed through legitimate managerial choice. As explained by Weick (1995:31), cultural change begins to happen 'when managers enact strategies and policies, they take undefined space, time, and action and draw lines, establish categories and coin labels that create new features of the environment that did not exist before'.

Micro-Communities of Knowledge or Role Formation Dimension

In conceptualizing organizations one has to acknowledge two distinct types of observable behaviour: interpersonal and group behaviour. Although both are social behaviours, their circumstances are substantially different. Thus, the distinction between intersubjectivity and generic subjectivity (Weick, 1995) which has already been referred to. Essentially, the former entails strictly dyadic (i.e. one-to-one) interactions while in the latter the dyadic dimension is lost. Generic subjectivity means individuals interact not as part of a dyad but as part of a group where each individual is given a role and an identity established by the group's inner dynamics. Hence at the generic subjectivity level roles and identities assume special relevance.

The concept of organizational role is well established in the management literature. Simon (1945/97) in his influential effort to set the agenda for a 'science' of administration and in identifying the organization as the prime locus for such undertaking, states that 'we are concerned with a role system known as organization' (p. 19). Katz and Kahn (1966:186), in one of the earliest authoritative texts on organizational behaviour, define human organizations as role systems, giving 'the role concept a central place in the theory of organizations'. Roles in organizations have a formal aspect (i.e. functional roles) usually under the form of a job description, but they also have an informal aspect, which is strongly influenced by the system of values prevalent in the organization. According to Selznick (1957:80) organizational roles are 'formal and informal patterns of behaviour associated with a position in the social system to which individuals are expected to conform'.

This is consistent with Fiol's (1991) notion of *identity* or contextual frames, discussed above. Fiol has suggested that because it is difficult to establish a one-to-one link between organizational values and behaviour, we need to find mediators between the unobservable components which form organizational contexts and the more overt forms of behaviour. Such mediators, which Fiol has collectively labelled as *identity*, are in fact the organizational roles, which make up the contextual frame of reference for the behaviour of the individual in the group.

The formation of meaning happens at the intersubjective level as well as the level of generic subjectivity. Intersubjective formation of meaning, through the interaction of dyads and the development of informal relationships, is the principal locus for the development of informal learning. Meaning formation through generic subjectivity, on the other hand, is more likely to be framed within the formal side of organizational relationships, leading to learning through *legitimate* participation. As proposed by Lave and Wenger (1991) knowledge exists in communities of practice, with group learning being an integral part of the generative social practice occurring as part of the work carried out within the community. *Legitimate (peripheral) participation* is put forward as a construct by Lave and Wenger to explain the incremental nature of engagement in social practice which entails the increased participation of newcomers from the periphery to the centre of the activity in question.

Such incremental participation, in turn, is intimately linked to the process of identity or role formation. In other words, as participation becomes more 'legitimate', so do the identities and roles of the participants become stronger.

Role formation and communities of practice, however, do not cover the whole universe of the group-level dimension. A community of practice implies that members of a group learn through imitation of existing practices and by gradually memorizing work tasks. Such conception of learning is restrictive in the sense that it does not leave much room for alternative or faster ways of learning, with innovation necessarily becoming a very long term aspiration. In many jobs in an increasing number of industries such long-term time spans are just not feasible. Employees are expected to learn fast and to contribute to results even faster. Hence, instead of communities of practice, the concept we have adopted, after von Krogh et al. (2000), is communities (or micro-communities) of knowledge. The prefix micro is intended to distinguish a small group of people (up to ten), focused on the same task or activity, from a large community sharing the same type of knowledge (e.g. the information systems community).

The key distinguishing feature between a community of practice and a micro-community of knowledge concerns the boundaries of the two concepts. The boundaries of the former are set by the task, the culture or the history of that community, whereas the boundaries of the latter are more dynamic and are set not only by task and culture but especially by the knowledge of the individual participants. In a micro-community of knowledge the focus goes beyond the notion of doing more of the same (as in a community of practice) but is intended to highlight the dynamic properties of creating new knowledge (von Krogh et al., 2000). Micro-communities of knowledge are characterized by face-to-face interactions, with members getting to know about each other's personalities, fields of interest and values and also about the type of behaviour that is or is not acceptable to the group. As suggested by Lewin (1947), the founder of the psychology of groups, the group creates its own dynamic. Through the sharing of knowledge, the commitment of the group's members is strengthened and as new knowledge is produced the group gradually develops its own *identity*.

The key point about micro-communities of knowledge, in terms of context formation, is that they constitute a very powerful means for the conversion of explicit into tacit knowledge. Tacit knowledge cannot be captured from formal training courses, documents or meetings; it can only be captured through socialization, and micro-communities are an ideal form of socialization. Shared tacit knowledge enables relationships among the members of the group to carry on for a long time, facilitates the assimilation of new members and helps to overcome the gaps left open by the departures of old members. Once a micro-community of knowledge is disbanded, much of the tacit knowledge is lost and this is why it is important to pay close attention to the maintenance of such communities and the retention of their members (von Krogh et al., 2000).

The narrative or storytelling approach (Boje et al., 1996) is crucial for an explanation of how the level of micro-communities of knowledge is operationally linked to the other levels in our three-dimensional model. Tenkasi and Boland (1993) have identified the making of narratives by organizational actors as the site for 'understanding processes of sensemaking, learning and change in organisations' (ibid., p. 80). By constructing narratives, individuals construct not only the organization in narrative, but they construct also their own selves (i.e. their identity) in the organization. By narrativizing their experience, organizational members construct not only how things work but also their roles (economic, social and moral) in the organizational group or sub-group where they spend most of their time.

According to the narrative approach, organizations can be conceptualized as sets of simultaneous discourses or stories, coming from the different micro-communities of knowledge. In the words of Boje (1995:1001):

> Organizations cannot be registered as one story, instead they are a multiplicity of stories and story interpretations in struggle with one another. People wander the halls and offices of organizations simultaneously chasing storylines – and that is the 'work' of contemporary organizations.

Hence, in the proposed three-dimensional model of organization, the unifying link among all three levels is conversational and narrative making in nature. From the level of intersubjective activity, organizational members bring to the level of micro-communities of knowledge the stories and their interpretations about the stories resulting from their interpersonal interactions. All the stories carry messages, of a personal nature, of an organizational nature or both. Each micro-community has its own stories and its own interpretations about the stories from the remaining micro-communities. The unifying factor comes from the level above, i.e. the level of cultural knowledge, through the conversations within the groups containing and conveying messages of an institutional nature and about the organization's institutional context.

CONCLUSION

This chapter is intended as a conceptual frame of reference for the chapters that follow, about the state of play regarding the old and the new paradigms of organization. In drawing attention to the operationally closed nature of systems, autopoiesis theory brings new meaning to *organizational learning*.

Thus, if organizations are essentially closed systems their internal growth in terms of knowledge and learning has to come from within, essentially. The environment as provider of new knowledge in the form of a constant flow of inputs into the system loses much of its previous relevance. In adopting a new paradigm upon which to model the organization and in accepting the essentially closed nature of such a systemic paradigm, languaging and the local recurrent conversational interactions of rules-driven organizational members become pivotal.

Complexity, autopoiesis theory and especially the notion of spontaneous organizational closure enable a better understanding of the order-generating, order-maintaining and renewal capacities of organizations. This means that closed networks of recurrent interactions are responsible for a complex social system's autonomous and self-referential behaviour. On the other hand, this is far removed from the view of an organization as an open system which copes with a turbulent environment by choosing an appropriate strategy, fitting its structure to align with the strategy and leveraging its core competencies, all of which presupposes clear cause and effect relationships (Broekstra, 1998).

In the chapters that follow, the ideas put forward about the new paradigm of organization synthesized into the three dimensional model will be used in the building up of a new theoretical framework for the organizational implementation of information systems. Within the context of the new paradigm, Chapter Five will focus on an innovative perspective on organizational strategy emphasizing managerial action; Chapter Six will be devoted to a review of intellectual perspectives on information systems implementation, with a final focus on an organizational and action-oriented perspective; Chapter Seven will be aimed at presenting a novel interpretation of strategic alignment of IS/IT founded upon IS/IT-related organizational values; and Chapter Eight will offer a number of suggestions towards the organizational implementation of information systems under a methodological umbrella by the name of *strategic development of IS/IT*.

5. Strategy as managerial action

Strategy implementation rather than strategy content differentiates successful from unsuccessful firms. It is simply much easier to choose an appropriate strategy than it is to implement it effectively. Moreover, successful strategy implementation is driven by employee strategic focus ...

(Becker et al., 2001:39)

INTRODUCTION

In this chapter we discuss organizational strategy. This discussion is important because strategy is the beginning of all things in organizations. Whether it is implicit or explicit there is a strategy behind everything an organization does.

There are two opposing camps in contemporary strategic management thinking: the rational view versus the emergent perspective. The first is represented, for example, by the writings of Michael Porter (1980; 1985) which hold that a firm can dominate and profit from a given competitive position by attending to the key factors that govern such an environmental position and by closing the gap between corporate action and the characteristics of the chosen competitive position. The opposite view, which has been championed by Henry Mintzberg (1990; 1994), describes strategy making as a natural process of emergence and of the interplay between deliberate and emergent processes. The rational view presents the realization of strategy as a process of imposing strategic intent and design through a mechanistic process of implementation which will not be challenged throughout its course. The emergent view focuses on strategies which come into being through a process similar to the crafting of an object by a handicraftsman, relying mostly on tacit knowledge which can never be made explicit.

In both cases, what seems to be missing are the answers to the implementation issue or the HOW question. Some examples of unanswered questions, firstly regarding the top-down camp: how to overcome barriers to the implementation processes?; how to overcome the gap between intent and realization?; how to test the strategic design in action? In what concerns the bottom-up camp, there are also some examples: how are emergent strategies integrated with existing strategies?; how should the organization cope during a period of revolutionary and emergent change?; how to dovetail an incrementalist mindset with concerns from shareholders about short-term results or from employees about security and stability? There are no clear-cut answers to any of these questions, but what seems to hold true regarding each of them is that the solution does not rest with one-off decisions or choices from individual managers, but with the existence of organizational contexts which will help people to deal with uncertainty and change. Such contexts, in turn, are built through managerial action.

Management and organization science have been theorized mainly through structural models; however, the usefulness of structural models stops at the level of description. In other words, we are able to describe and to analyse structures, functions and procedures of business or organizational activities but we cannot extrapolate from this level to the level of intelligent behaviour. And this is the level where the manager or the entrepreneur ultimately intervenes in the organization, either alone or through others. Thus, although structural and descriptive models are interesting and useful, they do not solve the problem, for example, of bridging the gap between intent and realization. This is a change problem which can only be solved through action and leadership.

In Chapter One, we talked about a *new modernist* type of management thinking as representative of a middle-ground position, between modernism or positivism on the one hand and postmodernism on the other hand. In the field of strategy, such a dichotomy is represented by the top-down and the bottom-up clash of ideas we have just outlined. In this chapter we are going to expand on this topic and explain how *middle-of-the-road* approaches to management and strategy embody many of the action-oriented characteristics of the new organizational paradigms discussed in Chapter Four and also how they contain many of the answers to the implementation issue.

In this chapter we also turn our attention to one of the key problems in management theory: how to turn strategic imperatives into business results? As we will see, in current strategic management ideology it is recognized that (organizational) knowledge is *the* factor in the solution of such an equation, that is, knowledge is the only factor which will guarantee long-lasting success in terms of organizational effectiveness and competitive differentiation. Hence, knowledge has become *the* strategic imperative. Such a turn in strategic management theory has come about through the resource-based approach, a theoretical body of knowledge which is gaining ground in both strategy and business economics as a fresh view on firm growth and on competitive advantage between firms (Wernerfelt, 1984 and 1995; Conner, 1991; Barney, 1991; Grant, 1991; Mahoney, 1995; Conner and Prahalad, 1996).

STRATEGY: A COMPOSITE DEFINITION

Concepts of strategy differ widely as has been insightfully illustrated by Mintzberg with his *5 Ps of strategy* (Mintzberg and Quinn, 1991). Strategy is sometimes regarded as a military-style *Ploy*; other times it is interpreted as a long-term *Perspective* on the business; very often it is (wrongly) perceived as synonymous with *Planning*; since the eighties it has been understood as competitive *Positioning*, and lately it is professed by a growing number of people as *Pattern* (of action). Thus, a definition of strategy has to be a composite effort, featuring concepts and emphasis from different authors. The following definition represents such an attempt:

> Strategy is:
> (1) a coherent pattern of action that consciously intervenes in the ongoing evolution of the organization (Van Der Heijden, 1996:274);
> (2) aimed at creating situations for economic rents to be produced and sustained (Rumelt in Mintzberg and Quinn, 1991:16);
> (3) by means of defining a company's position, making trade-offs and forging fit among activities (Porter, 1996:77).

Working from back to front and starting from part (3), we will expand on the various concepts of strategy contained within this definition, explaining their interrelated evolution and how the new paradigms of organization and managerial action are two complementary pillars of a theory of strategy.

BASIC CONCEPTS OF A THEORY OF COMPETITIVE POSITIONING

Strategy is not a new concern nor is it a concern of profit organizations only. Ever since management became a discipline, long before strategy became fashionable, writers have strived to provide theories, rules or guidelines whose final aim has been to make organizations more effective. If we look at Table 5.1 we will see how the attainment of organizational effectiveness has remained a key concern throughout the last 90 years of management history. As strategy becomes a discipline in own right, effectiveness is absorbed by the new discipline, but with decreasing relevance as a managerial concern as strategy grows in popularity. In spite of Porter's (1996:61), assertion that 'effectiveness and strategy are both essential for superior performance', organizational effectiveness is often regarded as a fairly minor component of the higher ambitions of strategy.

The reason for this is that strategy is mistakenly taken to mean the same as competitive advantage and given that most of the literature on competitive advantage takes effectiveness as a given, the topic does not merit the attention it deserves. According to Porter (1991:102) competitive advantage 'results from a firm's ability to perform the required activities at a collectively lower cost than rivals or perform some activities in unique ways that create buyer value and hence allow the firm to command a premium price'. Performing activities at *lower cost* than rivals or performing some activities in *unique ways* requires high levels of organizational effectiveness. Hence, it can be said that the issue of organizational effectiveness, which affects all organizations – profit and not-for-profit – is the root concern of strategy.

The ultimate objective of any organization is to stay in the market. In business organizations to stay in the market usually means to remain competitive, but in non-business or not-for-profit organizations there is also a concern regarding survival in the market. The only difference between profit and not-for-profit organizations in this respect is the time span which has to be considered. In profit organizations the time span over which an outcome can be expected regarding staying or leaving the market is usually shorter than in not-for-profit organizations. Universities, for example, also wish to stay in the market in a world where competition in higher education grows stronger every year. While this issue may not be a problem for university authorities on a daily basis, it will be a problem in the long run if the university starts to lose students because of stronger competition.

Thus, the basic premises of competitive success are also the outcome of the application of models and frameworks of competitive positioning. Such an outcome, which can be seen in the upper section of Figure 5.1, is *lower cost* and *higher quality* than rivals achieved through performing organizational activities with high levels of *organizational effectiveness*. The diagram, which integrates into a simple model the various elements of a theory of competitive positioning, is founded upon the work of Michael Porter (1980, 1985, 1991) on competitive strategy.

The figure highlights two different levels of analysis leading to the final outcome, which has just been discussed. These levels, which constitute useful categories for describing and discussing organizational strategy, are the cross-sectional or short-term approach and the longitudinal or long-term approach. Let us describe each in turn.

Included in the short-term view there are the elements which are better known from Porter's (1980; 1985) earlier work, namely, the techniques for environmental analysis and competitive positioning. Environmental analysis is aimed at determining the relative attractiveness of a given industrial sector and is achieved by means of the well-known *five forces model*. The model is aimed at analysing industry structure in terms of (1) bargaining power of clients; (2) bargaining power of suppliers; (3) barriers to new entry into the industry; (4) threats from substitute products or services; (5) rivalry amongst

Table 5.1 The historical search for organizational effectiveness

Management orientation	Representative thinkers	Effectiveness philosophy highlights	Typical effectiveness attributes
Scientific Management	Frederick Taylor (1911)	Time and motion studies. Importance of standards, planning, control and cooperation. Functional organization. 'One best way'.	Production maximization. Cost minimization. Technical excellence. Optimal utilization of resources. Task specialization.
Principles of Management	Henri Fayol (1949)	First 'complete' inductive management theory. Based on rules and principles. Views management as a teachable skill.	Division of work. Clear authority and discipline. Unity of command and direction. Order, equity, stability and initiative. Esprit de corps.
Human Relations	Elton Mayo (1933)	Importance of emotional factors. Sociological concepts of group endeavour. Satisfied workers are productive workers. Need for managerial diagnostic and interpersonal skills.	Productivity through employee satisfaction, obtained through attention to workers' physical and emotional needs.
Functions of the Executive	Chester Barnard (1938)	Organizations as cooperative systems. The role of managers and of managerial leadership as the key shapers of organizational contexts.	Internal equilibrium and adjustments to external environment achieved through executive action and example and through the work 'ethos'.
Decision-Making School	Herbert Simon (1947)	Effectiveness subject to bounded rationality. Input/Output efficiency criteria. Organization modelled upon an information-processing machine.	Resource savings through rational development of goals. Efficiency of information processing.
Socio-Technical School	E.L. Trist and K.W. Balmforth (1951)	Joint resolution of social and technical organizational demands. Social systems and open systems theory applied to organizations.	Degree of social/technological 'fit'. Congruence of internal processes.

Strategic Management	Alfred Chandler (1962)	Structure follows strategy. Rationalization of resource utilization and vertical/horizontal integration.	Structure/strategy congruence manifested as organizational growth, competitive attainment, environmental control and flexibility/adaptation.
Human Resources	Douglas McGregor (1961) Rensis Likert (1967)	Focus on organizational needs vs. organizational demands. Power equalization. Participative management. Concurrent satisfaction of competing demands: productive workers are satisfied workers.	Employee satisfaction, productivity, cohesion, loyalty, open communication.
Contingency Theory	P.R. Lawrence and J.W. Lorsch (1967)	Organization design based on environmental factors. 'Best way' contingent on a variety of conditions and situations.	Differentiation error vs. integration error. Organization/environment 'fit'. Ability to implement change in a timely manner. Leadership/contingency fit.
Culture	T. Peters and R. Waterman (1983)	The 7-S framework: strategy, structure, systems, skills, style, staff and shared values.	Bias for action; closeness to the customer; autonomy and entrepreneurship; hands, value-driven philosophy; stick to the knitting; simple form; lean staff; simultaneous loose-tight properties.
Competitive Strategy	Michael Porter (1980; 1985)	The five-forces model: bargaining power of suppliers and buyers; threat of new entrants; threat of substitute products; rivalry among competitors. Value chain analysis.	Environmental analysis and market positioning are the keys to competitive advantage. Generic strategies: cost leadership, differentiation and focus.
Resource-Based Theory	R. Rumelt (1984; 1987) J. Barney (1991)	To be valuable resources must be difficult to imitate. Imitation barriers are: time compression diseconomies; historical uniqueness; embeddedness of resources; causal ambiguity.	Firm-specific intangible resources such as competencies, organizational knowledge as the drivers of efficiency and competitive advantage.

Source: Adapted and updated from Lewin and Minton (1986).

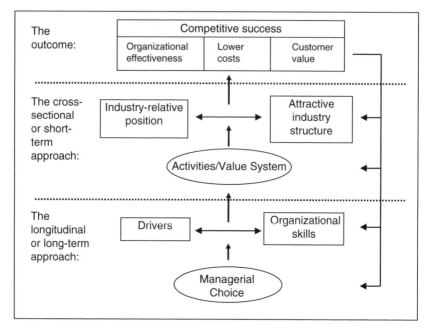

Source: Porter (1991).

Figure 5.1   Outline of a theory of competitive positioning

existing competitors. Following such analysis, the firm positions itself so as to outcompete its rivals. Hence, industry structure is partly exogenous and partly subject to the influence of a firm's actions over time. Although such categories and their interrelationships are an over-simplification of the reality in the field, they are 'a useful simplification for analytical purposes' (Porter, 1991:100).

Holding industry structure constant, a successful firm is one with an attractive relative position. Why or how does an attractive position arise? The answer lies in the sustainable competitive advantage the firm manages to build over and above its rivals. Superior profitability can only arise from commanding a higher price than rivals or enjoying lower costs. Thus, holding industry structure constant, a business organization has to choose an adequate competitive position in relation to the other players in the market; this is achieved through the use of the framework known as the *three generic strategies*, namely (1) differentiation, (2) overall cost leadership and (3) focus. The managerial decisions regarding such strategies have a relatively short-term impact on the performance of the firm and they can be altered so as to suit changing environmental conditions. However, it is in the long term that the conditions are established for the organization to create an internal environment supportive of competitive advantage, in a sustainable manner.

According to Porter (1991) the basic unit of analysis of competitive advantage is the discrete activity: 'a firm is a collection of discrete but interrelated economic activities, such as products being assembled, salespeople making sales visits and orders being processed. A firm's strategy defines its configuration of activities and how they interrelate' (ibid., p. 102). An activity can be anything to which a cost can be attributed and the way of performing discrete activities determines the firm's costs. The firm as a whole can be seen as a collection of interrelated activities such as, for example, 'buying input A', 'manufacturing component B', 'advertising product C', 'selling service D' or 'making an after-sales visit regarding product E'. The strategy of an organization, broadly understood as an overall pattern or disposition for behaviour, can be seen as both cause and consequence of the configuration and interrelationships of such discrete activities, usually formalized as the firm's organizational structure.

The value system is an alternative way of approaching the firm's collection of activities. Instead of being represented as costs, activities can also be represented as value for the customer, in such a way that the whole company's activities can be schematically arrayed in a series of value chains (Porter, 1985). Not only can the company's own activities be arranged on a value chain, but the company's suppliers' and the company's customers' activities can also be displayed as value chains, thus providing a useful checking system for the sources of buyer and customer value. A value chain provides a template for understanding cost position as well as the sources of buyer value, for example 'by understanding how households perform activities related to a product (procurement, storage, use, disposal, etc) the sources of differentiation can be better understood' (Porter, 1991:102).

Performing activities requires tangible assets or 'working capital' and intangible assets or 'intellectual capital', embodied in human resources and in the technology. Some tangible and intangible assets are internal to the company and some are external (for example, contracts and brand images). But performing activities not only requires assets as it also creates intangible assets 'in the form of skills, organizational routines and knowledge'. And 'while the tangible assets normally depreciate, the intangible assets involved in performing activities can cumulate over time' (ibid., p. 102). In reaching these conclusions, the model moves from the cross-sectional to the longitudinal approach. Moving to the longitudinal approach means that one's concerns change from questions such as 'What specific activities and drivers underlie the superior competitive position?' to questions such as 'Why do some firms achieve favourable positions vis-à-vis the drivers in the value chain?' In information systems implementation, this is precisely the question that we ask when approaching implementation from an organizational and, therefore, longitudinal perspective, i.e. *why do some firms achieve much better results from implementing IS/IT, as reflected in the drivers in the value chain?*

Porter's longitudinal approach contains the answers to what that author calls the 'origin of origins' of competitive advantage. The 'drivers' of competitive advantage are the 'structural determinants of differences among competitors in the cost or buyer value of activities' and they range from attributes such as 'cumulative learning in that activity' and 'ability to share activities' to attributes like 'the activity's location', 'the timing of investment choices' or 'the firm's policy choices about how to configure the activity independent of other drivers' (ibid., p. 104). So, the notion of drivers contains a mixture of *choices* that the company's managers make and of *skills* that the firm accumulates and which gives it an edge over the competition. The notion of 'drivers' is a similar notion to 'competencies' (Prahalad and Hamel, 1990) but 'drivers' is broader in scope in that it contains more static attributes such as, for example, 'the activity's location' which is a result of managerial choice.

While Porter's contribution to a theory of strategy as competitive positioning is a useful step forward, it stops short of the issue of *how* or the *implementation question*. Bringing in 'managerial choice' at the bottom of the causal chain is a positive development in relation to previous formulations by the same author where environmental forces were the sole force dictating the outcome of business competition. But 'pure' managerial choice, as Porter puts it, does not solve the implementation issue. Bottom-up and emergent events often cause managerial choices to be changed, delayed or aborted and managerial action becomes as important or even more important than managerial choice for the final outcome of competitive positioning. Managerial choice and managerial action are two sides of the same coin and it does not make sense to talk about the one without talking about the other.

THE RESOURCE-BASED APPROACH

Now let us turn our attention to the middle section of the composite definition of strategy suggested at the outset, i.e. 'aimed at creating situations for economic rents to be produced and sustained'. This section is supported by the latest trend of strategic management thinking – the resource-based approach.

In view of the ambiguity associated with definitions of profit, the academic literature increasingly utilizes the expression 'rent' to refer to 'economic profit'. Rent is the surplus of revenue over the real or 'opportunity' cost of the resources used in generating that revenue. The opportunity cost of a resource is the revenue it can generate when put to an alternative use in the firm or the price that the resource can be sold for. Such an interpretation of 'rent' is also known as Ricardian rent. When applied to the resource-based view of strategy, a Ricardian rent means the returns to a given resource (e.g. managerial skills) which confer competitive advantage to the firm over and above the real costs of such a resource (Grant, 1991).

The resource-based approach has emerged, partly as a reaction against a degree of environmental determinism which we have just alluded to. Since the appearance of strategy as a systematic area of study and activity (Chandler, 1962), a belief has formed amongst the management community that all major decisions are taken as a consequence of the workings of the business environment and of the outcome of various product-market formulae. Such formulae have been conceptualized in different ways over the years, such as Ansoff's (1965) product-market matrices, the Boston Consulting Group growth-share matrix (Henderson, 1970) or Porter's (1980) five forces model of industry, all strongly emphasizing the environmental component of business strategy.

The main criticism of these environmentally-oriented views of strategy is that it makes the role of management and of managerial choice and action negligible or virtually non-existent. In a large study of competitive performance of British firms, Pettigrew and Whipp (1991:26) make the following comment:

> Even allowing for the popular handbooks of business success, little analytical weight in the prevailing accounts of competition has been attributed to the *capacity of management* to adjust to external change. In spite of the recent speculation on supply side improvements in the UK economy, most policy discussion of competition has concentrated on policies at the expense of processes.

Another criticism of the product-market and environmental analysis models of competitive advantage is that the business advantage which is eventually gained is often short-lived because products or services are easy to imitate or to replicate. Valuable resources may resist imitation by competitors if protected by imitation barriers. Rumelt (1984) discusses some of such barriers or 'isolating mechanisms':

1. time compression diseconomies – the time factor may be important in achieving uniqueness in a particular resource, if learning, experience or trained proficiency in a particular set of skills can be accumulated in a span of time shorter than normal.
2. historical uniqueness (first-mover advantage) – some resources are inher-

ently unique due to either the non-replicability of the conditions under which they were acquired, such as a distinctive location or the advantages gained from being the first mover, such as brand loyalty or the power to establish industry standards.

3. embeddedness of resources – the value of a resource may be inexorably tied to the presence of a complementary resource and the two resources together make up a combination which is non-imitable.

4. causal ambiguity – the connection between a particular firm's resource portfolio and its performance may be difficult to determine, making the imitation of competitive advantage factors more costly.

Such thinking by Rumelt introduces the key issues of the new theory which, as a school of thought in industrial economics, is not entirely new. It can be traced back to Penrose (1959/1995) and to the notion that what makes a firm grow is the accumulated experience and knowledge from within the company and not the price mechanism from the market. However, the approach suggested by Penrose's writings in the late 1950s stayed dormant until the 1980s, probably due to a period of fast economic growth that followed in the 1960s and part of the 1970s. It has been the work on evolutionary economics by Nelson and Winter (1982) and a paper by Wernerfelt (1984) which have provided renewed foundation for the resource-based view to develop from.

The resource-based approach analyses firms from the resource side rather than the product side, as Wernerfelt (1984:171) explains:

> For the firm, resources and products are two sides of the same coin. Most products require the services of several resources and most resources can be used in several products. By specifying the size of the firm's activity in different product markets, it is possible to infer the minimum necessary resource commitments. Conversely, by specifying a resource profile for a firm, it is possible to find the optimal product-market activities.

Resources can be anything that might be considered as a strength or a weakness of a given firm, the internal part of a SWOT (strengths, weaknesses, opportunities and threats) analysis as opposed to opportunities and threats which are the foci of the external part of SWOT. Resources are the tangible and intangible assets which are tied semi-permanently to the firm and they can be classified under three categories: physical capital resources, human capital resources and organizational capital resources (Barney, 1991). Physical capital resources include the physical technology, a firm's plant and equipment, its geographic location and its access to raw materials. Human capital resources include the knowledge of individual workers, namely, their skills, experience and contacts. Organizational capital resources include the formal and informal organizational structures as well as the relationships among individuals and groups within and outside the firm. Examples of resources are: brand names, trade contacts, machinery, capital, in-house knowledge of technology, etc.

Table 5.2 *The resource-based approach compared with the neo-classical school of business economics*

	Definitions	**Assumptions**
Neo-classical school	• Firms exist to combine resources to produce an end product • Firm size is determined by the price mechanism, which in turn is influenced by technological and managerial scale factors (i.e. increasing average costs past a production level, which is small relative to the size of the market)	• In the production process: (1) the right input mix can be readily ascertained; (2) marginal contribution of each input is easily calculated; (3) all parties have perfect and complete information; (4) resources are completely mobile and divisible
Resource-based theory	• Firms as opposed to markets exist for reasons primarily related to 'creating positives' with or without opportunistic considerations • Firms are made up of heterogeneous asset bases, which are costly-to-copy sources of economic rents • Firms are social institutions with a social responsibility	• The only limit to the growth of the firm is its internal capability for generating new knowledge • Performance differentials between firms depend on possession of unique inputs and capabilities • Firm's performance results from (1) the firm's own asset base; (2) the asset bases of competitors; (3) constraints emanating from the broader industry and public policy environments

Source: Adapted from Conner (1991).

The key differences between the neo-classical school of business economics of the resource-based school can be seen in Table 5.2 above.

An important part of the literature on the resource-based approach includes the theories on organizational skills and competencies. Prahalad and Hamel (1990; Hamel and Prahalad, 1994) explain the relevance of the concept of core competence as follows:

> Of course, it is perfectly possible for a company to have a competitive product line up but be a laggard in developing core competencies – at least for a while. If a company wanted to enter the copier business today, it would find a dozen Japanese companies more than willing to supply copiers on the basis of an OEM (Original Equipment Manufacturer) private label. But when fundamental technologies changed or if its supplier decided to enter the market directly and become a competitor, that company's product line, along with all of its investments in marketing and distribution, could be vulnerable. Outsourcing can provide a shortcut to a more competitive product, but it typically contributes little to building the people-embodied skills that are needed to sustain product leadership (Prahalad and Hamel, 1990:84).

The development of core competencies inevitably requires an understanding of organizational behaviour in view of the fact that competencies are not only task-related but are also related to the building and maintenance of relationships in the workplace. Other authors writing in support of the resource-based approach such as Barney (1986) or Fiol (1991) have stressed the relevance of behaviour-related issues, such as organizational 'identity', 'culture' or 'context', as key organizational resources. However, be it in the case of core competencies or in what concerns organizational culture or contexts, all the questions related to individual and collective behaviour still seem to be missing. In other words, although attaching great importance to intangible assets as the drivers of strategy, the resource-based approach still stops short of the people-related implementation issues.

The failure to address the implementation issue has its roots (once again) in the positivist, rationally-centred paradigm of the economics discipline. Winter (1987), one of the founders of the resource-based approach, recognizes that although the management of knowledge is necessarily tied to individual behaviour issues, convincing fellow economists of the non-deterministic and unpredictable nature of organizations, is no easy task:

> The tradition of viewing the firm as a unitary actor with well-defined preferences has long been challenged by organization theorists and social scientists outside of economics, and by a few economists of heretical bent (...) there are indeed some key issues in the strategic management of knowledge assets that relate to whether the firm can hold together in the face of conflict among the diverse interests of the participants (Winter, 1987:164).

What Winter is highlighting in this passage is a key divergence between two ways of looking at organizations which bear important consequences for the respective approaches to strategy. On the one hand there are the theories of behaviour (i.e. organizational behaviour) and, on the other hand, there are the theories of structure (i.e. the structure of industrial/business effectiveness and competitiveness), of which Porter's theory is one example. Although the resource-based approach turns the spotlight on some behaviour-related issues, such as skills or internal processes, it is still too structure-oriented to be able to articulate the management practices that enable firms to earn rents more efficiently. But, on the other hand, process-oriented models inspired by theories of organizational behaviour are also incomplete because they cannot make the distinction between what is strategically relevant and what is strategically irrelevant.

The solution would rest upon the development of a new theory which is able to explain how strategically positioned core competencies, managerial skills along with other firm resources, may be put to work and produce value for the stakeholders. Mahoney (1995) makes an interesting suggestion to this end, in the form of a *resource learning theory*, i.e. a synthesis of the resource-based approach and of organizational learning theories, focusing on the development of human resources and of organizational resources in tandem. Mahoney's formulation of the problem does highlight the importance of the middle ground, between top-down rational policy formulation and the bottom-up strategic emergence through collective action. This is the basis of the approach we will be discussing next, the managerial action approach.

THE 'MIDDLE-GROUND' IN MANAGERIAL THOUGHT

Action-based strategy, the middle-ground position or the *new modernist* management theory has its origins in the pragmatic approaches to managerial leadership from pioneers such as Mary Parker Follet (1924), Chester Barnard (1938), Peter Drucker (1955), Philip Selznick (1957) or Burns and Stalker (1961). More recently, Bartlett and Ghoshal (1993) and Ghoshal and Bartlett (1994; 1998) have taken up this school of thought and have contributed to operationalizing the dual notion of managerial action versus organizational context. In returning the figure of *the manager* to centre-stage of the theorizing about management, this school of thought places behaviour and action at least on the same level of importance as planning, choice or structure.

But the middle-ground position and, therefore, the [managerial] action approach has another set of very influential origins in the writings of Chris Argyris and Donald Schon (1978; 1996). These authors claim that by leaving out what actually happens during the implementation of strategy (within the rational view) or during the integration of emergent strategy (within the emergent view) 'both perspectives tend to ignore a crucial element of strategic management: the *realtime* microactions through which managers respond to the challenges to implementation or to integration' (1996:255). Furthermore, they state that 'The action proposals of the authors on both sides seem to have been afterthoughts of theorizing; they are described as though they were self-evident, if only the right prescriptions were followed or if only managers were able to manage without interference' (1996:253). In Chapter Three we have already touched upon the writings of Argyris and Schon. In this chapter we will explore these in greater depth.

Let us begin with the first set of authors. Mary Parker Follett (1924), a relatively unknown pioneer of management, had some extraordinary insights into the idea that managerial action is central to the whole process of managing organizations. The idea is centred upon the notion that action implies 'enaction'. In other words, when we do something we immediately create something else and that something else inevitably affects what we do next. Formulated in a different way, Follett's view of cognition is that people receive stimuli as a result of their own activity. Such a view, expressed back in the 1920s, is identical to that expressed much more recently by authors in the field of the cognitive sciences (Varela et al., 1991) and in the organization sciences (von Krogh and Roos, 1995) and which have already been referred to in Chapter Three. Weick (1995) claims that Follett was the first author to study and apply an 'enactive' approach to cognition in organizations:

> The activity of the individual is only in a certain sense caused by the stimulus of the situation because that activity is itself helping to produce the situation, which causes the activity of the individual. In other words, behaviour is a relating not of 'subject' and 'object' but of two activities. In talking of the behaviour process we have to give up the expression 'act on' (subject acts on object, object acts on subject); in that process the central fact is the meeting and interpenetrating of activities. What physiology and psychology now teach us is that part of the nature of response is the change it makes in the activity, which caused so-to-speak the response, that is, we shall never catch the stimulus stimulating or the response responding (Follett in Weick, 1995:32).

Chester Barnard (1938/68) was the first organizational theorist to come not from academia but from the world of management practice. This gives his writing a true 'managerial' flavour in the sense that he makes a strong case for the responsibility of the company's executive in creating a 'work ethic', which will lead people to cooperate willingly and for the benefit of the organization. The 'vitality' of organizations depends upon the willingness of individuals to contribute their efforts towards the cooperative system, that is, to the organization. Barnard emphasized the point that what constitutes organizations are not people but the acts or actions or influences (i.e. the 'forces') of persons. He compares the organization to an electromagnetic field: people are to the organization the same as electromagnetic forces are to the electromagnetic field. The electromagnetic field can only be identified when an electromagnetic force is applied to it, otherwise the electromagnetic field does not exist. Similarly, the organization is only identifiable when people apply their energies (actions) to it or when certain phenomena occur as a direct result of such application of energies.

In his writing, Barnard has captured the essence of the intangible nature of organizations. The following passage is one example:

> The actions which are evidence of organization forces include all actions of contribution and receipt of energies, so that a customer making a purchase, a supplier furnishing supplies, an investor furnishing capital, are also contributors. What they contribute is not material but the transaction, the transfer, the control of things, or actions upon physical things themselves (1938/68:77).

Together with the 'willingness to serve', Barnard singles out 'purpose' and 'communication' as the key elements of organization as a 'cooperative system'. Regarding purpose, he makes a clear distinction between organizational purpose and individual motive and claims that with rare exceptions the two are not identical. In order to get individuals to cooperate, organizational purpose must be translated into inducements or motivating factors, which will enable organizational members to find satisfaction of some of their personal needs in helping the organization achieve its aims. Another key mechanism that is offered as a means of bridging the gap between organizational purpose and individual motive is communication, which is not just about the spoken word. He stresses the fact that perhaps the most important part of communication is unspoken and is dependent upon mutual understanding or mutual acceptance. Barnard talks about an 'observational feeling', which he describes as 'the ability to understand without words, not merely the situation or conditions but the *intention*' (1938/68:90).

Burns and Stalker (1961) became well known for their work on technical innovation and the conceptual distinction between mechanistic and organic management systems. It is worth recalling such a dichotomy, not only because it is still relevant today but especially because the organic system which, back in the 1960s, seemed to be the most appropriate for turbulent and fast-changing environments, in the environmental conditions of the late 1990s is the only system that makes sense. There are two important points about Burns and Stalker's writings: (1) they emphasize that the mechanistic versus the organic distinction does (or did) in fact exist in real companies, that is, it is based on extensive empirical work and it is the result of speculation by sociology theorists; (2) more importantly, they claim that each of those management systems would establish itself as a 'code of conduct' in the company and determine the kinds of formal and informal relationships which developed as the result of the day-to-day functioning of the organization. This notion, very similar to Barnard's (1938/1968) notion of the 'work ethic' is also very close to the modern-day and perhaps lighter constructs of organizational contexts, which Bartlett and Ghoshal (1993) and Ghoshal and Bartlett (1994) refer to as the 'feel of the place'.

These authors argue that the general environment for large (and small) firms has changed beyond recognition and a new approach to the roles of management is needed. They base their argument on the general macro-trends which have been affecting companies more acutely in the last 10 to 15 years. Such trends are (1) a fundamental change from a suppliers' market to a consumers' market; (2) serious overcapacity in production due to a slowing-down of market growth; (3) profound changes in the traditional structures and boundaries of many industrial sectors due to deregulation and also to general technological developments; (4) deep internal changes in the work processes and roles in organizations due to ever more powerful and diversified information-processing and communication technologies, among others.

The combined impact of these changes has led to a major shift in the strategic emphases of many companies. The principal strategic task is no longer allocating capital, but managing the existing human capital, namely, managing the company's knowledge and learning capabilities. The main production task is no longer to produce excellent products, but to be close to the customer. The key managerial task is no longer to devote time to elaborate planning, coordination and control systems, but to concentrate on adding value. This is the new management agenda, which companies can no longer ignore. Such an agenda is really the cause and the consequence of the customer-oriented and quality-focused programmes, such as BPR (Business Process Re-engineering) and TQM (Total Quality Management), which companies all over the world have been battling with for the last decade.

Bartlett and Ghoshal (1993) propose a fresh look at organizations and management, not emphasizing organizational structures and formal managerial roles, but managerial processes and their interrelationships. In the 'new model' top managers are the creators of organizational purpose and challengers of the status quo, as opposed to resource allocators or makers of strategy. Middle managers are horizontal integrators of strategy and capabilities as opposed to controllers or information brokers. Front-line managers are the organizational entrepreneurs as opposed to implementers of plans or problem solvers. The new model is a radical departure from the traditional management thought on the structuring of organizations. It is based on a new conceptualization of organizational endeavour whereby organizations are developed and managed on a principle of '*proliferation* and subsequent *aggregation*' of small independent entrepreneurial units from the bottom up, rather than on a principle of '*division* and *devolution*' of resources and re-sponsibilities from the top down (Bartlett and Ghoshal, 1993:42, italics added).

The second school of thought of the middle-ground position in manage-ment theory comes from the very influential writings of Chris Argyris and Donald Schon (1978; 1996) on organizational learning. These authors con-clude that both the proponents of the rational (top-down) and the emergent (bottom-up) views tend to be inattentive to the *defensive routines*, which are omnipresent in all corporate activities. Defensive routines, in turn, are de-fined by the *theory of action*, which is held by each player in any organizational interaction. The problem is that, to the majority of organizational members, their true theory of action is not known at a conscious level. The basis of Argyris and Scion's (1978; 1996) action theory is to surface and make known to each organizational members his or her true theory of action, so that defensive routines can be avoided. However, although very deep in psycho-logical reasoning and full of insights into interpersonal relationships, such theory cannot serve as a basis for an approach to *collective* action.

For Agyris and colleagues (Agyris, 1977; Argyris et al., 1985; Agyris and Schon, 1978; 1996) action means individual action and not group or collec-tive action. It means that each individual manager operates from one of two theories of action: an espoused theory or a theory-in-use, giving rise to two types of managerial behaviour: Model I behaviour, a consequence of an espoused theory of action and Model II behaviour, which results from a theory-in-use type of action. Model I behaviour is founded upon four basic 'governing variables' (Argyris, 1977): (1) that one must achieve one's goals as one sees them; (2) that one must win rather than lose; (3) that one must minimize eliciting negative feelings in relationships, and (4) that one must be rational and minimize feeling or showing emotions. Such governing variables lead to behaviour which makes one feel safe, in control of others, and requir-ing minimal confrontation and emotionality.

From the studies carried out by Argyris and colleagues by means of inter-views with hundreds of managers, it was shown that overt behaviour was not only non-confrontational but also in direct contrast with the person's inner feelings. However, because subordinates too conceal their true feelings and emotions in interacting with the manager, the end result is a guessing game of who is feeling what, with both the manager and the subordinate trying to manipulate the situation as best they can. Model I behaviour is 'self-sealing' and leads to single-loop learning, that is, people set up the situation to confirm their own premises. This is in accordance with the organizationally closed characteristics of enactive cognition and of self-referential social sys-tems, as discussed in Chapter Three.

Model II behaviour is put forward as the solution to single-loop learning. Argyris' proposition is that if managers could adopt a different set of premises about human relationships, organizations would be more effective because learning in them would be enabled. The proposed new premises for organizational action, then, are as follows: (1) it should be based on valid information; (2) it should be based on free and informed choice; (3) it should be based on internal commitment to the choice and on the permanent monitoring by each individual of his or her own efforts to implement such a choice. This is the recipe for the so-called double-loop learning or the 'learning how to learn' techniques, typical of the American-style Organization Development interventions designed to build up interpersonal competencies (French and Bell, 1995).

Argyris's theory of action is less useful for prescribing organizational learning and organizational change than it is in drawing attention to the emotional basis of theories-in-use and to the difficulties involved in changing cultural values. Behind organizational values, there are human emotions and emotions are the building blocks of social organizations, as Maturana (1988) has shown. The problem of espoused theories versus theories-in-use and of the games of concealment of feelings and guessing of intentions in organizations, all have to do with the rationalist ethos. In Western societies, we have evolved in a paradigm which encourages the separation of logic from emotion and this, in turn, can only give rise to hypocrisy or insincerity. However, a social system will continue to exist in spite of hypocrisy:

> A social system can persist in the presence of hypocrisy of some of its members as long as these continue performing the actions of mutual acceptance, but it is unstable because insincerity always shows up in conflicting actions due to the emotional contradictions entailed in hypocrisy. In other words, it is the behaviour of mutual acceptance between the components of a social system, not their sincerity that is essential for its continued realization (Maturana, 1988:68).

Another problem with the approach put forward by Argyris and colleagues is the issue of organizational power. Although it correctly highlights a situation which is directly related to power relationships (Model I behaviour), the suggestion that once all the managers have been changed into Model II-type of behaviour, then the organization as a whole will follow suit, just cannot happen in such a way. This is due to the fact although interpersonal relationships can be changed in the psychologically secure environment of a consultancy meeting, when individuals are put together in real-world groups, a host of new (power) relationships is continually emerging and future behaviour becomes impossible to predict. Defence mechanisms can be down at one point in time but they will be up again as soon as a new element is introduced in the organization's power network and that can happen at any time. As observed by Introna (1997:144) 'the manager, as a manager, is already one of the prime effects of power. The manager can never get out or distance herself from the circular grid of power. To rise above power is a useless abstraction'.

According to this conception of organizational power as a network of force relations, power relationships exist irrespective of managerial will and the answer seems to be to accept power as something endogenous to the organization, which can never be fully analysed, dissected or controlled. However, this is not entirely so. In order to achieve partial control over the never-ending organizational power games, managers can do a great deal by constructing their own *legitimacy*. This has been described as a 'process of symbol construction and value use designed to create legitimacy for one's ideas, actions and demands, and to delegitimate the demands of one's opponents' (Pettigrew, 1987:659). According to Pettigrew, the *legitimacy* process is the link between the cultural and political analyses of organizational life, that is, how the creation of a strong work ethic and a strong drive towards cooperative action through organizational values, can '*shape* and not merely reflect organizational power relationships' (p. 658, italics added).

Hence, the issue that managers should focus their attention on is not on how open or truthful each organizational relationship is but on something which hangs above all organizational (power) relationships like a large umbrella: the organization's *constitution* (Normann, 1985), the organization's *work ethic* (Barnard, 1938/1968), the organization's *codes of practice* (Burns and Stalker, 1961) or the organizational *context* (Bartlett and Ghoshal, 1994). This is one of the foundational arguments of the managerial action approach.

TOWARDS A THEORY OF MANAGERIAL ACTION

In their theory building, Bartlett and Ghoshal defend the notion that improved organizational performance depends, primarily, on the organizational contexts (or climates) that managers are able to build in fulfilling their managerial roles and processes. Context can be understood as the situation in which the individual, the work team or the department finds itself, exerting a powerful influence on internal and external interpersonal relationships and, ultimately, on the quality of the management that holds the organization together. This idea is further reinforced by Kakabadse and Kakabadse (1999:7):

> the power of context is substantial, for context helps form the attitudes and perspectives individuals hold about life, work, people and organization.

As the outcome of their research into the practices of successful companies, Ghoshal and Bartlett (1994) have identified a number of value-oriented characteristics of managerial action. Organizational values are the 'ideas, beliefs or principles, which have been socialized by organizational members and which are behind the way individuals in the organization think or feel about a given situation and about the way that "things should be done" in that particular organization' (Bowditch and Buono, 1997). Such values can also be understood as the key dimensions for quality management, that is, a type of management which induces the creation of a favourable or supportive organizational context for improved organizational performance.

Ghoshal and Bartlett (1994) have grouped organizational values into four key dimensions – Stretch, Discipline, Trust and Support – which are defined as follows:

- Stretch – The attribute of an organization's context that induces its members to voluntarily strive for more rather than less ambitious objectives (e.g. the development of a collective identity or the establishment of a shared ambition).
- Discipline – The attribute of an organization's context that induces its members to voluntarily strive for meeting all expectations generated by their explicit and implicit commitments (e.g. the establishment of clear standards of performance or the consistency in the application of sanctions).
- Trust – The attribute of an organization's context that induces its members to rely on the commitment of each other (e.g. the involvement of individuals in decisions and activities affecting them).
- Support – The attribute of an organization's context that induces its members to lend assistance and countenance to others (e.g. freedom of initiative at lower levels or personal orientation from senior staff).

Conceptualizations about behaviour in organizations depend very much on how managers themselves view the nature of organizations and of the people who work in them. This point has been made in the organizational behaviour literature by several authors. Among the better known are McGregor (1960) with the opposing theories X and Y, and also Burns and Stalker (1961) with their organic versus mechanistic organizational modes. Ghoshal and Moran (1996) address these issues in the context of a theory of the firm. Why organizations exist and why human beings work in organizations are fundamental questions, which can be answered in accordance with theory X's organic disposition or in line with theory Y's mechanistic mode. In the first instance, the role of human emotions is recognized; in the second instance, the prevailing discourse is one of logic and rationality, and the role of emotions and therefore of human and organizational values is consistently played down. This is the reason why organizational context has never been afforded the role and the relevance it deserves.

There are a couple of important points to be made about Bartlett and Ghoshal (1993) and Ghoshal and Bartlett (1994; 1998), very briefly summarized here. What makes the work from these authors different from that of many others in the field of strategic management is that in their theory development Ghoshal and Bartlett interrelate many previously held notions not openly recognized by the predominant approach in strategic management. Firstly, they interrelate the nature and function of organizations within the economy with the nature of organizations as social entities and the nature and function of management within the firm. Secondly, they are concerned with characterizing the *ethos* or the overall context of the organization, both for external purposes (the role of firms in the economy) and for internal purposes (the role of workers and of management in the firm). Thirdly, they highlight emotional knowledge (as opposed to factual knowledge) as a key factor in the construction of successful organizations and put forward four major organizational value dimensions which make up the contexts of such organizations.

As the reader will have appreciated by now, Ghoshal and Bartlett's theory is wholly in tune with many of the characteristics of the new organizational paradigm we have discussed in the preceding chapter, especially with the notion of organizations as living cultures, made up of climates or contexts. So, the model of organizational context formation put forward in Chapter Four is the same model which would support Ghoshal and Bartlett's proposals of organizational context formation vis-à-vis managerial action. The model also assumes that treating the concepts of organizational climate, context, culture and knowledge as separate concepts is unhelpful and even confusing. Therefore, we have proposed, after Sackmann (1991), the expression *organizational cultural knowledge*, as a unifying concept capable of bringing together all the sub-themes and supporting the notion of organizations as living cultures.

Supported by the enacted view of cognition, as well as the social theory of structuration, the managerial action approach brings together several strands of managerial knowledge. It is an attempt at integrating existing building blocks, rather than a proposal for a totally different approach. It recognizes that *managerial choice* and *action* (the top-down perspective) has a fundamental role in the final outcome of implementation, but it is also aware of the emergent properties of *collective action* (the bottom-up perspective). The interaction of managerial choice/action and of collective/emergent action creates a dialectic, which can be considered as the basis of the constitution of organizational climates or contexts, culture or knowledge.

These epistemological approaches help to explain the dialectic relationship that exists between the top-down and the bottom-up views of strategy. According to these perspectives, organizational context and managerial action are co-determined, that is, one exists always in the light of the other. Furthermore,

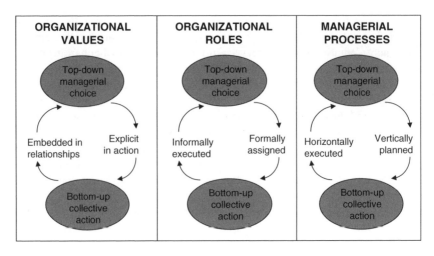

Figure 5.2   Enacted cognition and structuration applied to managerial action

they provide a good explanation for the influence of organizational values on the transformation of organizational roles and processes. Some examples of such co-determination are depicted in Figure 5.2.

In this figure we suggest that organizational values are introduced to the organization by means of managerial choice, through explicit action. After a while, and through collective action, such values become embedded in the interpersonal relationships which make up the organization. Similarly, roles are formally assigned to organizational members by managerial choice, but soon their formal content is replaced by their informal interpretation, as parts of the organization's autopoietic processes. Given a supportive (i.e. learning) organizational ethos such informal roles will develop characteristics akin to cooperation and self-initiative.

Finally, the notion of 'managerial processes'. Most processes in organizations are vertical, that is, they are a direct consequence of the traditional functional form which is (still) adopted by the majority of organizations. However, there is also increasing recognition that real added value is not achieved through the vertical organization but through horizontal processes. Such recognition has fostered the appearance of the matrix form, which should be perceived more as a 'state of mind' (Bartlett and Ghoshal, 1990) than as a tangible structural device. Thus, although most organizational processes are planned (managerial choice) as part of vertical functions, a conducive ethos (collective action) will allow such functions to develop many informal features, essential for the horizontal organization to flourish.

Managerial action is a theory of strategy which addresses the implementation issue while addressing also the top-down imperative of strategy formulation and the bottom-up recognition of knowledge emergence. Hence, while accepting definitions of strategy as planning and positioning and strategy as ploy and perspective, the managerial action position emphasizes strategy conceived, above all, as a *pattern of action*. Although written against a military background, Clausewitz's views on war represent another theory which, perhaps surprisingly, is also aligned with the perspective of strategy as a *pattern of action*. Clausewitz's magnum opus *On War*, which has been applied by several authors to the fields of strategy and management, has been given a phenomenological reading by Ilharco (2003). This interpretivist (as opposed to positivist) analysis of *On War* is another contribution towards the managerial action perspective, as outlined in this chapter.

In Figure 5.3 we have sketched our own interpretation of Ilharco's (2003) analysis of Clausewitz's theory on war and strategy. The relationship between war and strategy lies in the fact that they are both instruments of policy. Policy evolves and is the target of planning on the basis of past experience but, above all, policy is the result of external influences. Both in war and in business strategy, the external environment plays a dominant role in the crafting of policy. Theory is another important component of war and strategy to the extent that, in order to implement policy with a degree of effectiveness, somehow past experience must be organized systematically. Rules, principles or models (in the case of present-day business strategy)

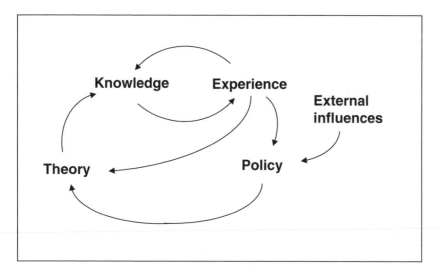

Figure 5.3   An action perspective on Clausewitz's theory of strategy

make up the theory which, according to Clausewitz, should be taken as a device to enhance intuitive or analytical judgment and not as a set of more or less static guidelines.

But the focal point of Clausewitz's thinking lies in the pattern of action of the officer (or the manager). War is about fighting, in dangerous and unpredictable circumstances and it cannot be fully understood until it is experienced. Strategy is not about fighting but it is about acting in equally unpredictable (and sometimes dangerous) circumstances. In war, theoretical or explicit knowledge becomes much less important than tacit knowledge made up of instinct and tact, in order to overcome the plentiful minor obstacles which emerge every step of the way. An officer who can recognize the obstacles and deal with them appropriately, through instinct and tact, is a knowledgeable officer. Likewise, the knowledgeable organizational strategist is not the one who knows the business policy manual by heart but the one who can deal appropriately with emerging events. Hence, in both war and strategy, there is a closely knit, dual relationship between knowledge and experience, which is summed up in action.

Finally, for Clausewitz, the psychological, motivational and emotional issues are central in a theory of war. Although they are recognized as being the most difficult issues to theorize about, they have to be acknowledged and well understood. In the world of strategy, although theorists of a positivist theory of administration have praised values and moral choice, conventional management education and training have not converted such theory into practice. Thus, logic and rationality keep being presented as something quite alien to emotions. Back in the 1950s, Selzinck (1957) was one of the few theorists to denounce such a duplicity by saying 'the importance of values is affirmed but the choice of goals and of character-defining methods is banished from the science of administration' (ibid., p. 80).

However, such a situation is changing. The fields of management and strategy cannot stay detached for much longer from the quiet revolution going on in all fields of science through the unfolding of the Complexity archi-paradigm. At the dawn of the 21st century, we believe there are signs that there is renewed recognition of the major changes under way concerning the perceived importance of intangible elements in the workplace, such as attitudes, feelings, emotions and values. One example is the latest interest in the topic of *emotional intelligence*, which is well in line with the enacted or pragmatic view of human cognition, regarding the role of emotions. Emotions form the background of the embodiment of all our knowledge and cannot be separated from logical thought in everyday action but, above all, they are also *the* ingredient, which makes all social phenomena possible, through mutual acceptance (Maturana, 1988).

CONCLUSION

Managerial action is the generative mechanism which underlies the formation of organizational contexts. Such mechanism is found in the action of organizational actors, with special emphasis on the managerial cadre. Why the emphasis on the managerial cadre? Simply because organizations have to be managed and everything in organizations starts with decision making and managerial choice (Porter, 1991). Through such choice (which cover formal as well as informal aspects) managers are responsible for the process of 'enacting' the organization's internal and external environments (Weick, 1995). This means that, because managers have the authority invested in them by whoever owns the organization, they are in a position to make policy decisions, infuse and diffuse management and leadership values and establish organizational systems and structures, thus setting the conditions for people to interact and for work to take place. This, in essence, is the top-down view of strategy and management.

Management and leadership values, through interpersonal and group relationships, form organizational contexts which, in turn, confirm or reinforce individual action throughout the organization. Organizational contexts supply the backdrop against which organizational members interpret or make sense of formal roles, thus opening up the way for the formation of informal roles and relationships. Organizational contexts, formal and informal roles and relationships are the basic ingredients for the creation of new knowledge. New knowledge, in turn, feeds back on organizational contexts, reinforcing or confirming values which are no longer just management and leadership values but which have become organizational. This, basically, is the bottom-up view. The dual relationship between managerial action and organizational contexts is similar to the 'Yin and Yang' dialectic found in oriental philosophies, such as Tao, competently explained by master Ma-Tsu as follows:

> The Tao has nothing to do with discipline. If you say that it is attained by discipline, finishing the discipline turns out to be losing the Tao ... If you say there is no discipline, this is the same as ordinary people (Rowan, 1976:19).

From this, what final conclusions can be drawn about strategy as managerial action? We submit the following:

1. There is a pragmatic gap between top-down approaches of competitive positioning and bottom-up theories of emergent strategy, comparable to the conceptual gap between mind and body in the cognitive sciences or between objective and subjective reality, in sociology.

2. As in the cognitive sciences or sociology, such a gap can only be filled if the rival approaches are seen as one dual relationship of recurrent action and reaction between managerial values and organizational contexts.

3. The top-down approach results, in its ultimate outcome, as the delivery of managerial action (including managerial values) while the bottom-up theory presents, as its final consequence, the formation of organizational contexts.

4. Managerial action and organizational contexts form the dual relationship which lies at the heart of the rationale between action, knowledge, theory and policy, the grounding of a theory of strategy.

6. Evolving perspectives on IS/IT implementation

> Whilst a great deal of effort has gone into devising standard ways of designing and developing information systems from analysis through to delivery of the system to the user, the process of systems implementation has been somewhat neglected (...) Given the importance, for the ultimate success of the system, of having a good implementation process, the lack of research effort in this area has to be regretted.
>
> (F. Land, 1992:145)

INTRODUCTION

In the research literature, IS/IT implementation is not neatly classified into this or that approach, and usually the same paper will contain two or more approaches to the implementation phenomenon. To the best of our knowledge, nowhere in the IS/IT literature is there a single framework bringing together all the IS/IT implementation approaches to be found. This makes it difficult to give the reader a quick overview of the field. Trying to bring together all the existing views on IS/IT implementation is almost as difficult as trying to put together an overview of definitions of information systems. In fact the two issues are related, meaning that one's view of IS/IT implementation will change in accordance with the definition of information system that one adopts. And because the number of definitions is countless, trying to pinpoint IS/IT implementation becomes a difficult task.

The term *implementation* is used in the literature with many different meanings in the context of IS/IT research and practice which, inevitably, causes a great deal of confusion in the field. In the words of an IS/IT researcher 'the word implementation often causes problems. To a programmer or software engineer it means taking design specifications and writing programs. To an information systems analyst it means taking the programs and other components and setting them to work in the real world' (Cornford, 1995:45). To solve the problem, that particular writer suggests the use of the word *construction* to mean software development and the word *changeover* to name the stage of software installation, instead of implementation.

So, what does implementation actually mean? Let us start by looking at what the dictionaries say about the word. Turning to the *Oxford English Dictionary* (1989) we find:

> Implementation: The action of implementing; fulfilment.
> Implement: 1. To complete, perform, carry into effect (a contract, agreement, etc.); to fulfil (an engagement or promise). 2. To complete, fill up, supplement.

Meanwhile, the *Webster's Third New International Dictionary of the English Language* (1961) reads as follows:

> Implementation: The act of implementing or the state of being implemented
> Implement: 1a. To carry out; to give practical effect to and ensure of actual fulfillment by concrete measures. 1b. To provide instruments or means of practical expression for.

From these dictionary definitions, we see that the notion of *implementation* carries with it a semantic load indicating 'completing', 'fulfilling' and 'giving practical expression' to something. But, in the specific case of implementing IS/IT, how can such expressions be operationalized, in other words, when can we say that *we have implemented IS/IT*?

The conventional views on information systems (IS/IT) implementation are usually very partial and do not encompass the whole problem of the infusion and diffusion of new information technologies in the organization, as discussed in Chapter Two. Orlikowski and Gash (1994), using concepts from structuration theory (Giddens, 1984) argues that the problem of implementing IT in organizations cannot be seen as a 'one-way' process. On the one hand, there are the technological structures inherent in the design of the hardware and of the software applications and, on the other hand, there are the structures that *emerge* in human action as people interact with the technology. This theoretical viewpoint, illustrative of the diffusion dimension, is one type of perspective on IS/IT implementation (Orlikowski, 1992; Walsham, 1993; De Sanctis and Poole, 1994).

Another type of perspective on IS/IT implementation, but now illustrating the infusion dimension, is the perspective which highlights the strategic context. Strongly influenced by the writings of Porter (1980; 1985) on competitive advantage, such a perspective has given rise to the publications of many books and articles on IS/IT-induced competitive advantage (McFarlan, 1984; Cash and Konsynski, 1985; Porter and Millar, 1985; Bakos and Treacy, 1986; Ives and Learmonth, 1984; Wiseman, 1988; Earl, 1989; Galliers, 1991; Cash et al., 1992; Ward et al., 1990; Ward and Griffiths, 1996; Applegate et al., 1999). During the 1980s and the 1990s much of the information systems literature was dominated by this perspective and by the notion that strategic planning methodologies and frameworks were the key to implementation success.

So, what to make of IS/IT implementation? Boje et al. (1996:91) states that 'every body of knowledge has some particular epistemological and ontological assumptions that ultimately shape our existential, social, political and economic relations'. This means that when researchers and practitioners talk about IS/IT implementation they start from a set of epistemological and ontological assumptions. 'What are the strategic, technical, social and organizational processes which underlie the IS/IT organizational implementation phenomenon' are questions of an epistemological nature. And 'how do such processes interact and why' tend to be issues of the ontological realm. Behind each ontological domain there is an epistemological foundation but sometimes the distinction between the two domains becomes blurred and it is difficult to say where ontology stops and where epistemology begins.

There being no purpose in embarking on a philosophical discussion about the definition of such concepts, we wish to emphasize that it is important to go to the roots of the IS/IT implementation phenomenon and not merely describe the phenomenon. We wish to discuss and to question the theoretical assumptions, behind the activities conventionally known as *IS/IT implementation*, and to propose some new intellectual avenues for the field, in line with the analyses carried out so far but with special emphases on Chapters Two and Four. The method we have used to discuss the theoretical assumptions behind IS/IT implementation is to review existing classifications of theoretical perspectives on IS/IT implementation which we have rearranged into four strands: *Technological Optimism, Strategic Rationality, Socio-Technical Interactionism* and *Organizational Holism.*

The focus of attention, however, will be on the *Organizational Holism* perspective, in line with the intellectual approaches to organization and strategy expounded so far in Chapters Four and Five respectively. Such a perspective is favoured because the causes and consequences of applying information systems to organizations cannot be reduced to a series of single events or analytical snapshots, but have to be seen as a holistic phenomenon with pervasive and continuous consequences which must be analysed through longitudinal lenses.

Implementation should not be seen as a 'one-off' event, which is finished when the information systems development cycle is complete. Rather than a single step in the methodological frameworks popularized by the technical or the strategic approaches, IS/IT implementation is a process more akin to organizational growth, learning and change. Viewing IS implementation as a process of organizational change is supported by various well-respected writers in the field. In one of the earliest textbooks on MIS (Management

Information Systems) Davies and Olson (1985:593) state that 'the implementation of information systems is a process of organizational change'.

Land (1992) argues that planning for IS implementation *is* planning the organizational change process and identifies six factors, essential in the change management process and which determine the successful linkage between the strategic and the tactical levels of IS/IT implementation: (1) motivation for introducing the new system; (2) commitment to the system; (3) organizational culture; (4) management of the implementation process; (5) the 'distance' between the existing system and the replacement system; (6) the technology itself. Lucas (1990:397) agrees that 'implementation is part of the process of designing a system, and it is also a component of organizational change'. And Checkland and Holwell (1998) are also quite clear in the argument that the whole process of IS implementation is, in fact, a process of organizational change.

Although there has been an intellectual recognition that the installation of new information technology applications does bring about change in organizational procedures, processes and behaviour, the actual outcome of thousands or perhaps millions of IS/IT projects over the last 20 years do not, however, bear evidence of such a recognition.

THE FOUR IS/IT IMPLEMENTATION PERSPECTIVES

The different perspectives on IS/IT implementation which will be discussed can be seen in Table 6.1. It must be noted that this table reflects a historical evolution of the field of information systems research. With time there has been a cross-fertilization effect among the four strands, especially in what concerns the development of practical implementation methodologies. In the main, these perspectives have been evolving cumulatively, meaning that a degree of convergence exists in the field. Nevertheless, there are still very marked differences in the way that IS/IT implementation is approached, especially in the realm of academia, and for this reason the discussion that follows does serve a useful purpose.

The variables which have been used to characterize each perspective (in the first column) are explained below.

(1) Methodological Approach

The methodological approaches considered can be represented in relation to three axes (see Figure 6.1). The first axis goes from an engineering paradigm to a social science paradigm. If IT is understood to be at the heart of the implementation problem, then the approach must answer the requisites of a typical engineering project, i.e. materials, design and construction. If people are understood to be the central concern, then the approach must answer the requisites of a typical social science project, i.e. perception, motivation, attitudes, individual behaviour and group behaviour.

The second axis ranges from hard systems methodologies to soft systems or interpretive approaches. Checkland and Holwell (1998, p. 48) make the following distinction between these two systems thinking epistemologies: in hard systems 'the world is assumed to be systemic', while in soft systems thinking 'the process of inquiry into the world is assumed to be capable of being organized as a system'. The concept of information system naturally varies in relation to each paradigm. According to the hard systems convention, an information system is 'an aid to decision making in pursuit of goals', while for the soft systems tradition, an information system is 'a part of interpreting the world and making sense in respect to it' (ibid., p. 48).

Being a discipline associated with the hard sciences, engineering is informed, above all, by a positivist research epistemology and hard systems thinking methodologies. A research framework can be considered as *positivist* when formal propositions, quantifiable measures of variables, hypothesis testing, and the drawing of inferences about a phenomenon from a representative sample to a stated population are used. A research framework can be classified as *interpretive* when there are no predefined dependent and independent variables but the focus is on the complexity of human sensemaking as the situation emerges. Interpretive research attempts to understand the phenomena through the meanings that people attribute to them, enabling an understanding of the social and organizational issues related to the adoption and integration of IS/IT in organizations. Although information systems is a multidiscipline trying to find its territory between engineering and the social sciences, Orlikowski and Baroudi (1991) have identified that about 97 per cent of research articles in the discipline fall under the positivist paradigm.

The final axis goes from an operational to a strategic focus. As Mason (1993) explains, the role of IS/IT in organizations has been reversed. Primarily, it served as an enabler for administrative tasks and was shaped by the necessity to maintain records of economic activity. Information was used to report on the transactions of the business, performing a function of keeping track of 'what things are where' and 'who owes what to whom'. Since the 1980s, however, information processed by IT systems is not only used to guide business decision making, but it has become an integral part of the product or service that the business offers to its clients. Through IS/IT, businesses have been able to get much closer to the customer and, for that reason, IS/IT have become part of product or service planning activities. In many organizations (but by no means all) IS/IT implementation is no longer treated as an operational issue but as a strategic one.

Table 6.1 *Perspectives on the implementation of information systems*

	Technological Optimism	Strategic Rationality	Socio-Technical Interactionism	Organizational Holism
Methodological approach	Hard systems engineering approach with operational focus	Hard systems organizational approach with strategic focus	Soft systems organizational approach without managerial focus	Soft systems organizational approach with managerial focus
Implied implementation strategy	Unclear. Sometimes top-down	Top-down	Bottom-up	Mixed, Eclectic
Likely outcome of implementation	Efficacy and efficiency leading to more rational decision making	Efficacy, efficiency and effectiveness in line with strategic objectives	Efficacy and efficiency on the technical side balanced with emergent phenomena on the social side	Efficacy, efficiency and effectiveness in line with organizational imperatives
Infusion vs. Diffusion Focus	Emphasis on Infusion contents and process. No concerns over Diffusion	Emphasis on Infusion context. Diffusion addressed only as a planning problem	Emphasis on Diffusion context, contents and process. No concerns over Infusion	Emphasis on Diffusion processes. Attempts at integrating Infusion and Diffusion concerns

Morgan's organizational metaphor	Machine	Brain	Organism	Culture. Flux and Transformation
Examples from the literature	De Marco (1979); Jackson (1983); Yourdon (1989); Finkelstein (1989); Benyon (1990); Cooprider and Henderson (1990); Avison & Wood-Harper (1990); McFadden and Hoffer (1994)	McFarlan (1981); Porter & Millar (1985); Wiseman (1988); Ives and Learmonth (1988); Martin (1989); Ward et al. (1990); Galliers (1991); Cash et al. (1992); Galliers & Baker (1994); Ward and Griffiths (1996); Earl (1989, 1996); Applegate et al. (1999)	Mumford & Weir (1979); Kling (1980); Mumford (1983); Orlikowski (1992); Walsham (1993); De Sanctis & Poole (1994); Mumford (1996)	Markus (1983); Kwon and Zmud (1987); Swanson (1988); Walton (1989); Cooper and Zmud (1990); Saga and Zmud (1994); Land (1992); Ciborra & Lanzara (1994); Markus & Benjamin (1997) Introna (1997); Checkland & Holwell (1998)

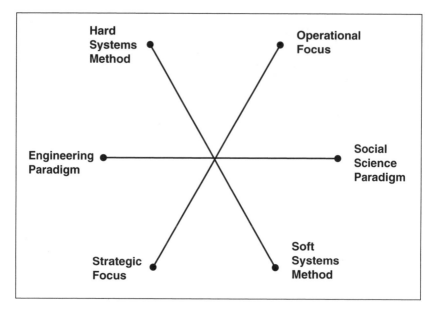

Figure 6.1   Methodological approaches to IS/IT implementation

(2)   Implied Implementation Strategy

De Jong (1994:153) uses four interesting metaphors to illustrate the implementation strategies which might be implied in each of the four perspectives:

1.   No strategy. Metaphor: *Let a thousand flowers bloom*. This is the typical situation of the early development of computing in organizations where information technology artefacts were acquired with no strategic guidance and following the notion of *the more the better*. It is also representative of a situation, still very real in many organizations, of an almost total lack of methodological guidance regarding the actual implementation/development process.
2.   Top-down strategy. Metaphor: *Design and construction of a (routine) building project*. The hallmark of any engineering project following a strict hard systems thinking methodology. In IS/IT implementation this type of strategy ranges from methods which focus more heavily on strategic analysis and design to methods whose main focus is the consistency of the actual implementation/ development framework.
3.   Bottom-up strategy. Metaphor: *Playing chess without a strategy*. Typical of a path followed by some organizations where the end users have a dominant role and the option is to acquire and develop information

technology artefacts in line with their needs. Also representative of a research strategy which emphasizes the emergent effects of IS/IT implementation.

4.   Mixed or eclectic strategies. Metaphor: *Crossing a river by searching useful stepping stones on a sketchy migration path.* This type of strategy is representative of the recognition that IS/IT implementation is, above all, an organizational issue and that, as such, cannot be approached by means of one type of methodology only. It is a new type of contingency strategy which has to mix theories and methodologies from two different fields of knowledge: information technology and organization.

(3)   Likely Outcome of Implementation

As regards the outcome of the implementation exercise, in the table above we make use of the distinction, already mentioned in Chapter Two, between efficacy, efficiency and effectiveness (Checkland and Holwell, 1998). By efficacy, one tries to answer questions such as 'are we doing what we are supposed to be doing?' or 'do the means work well?'. By efficiency, one addresses the issue of the use of resources and attempts to answer the question such as 'are we doing what we are supposed to be doing in the cheapest and quickest way?' or 'is the minimum possible level of resources being used?' Finally, the effectiveness dimension addresses the question of the contribution of the proposed IS/IT implementation to the long-term aims of the organization, thus approaching issues such as 'did it pay in the long term to be doing what we were supposed to be doing in the cheapest and quickest way?'.

(4)   Infusion vs. Diffusion Focus

In Chapter Two we have introduced the distinction between *IS/IT Infusion* and *IS/IT Diffusion*. In this chapter, such a distinction is elaborated upon. *Infusion* is related to managerial choice in determining the company's levels of investment in IS/IT as a consequence of its strategic and operational requirements. It is also related to the actual processes involved in the introduction and implementation of IT artefacts in the organization. While the concept of *Infusion* addresses the problems of strategic relevance, decision making and decision implementation regarding IS/IT implementation, the concept of *Diffusion* is proposed as a measure for the level of deployment, internal use and management of the investments made in IS/IT within the organization. In other words, while the needs imposed by strategic positioning may lead companies in the same sector to carry out similar levels of investment in IT (i.e. similar levels of infusion), the deployment, use and management of those investments within the companies almost certainly is different. While infusion depends largely upon market forces, diffusion depends mainly upon the effectiveness of the organization's IS/IT corporate governance processes.

For the purposes of the present discussion on IS/IT implementation perspectives, the Infusion and Diffusion dimensions can usefully be broken down into and associated with three additional sub-dimensions: Context, Content and Process. Such sub-dimensions come from the work of Pettigrew and Whipp (1991) in their extensive research on strategic change (see Figure 6.2). The Context dimension emphasizes the external circumstances and the internal situation surrounding an episode of change. The Content dimension concerns the assumptions, the objectives, the methods, the techniques and the resources used to go about a particular implementation exercise. Finally, the Process dimension deals with the model of change itself, the contents of formulation and implementation stages, the pattern of change through time and the management of change.

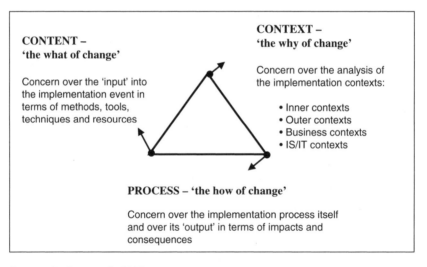

Source: Pettigrew et al. (1989).

Figure 6.2   Strategic change framework

From Table 6.2 below, it can be seen how IS/IT Infusion or IS/IT Diffusion can be analysed in terms of Context, Content or Process:

Table 6.2   IS/IT Infusion and Diffusion

	Context	**Content**	**Process**
IS/IT Infusion	Why do IS/IT need to be implemented? Issues related to the context surrounding the process of managerial decision taking regarding IS/IT implementation	What is being implemented in terms of IS/IT? Issues related to the actual IS/IT infrastructure (HR, hardware, software, communications)	How is IS/IT implementation going to be carried out? Issues related to IS/IT development/ implementation models, frameworks, methodologies
IS/IT Diffusion	Why does IS/IT-related change need to be addressed? Issues related to the context surrounding the process of IS/IT *organizational* implementation	What are the organizational issues related to IS/IT implementation that need to be addressed. Issues related to strategic repositioning, process reorganization, competence development, personal coaching, etc.	How will IS/IT-related change be carried out? Issues related to strategic/ organizational development models, frameworks, methodologies

(5)   Morgan's (1997) Organizational Metaphors

In preceding chapters we have already made references to Morgan's (1997) organizational metaphors. For the table above we have selected the five metaphors which best represent the four perspectives: Machine, Brain, Organism, Culture and Flux and Transformation. Their key defining features are highlighted below.

In the *Machine* metaphor the organization is seen as: a state of orderly relations made up of clearly defined parts and working in accordance with a pre-determinate order. As regards the *Brain* metaphor the organization is considered as an information-processing living mechanism with attention and interpretation capabilities which forms the basis of the organizational learning concept. Although organic in nature, the brain metaphor has been implemented in a mechanistic fashion in the management literature, the same being true of the organism metaphor. In the *Organism* metaphor the organization is depicted as a systemic entity which has to adapt to the environment in order to survive, capable of evolution through life cycles and subject to interacting factors which affect organizational health and development.

The *Culture* metaphor is characterized by a belief that organizations develop their own identity through an ongoing process of collective construction of common values and sensemaking capabilities which defines what the organization *is* as opposed to something that the organization *has*. Finally, in the *Flux and Transformation* metaphor the organization is regarded as a self-referential entity produced and reproduced through social interaction subject to evolution and growth coming essentially from within and in the form of new knowledge.

If we recall now the discussion about the old and the new paradigms of organization in Chapter Four and using some interpretative latitude, we suggest the following relative positions for these five metaphors:

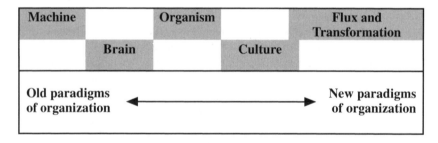

Figure 6.3   Relative standing of Morgan's organizational metaphors

(6)   Examples from the Literature

The examples provided are a selection taken from some of the best-known books and journals relevant to the information systems discipline.

PERSPECTIVE 1: TECHNOLOGICAL OPTIMISM

This first strand of perspectives on IS/IT implementation which we have labelled as *Technological Optimism*, is a derivation of labels such as *Techno-*

logical Determinism (Campbell, 1996), *Technology Imperative* (Markus and Robey, 1988), the *Determinist Perspective* (Symons, 1991) or the *Decision Making School* (DeSanctis and Pool, 1994). It is a perspective that views technology as an exogenous force which determines the behaviour of individuals in organizations and, therefore, as the principal force behind technology-related organizational change. This view is imbued with a sense that technology is intrinsically good and with an optimistic attitude in relation to effects of automation on organizations and society in general.

Under this perspective, we classify most of the approaches to IS/IT implementation which emphasize the actual methods, tools and techniques involved in applying information and communication technologies to organizational setups. The main stream of ideas has been based around the notion of information systems development methodologies, aimed at presenting the logical specification of the proposed information system. The methodologies, generally known as structured systems analysis, vary considerably, with one group emphasizing the study of the data that the system will handle, another group being oriented towards the investigation of the processes to be applied to the data, and a third group focusing its attention on the events which initiate decision processes and data transformations (Avgerou and Cornford, 1993).

One of the earliest and most influential development methodologies – the one proposed by De Marco (1979) – is still a common practice today, after undergoing a number of modifications. It starts by investigating the way that data travel is transformed within an information system using as its basic tool the data flow diagram (DFD). DFDs, which are used in a majority of methodologies, describe how data flow among processes, files and external inputs or outputs.

Another technique which has evolved from the DFD tool is the data analysis or data modelling technique (Yourdon, 1989; Benyon, 1990). The basis of data modelling is the entity-relationship model (E-R model), whose objective is to identify and structure the various items of data that the system will need to hold and to describe them in a manner which is independent of any particular database. In data modelling the starting point is to identify and name the main categories of items about which information will be stored – the entities – and the relationships among such items – the relationships. E-R models are used to convey information about the workings of the system from the systems analyst to the systems designer and to the programmer. Systems design includes database design and the variety of tasks it involves, such as specification of data organization, access methods, size and controls and the design of communication networks (McFadden and Hoffer, 1994).

In the information systems development literature, implementation is usually considered to be one or more of the stages of the information systems life cycle (ISLC), which is a model of planned change applied to IS/IT development. The IS/IT life cycle approach has its roots in the engineering disciplines and the major emphasis is on how to make the technology work, that is, how hardware, software and data can be utilized to serve a particular organizational need. There is a wide variety of ISLC models, with the number of stages ranging from four to seven or more. The basic steps are (1) Definition, which includes initiation, planning, requirements determination (i.e. analysis) and design; (2) Construction, which includes programming and/or the acquisition of software and testing; (3) Installation (or Implementation), which includes changeover, training and evaluation; (4) Operations, which includes maintenance, enhancements and further evaluation. In terms of iteration between the stages, with varying levels of dialogue between developers and users, ISLC models range from no iteration among stages as in the classic project life cycle to highly iterative prototyping models (Kappelman and McLean, 1994).

Prototyping can be used within the traditional life cycle models of IS development, as one of its stages of development or it can play a set of important roles as an alternative, evolutionary type of systems development. Prototyping can have an explanatory role, if used to explain or clarify features of the new system; it can have an experimental role when it is used to test new functionalities; it can play an evolutionary role if used as strategy for evolution from a more rudimentary to a more sophisticated version of the system or it can play a facilitatory role when used as a tool to cope with organizational change.

According to this perspective, implementation is guided solely by externally prescribed criteria, such as the deadlines or performance indicators from the implementation plan. The *Technological Optimism* perspective is dominated by an engineering worldview with the emphasis on technological and organizational performance measures, such as speed of response and better data for decision making. Implementation is regarded as a straightforward task where the human and the organizational components are given little priority in relation to the machines and the methods for making the transition from manual tasks to automated tasks. Huber (1990) is one example of this perspective, in suggesting a simplistic cause-and-effect relationship between the adoption of IT and improved organizational intelligence and decision making.

This approach has another set of origins in BSP (Business Systems Planning), a methodology created by IBM aimed at designing corporate-wide plans for IS/IT development. BSB has been further developed by many writers and consultants into a new sub-discipline known as information systems architecture (Zackman, 1987, 1997; Zackman and Sowa, 1992). The notion of architecture is very appealing to the information systems discipline, in view of the analogies which can be undertaken *vis-à-vis* the engineering profession (Lee, 1991). Information systems are designed by information systems architects but they are built by hardware and software engineers. On a more practical level, the key idea behind the notion of information systems architecture is that by adhering to good architectural principles, the whole IS/IT infrastructure should be capable of taking updates and enhancements with no need for drastic changes over the long term.

The architecture of a system is a comprehensive framework that describes its form and structure, that is, how its components fit together. It does not make a distinction between hardware and software since the system's architecture comprises both. In this sense, there is a close relationship between architecture and infrastructure. The former is a blueprint and the second is the implementation of the architecture. IS/IT infrastructure is generally understood as the ensemble of the organization's information management capabilities, which are intended to be shared, including the digital network, the hardware, the software, the databases, the standards as well as the competencies which allow IT and information to be used effectively (McNurlin and Sprague, 1998).

There are several types of IS/IT architecture. Firstly, there is the nontechnical architecture, also known as functional or applicational, which defines the breakdown of application functions into systems, sub-systems and lower-level functional areas, depending on the level of detail required. The hardware and network architecture shows the computers and networks involved in developing and processing the application. The software architecture, which includes the operating systems and the database management systems (DBMS), the middleware as well as the components of the application function itself. Lastly, there is the database architecture which defines the databases, their relationships, their location (on the hardware and on the network architectures) and their structure. Each of these architectural dimensions can be overlaid on any of the others, thus creating a complex grid for describing the whole IS/IT infrastructure.

Although the notion of IS/IT architecture is quite appealing in theory, in practice it becomes an extremely time-consuming exercise where the costs are very obvious but the benefits are hard to demonstrate. Also, many methodologies place a great deal of emphasis on data modelling and on designing the overall corporate data resource with questionable results in terms of the ever-changing information needs of the business. Given their engineering bias, most architectural methodologies show an almost complete lack of concern regarding organizational and people-related issues (Davenport, 1994).

In terms of Morgan's (1997) organizational metaphors this perspective views organizations as 'machines' where human behaviour is highly predictable and determined by clearly defined rules. The mechanistic mode has shaped the basic conceptions of what organizations are about as far as the technological deterministic perspective is concerned. The introduction of new technology does not pose a problem as long as the rules are in place. Shared goals, an apolitical view of organizational members, overall consensus and organizational stability are also characteristics of the machine organization.

In terms of an implied implementation strategy for the organization, the *Technological Optimism* perspective does not treat strategy as an issue, given its views on the nature of human beings and of the organization. Because human behaviour is predictable and organizations can be structured in such a way as to accommodate the future impact of new IT applications, implementation is simply the final stage in the technical process of getting the technology to work.

The *Technological Optimism* perspective has naturally evolved to the *Strategic Rationality* perspective as more and more systems development methodologies have began to include strategic analyses components, such as in the case of the so-called information engineering school (Finkelstein, 1989). Another evolution of *Technological Optimism* was in the direction of the *Socio-Technical Interactionist* perspective, with an increase of popularity of methodologies which include analysis and design of socio-technical systems. Avison and Wood-Harper's (1990) Multiview methodology is an example of this trend.

PERSPECTIVE 2: STRATEGIC RATIONALITY

This perspective on IS/IT implementation has many roots, but it can be argued that its earlier influence is Simon's (1945;1997) so-called information processing model of the organization, already discussed in Chapter Four. According to Simon, the organization is similar to a black box whose task it is to turn inputs into outputs. In order for the black box to produce efficient results, the actors within it should always take rational decisions; however, Simon recognizes the reality of organization is such that the rules of rationality often do not work. So, when it comes to decision making, managers have to act according to rules of 'bounded rationality'. Given that human decision makers have to operate under such conditions, the decision-making processes have to be clearly identified, so that for each decision all the variables are accounted for and the information that has to be processed by the decision maker can be reduced to a minimum. In spite of the recognition of such limitation in human decision making and its rationalist imperative, Simon's work has been important in establishing the organization as the centre of attention. Hence the label *Organizational Imperative* created by Markus and Robey (1988) to characterize this perspective on IS/IT implementation.

In terms of Morgan's (1997) organizational imagery, this perspective views organizations as 'institutionalized brains that fragment, routinize and bound the decision-making process to make it manageable' (p. 79). However, the notion of organizational learning derived from the information-processing metaphor of organizations tends to be abstract and mechanistic. To give an example: in an interesting application of organizational learning to information systems, Pentland (1995) explains how IT might be absorbed into the organization's knowledge system by using a five-step process of construction, organization, storage, distribution and application of knowledge. At each of those steps, IT applications play a role, which, in turn, has an effect on the organization's knowledge system. Although useful, mainly for purposes of description of events, this type of approach treats the organization as a black box in the sense that it fails to consider the people, the groups, the culture or the leadership, which is necessary for the actual absorption or the learning to take place.

This perspective, which has also been labelled *Managerial Rationalism* (Campbell, 1996) has a different set of roots in the influential school of strategic management, born of the work of some of the best-known American business schools (Chandler, 1962; Ansoff, 1965; Andrews, 1971). The basic assumption of this school of thought is that, through a carefully designed strategic plan, organizations will become more effective and more efficient. Applied to IS/IT implementation, one of the key assumptions of the Strategic Rationality perspective is that management has unlimited options over the choice of technologies as well as unlimited control over the consequences of their application in the organization.

In the information systems literature the influence of the strategic planning school was also felt, especially after the writings of Porter (1980;1985) on competitive advantage. Porter's models of industry analysis and of generic strategies have given rise to the publications of many books and articles on IS/IT-induced competitive advantage (McFarlan, 1984; Cash and Konsynski, 1985; Porter and Millar, 1985; Bakos and Treacy, 1986; Ives and Learmonth, 1984; Wiseman, 1988; Earl, 1989; Cash et al., 1992; Ward and Griffiths, 1996; Galliers, 1991). During the 1980s and the 1990s much of the information systems literature was dominated by the notion that strategic planning methodologies and frameworks were the key to success.

This movement gave rise to a number of methodologies, collectively known as Strategic Information Systems Planning (SISP). SISP methodologies present a dual purpose. Firstly, they serve as a means to identify a portfolio of computer-based applications, which will enable the organization to realize its business plans and consequently to fulfil its business objectives; secondly, SISP can also be used in the analysis of the competition and in the search of applications, which will create business advantages for the organization

(Lederer and Sethi, 1988). The SISP movement and its emphasis on the influence of the external environment upon the organization justifies the labelling of this perspective as the *Systems Perspective* (Symons, 1991).

These methodologies are typically top-down in the sense that they all start from the statement of the organization's business strategies and objectives and, with varying degrees of emphases, go through the following steps: (1) from the business strategy, formulate a clearly defined information policy; (2) proceed to the identification of business needs and business processes, eventually to be represented in the form of an information architecture; (3) the information architecture, in turn, becomes the basis for the formulation of the organization's information systems and information technology strategies and policies. The outcome of a SISP exercise is a priority list of computer applications to be built or updated, taking into account important factors such as cost–benefit considerations, the organization's legacy in terms of its technological architecture, the market trends in the relevant technologies, the potential risks involved and, sometimes, an implementation plan.

In the SISP literature the word 'implementation' is often mentioned but always as something which will follow the planning stage. In other words, IS/IT implementation is not seen as a problem or, at least, not as an important a problem as IS/IT planning. IS/IT implementation issues are assumed to follow from an analysis of the factors which may hinder success in the implementation effort (Lederer and Sethi, 1988; Galliers, 1991). Galliers (1991), for example, writes about 'guidelines for successful implementation' of SISP but does not define the scope of the word 'implementation'. The guidelines are as follows: (1) appropriate commitment and involvement from top and senior management; (2) appropriate choice of strategy; (3) adequate assessment of the benefits of SISP from the point of view of the various stakeholders involved, and (4) successful linkage with business strategy. Judging by this list of factors, implementation success is limited to the strategic level of the organization and does not include success at the operational levels. Conceivably, this could mean that an organization might have success at the SISP level, but fail in successfully implementing the resulting applications at the tactical or operational levels (Land, 1992).

A second trend in the strategic rationality perspective applied to IS/IT implementation concerns the strategic alignment models. The notion of IS/IT strategic alignment was introduced in the IS/IT literature through the study carried out by the MIT *Management in the Nineties* (Scott Morton, 1991) and the 'SAM' – (Strategic Alignment Model). For the contributors to this study the overall effectiveness of IS/IT implementation was attributed to the quality of the alignment achieved between the strategies for IS/IT and the organization's strategies. For the MIT team, IS/IT alignment is a mechanistic process achieved by a series of iterations between four alignment domains repre-

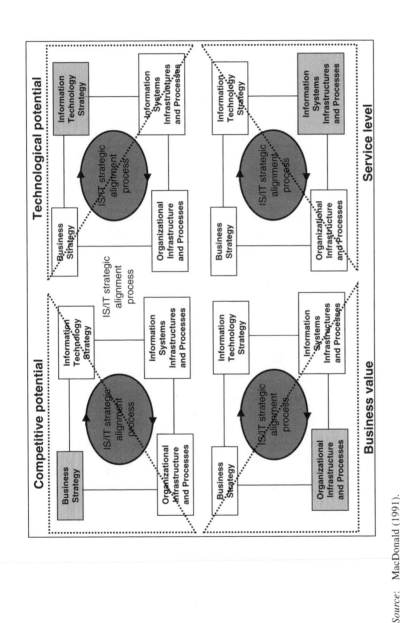

Source: MacDonald (1991).

Figure 6.4 SAM: the interacting triangles

sented in Figure 6.4 by four rotating triangles: competitive potential, technological potential, business value and service level.

In the corners of each triangle there is a component of the alignment domain. The components are as follows: 'anchors', 'pivots' and 'impacts'. Domain anchors provide the change forces (e.g. the IT strategy), domain pivots are the problem areas being addressed in that particular iteration (e.g. the business strategy) and domain impacts are the components affected by changes to the domain pivot (e.g. the organizational infrastructure and processes). According to this model, alignment is achieved by taking each triangle in turn and analysing the impacts, the transformations, the embedded technology or the required IS/IT services, in accordance to the domain being analysed. The key problems to be addressed in using the model and according to its creators are where to start the iterations, the direction of rotation (e.g. from the IT strategy domain to the business strategy domain or viceversa) and how many times to go around the four different domains (MacDonald, 1991).

Other alignment models have followed (Henderson et al., 1992; Earl, 1996; Burn, 1997; Yetton, 1997), exhibiting different methodological designs but sharing some common characteristics, namely:

- A preoccupation with the order in which alignment should occur, thus giving the exercise a rational, mechanistic tone.
- Conceptually elegant models but lacking completely on implementation issues.
- Processes, roles and relationships are presented as abstract generalizations, but never specified in terms of contents.

These rationalist notions of IS/IT alignment have been severely criticized by European IS/IT researchers (Ciborra et al., 2000) on the grounds that when a complex problem such as IS/IT alignment is reduced to a set of simple geometrical drawings, we may be tempted to take the model as being the same as the *actual* variables it intends to represent. In reality, and as far as we are aware, such alignment models have never been put to any practical use, be it in research or in professional practice, and they remain what they have always been, i.e. very faint representations of the real world of IS/IT implementation.

In Chapter Seven we will return to the issue of IS/IT alignment but to present a very different approach, based on the action-oriented view of organization and strategy we have been discussing in preceding chapters.

PERSPECTIVE 3: SOCIO-TECHNICAL INTERACTIONISM

The strategic dimension of IS/IT implementation is not limited to the top-down view of IS/IT strategy. Using the resource-based approach to business strategy as the key theoretical argument, Ciborra has been one of the champions of the bottom-up approaches to IS/IT strategy (Ciborra, 1994; Andreu and Ciborra, 1994; Ciborra et al., 1995). Starting from a revisitation of some well-known strategic information systems cases – Baxter's ASAP, McKessons' Economost, American Airlines' SABRE and the French Teletel system – Ciborra states 'these cases emphasize the discrepancy between ideal plans for SIS and the realities of implementation, where chance, serendipity, trial and error or even gross negligence seem to play a major role in shaping systems that will, but only after the fact, become textbook or article reference material' (1994:10).

The top-down approaches to IS/IT implementation have also been subject to the same criticisms as the top-down strategic planning methodologies criticized by Mintzberg (1990) under the label of 'design school' of strategy. Ciborra (1994) and Davenport (1994) argue that the top-down, highly structured approaches typical of the strategic rationality perspective do not lead to the development of effective information systems. The business environment is changing fast and such methodologies are very slow in producing results. By the time that the various stages of the methodology have been completed, the initial assumptions made about the business will have been out-of-date. Gaining a competitive edge over the competition does not depend on the planning and implementation of information systems, but on the overall management of the firm, which is capable of using information systems (old and new) to build a competitive edge. Hence, the top-down approach has failed to deliver the expected results. According to (Ciborra, 1994:18) 'what is required is a novel approach to technological and organizational innovation in a rapidly changing context'.

Ciborra's approach to the strategic dimension of IS/IT implementation is based on the 'grassroots of IT' and emphasizes the emergence of a disposition in the organization, regarding IT-related knowledge, hinging on two factors: 'bricolage' and radical learning. By 'bricolage' it is meant that tinkering with IT at the operational level should be encouraged, that is, known IT tools should be made use of, to try and solve new problems at the local level. This view of the potential of the small local groups in the workplace for the informal learning of office automation tools, as opposed to a learning mostly centred around institutional arrangements, is confirmed by empirical evidence produced by George et al. (1994). Radical learning entails the intentional challenging or 'smashing', by management, of old routines, especially those which involve learning by doing, in order to create better conditions for both managers and IT users to devise new strategies in a restructured context.

Ciborra's bottom-up approach is not common among authors writing from a strategic management perspective. Rather, it is an approach favoured by authors whose foci of interest are the consequences of IT in organizations from the point of view of social theory. Under this trend we find labels such as *Emergent Perspective* (Markus and Robey, 1988), *Interactionist Perspective* (Symons, 1991), *Social Technology School* (DeSanctis and Poole, 1994) or *Social Interactionism* (Campbell, 1996). We have selected *Socio-Technical Interactionism* as our own label because it encapsulates better the various trends grouped under this category.

Although still dominated by an engineering mindset present-day IS/IT development methodologies take more notice of the organizational and of the human aspects involved in applying information technology to the workplace. This has been achieved by a progressive introduction of socio-technical systems thinking in IS/IT implementation. Socio-technical systems design, which was introduced as a way to decrease the number of failures in IS/IT implementation (Bostrom and Heinen, 1977), has been applied to IS/IT development in a more general way, mainly through the work of Enid Mumford (Mumford and Weir, 1979; Mumford, 1983, Mumford, 1996).

As can be seen in Figure 6.5, in socio-technical systems design, the technical and the human aspects of IS/IT development run in two parallel and

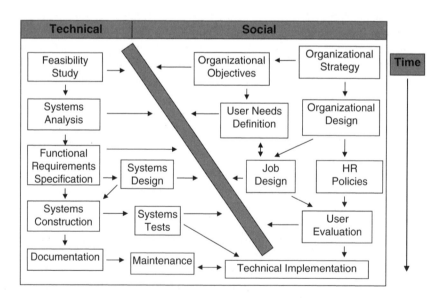

Source: Adapted from Eason (1988).

Figure 6.5   Socio-technical systems design

interacting streams and thus, it was possible to talk of an 'organizational' dimension of IS/IT implementation, as a linking theme (Walsham, 1993) running through the social and technical aspects of IS/IT development. Socio-technical systems design methodologies are built on the assumption that organizations are unlikely to achieve real benefits from information technology (IT) unless the human and organizational changes that follow from the introduction of any IT application are also planned and designed for alongside the technical changes. Eason (1988) puts forward three principles which are behind the application of a socio-technical design methodology:

1. The successful exploitation of information technology depends upon the ability and willingness of the employees of an organization to use the appropriate technology to engage in worthwhile tasks.
2. The design target must be to create a socio-technical system capable of serving organizational goals, not to create a technical system capable of delivering a technical service.
3. The effective exploitation of socio-technical systems depends upon the adoption of a planned process of change that meets the needs of people who are coping with major changes in their working lives.

Socio-technical systems thinking has provided the first clues regarding the fact that implementing IS/IT was more than just putting together a number of technical devices and organizational procedures and that there was a need to look for other variables within the organization, which might also influence the ultimate success or failure of the implementation effort. In fact, the *Socio-Technical Interactionist* approach places a strong emphasis on the bottom-up consequences of the introduction of new IT applications. It highlights the fact that the long-term success of IS/IT implementation depends, to a large extent, on how IT-based work tasks are managed at the local level. In other words, it emphasizes the fact that the *informating* capabilities of IT can only be maximized if the local management style is also aware of such capabilities and is willing to take advantage of them, as part of the implementation process (Zuboff, 1988).

Orlikowski (1992), using concepts from Giddens's (1984) structuration theory, argues that technology has a dual nature. On the one hand, technology has objective reality in the sense that it has embedded in it objective features, such as the design of the hardware or of the software; but on the other hand, technology is also a socially constructed product in the sense that new structures *emerge* in human action as people interact with the technology. That author puts forward a structurational model of technology (see Figure 6.5), which is intended to throw new light on key aspects of the phenomenon of

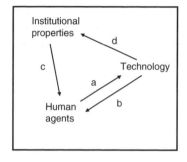

Arrow	Type of influence	Nature of influence
a	Technology as a product of human action	Design, development, appropriation and modification of the technology
b	Technology as a medium of human action	Facilitation or inhibition through interpretive schemes
c	Institutional conditions of interaction with the technology	Professional norms, state of the art in materials and knowledge, design standards
d	Institutional consequences of interaction with the technology	Reinforcing or transforming structures of signification, domination and legitimation

Source: Orlikowski (1992).

Figure 6.6 Structurational models of technology

integration of technology into organizations as well as suggesting typical relationships and interactions.

This approach is characterized by soft-line determinism (DeSanctis and Poole, 1994), meaning that, while expected relationships may be proven and tested empirically for certain organizations in certain historical and socio-economic conditions, causality may break down due to the emergent and unforeseen nature of human action, which can always 'alter the cycle of development, appropriation, institutionalization and reproduction of the technology' (Orlikowski, 1992:423). From this perspective, information systems are not just equipment, methodologies and policies, but they are also the result of individual sensemaking, that is, the perceptions and understanding of the role and value of the data and of the systems themselves (Symons, 1991; Campbell, 1996).

Broadly speaking, the socio-technical interactionist movement is inspired by the organism metaphor of the organization (Morgan, 1997). One of the great strengths of such a metaphor is the notion that in order for organizations to survive, special attention must be paid to the needs (technical as well as social) that have to be satisfied and which have to be balanced internally as well as in relation to the external environment. However, as pointed out by

Morgan (1997), the organism metaphor also has some major drawbacks, for example, the danger of the metaphor becoming an ideology. Much of the work carried out under this perspective follows the ideal of achieving perfect integration between the individual and the organization and in doing so it runs the risk of considering that all or the majority of the individual's needs can be satisfied through the organization. Thus, 'people become resources to be developed rather than human beings who are valued in themselves and who are encouraged to choose and shape their own future' (p. 71).

Another drawback is that interactionist approaches do not exhibit concerns over Infusion, i.e. the managerial decisions leading to the implementation of IT applications or the content of such implementation. They are essentially tools for analysis of Diffusion context and content. As regards Diffusion processes, they are quite adequate as tools for describing and understanding but they are rather poor as tools for acting and managing. And because acting is important in a discipline (i.e. information systems) that is so close to the *real* world of managerial practice, an interactionist approach must be complemented with other, more action-oriented tools. Ciborra and Lanzara (1994), who are critical of the interactionist approaches based on Giddens's (1984) structuration theory for being too general and too abstract, reinforce this point:

> How do such abstract frameworks come to bear when we come to the question of how a specific structure is actually *produced* (not simply described) or how a new system or organization is designed *in practice*? (p. 63)

PERSPECTIVE 4: THE ORGANIZATIONAL HOLISTIC PERSPECTIVE

The last perspective on IS/IT implementation – *Organizational Holism* – is also the perspective we adopt and support in this book. For that reason, this section is somewhat more detailed than the preceding three. In line with the exposition on the Complexity paradigm in Chapter Three, an information system implemented in an organization can be regarded as a complex adaptive system. To recap, a complex adaptive system is defined as 'a system of independent agents that can act in parallel, develop "models" as to how things work in their environment and, most importantly, refine those models through learning and adaptation' (Pascale et al., 2000:5). Similarly, an information system is a socio-technical object with multiple variables, all exerting their influence at the same time and causing many unintended consequences.

Thus, the *Organizational Holism* perspective represents an attempt at understanding and/or intervening in one or more of such variables, but taking as the level of analysis the organization as a whole. Because there are so many variables involved, often there is overlap between this perspective and one or more of the other three. For example, some variables may be contextual as regards the business and the IT market environments, thus turning one's attention to the tenets of the *Strategic Rationality* perspective. Others variables may emphasize the content of specific IS/IT implementation projects and attention is inevitably drawn to the *Technology Optimism* perspective. Meanwhile, if a project shows signs of serious problems regarding the actual implementation process and the project leaders are obliged to devote attention to the issues emerging from the bottom of the organization, they will probably be using concepts from the *Socio-Technical Interactionist* perspective.

In this section we will review firstly three trends which fit into the *Organizational Holism* perspective. They are: the political and organizational power trend, the organizational learning and culture trend and the organizational maturity and innovation trend. To conclude the chapter, a synthesis of the *Organizational Holism* perspective is presented.

Perspective 4a: The Political and Organizational Power Trend

The political aspect of IS/IT implementation was the target of early exploration by Keen (1981). That author views information systems development and implementation as an 'intensely political' process given that the introduction of a new information system always upsets the existing distribution of power within the organization. Keen considered the building of power coalitions as essential for implementation success and advised that the people responsible for the implementation process should be armed with a number of tools to counter the 'counterimplementation' tactics used by those resisting the project. Markus (1983) takes a similar view in the context of a case study about the implementation of a new accounting system, where the new technology had a strong impact on the existing power relationships. The practical conclusion was that the team in charge of the implementation process should predict all the potential foci of resistance and address them before they become problematic.

The political and power-related aspects of IS/IT implementation have not been a particularly trendy topic over the years, especially in view of its non-deterministic and abstract nature. The work by Introna (1997), supported by theories from sociology from thinkers such as Foucault, Callon and Latour and building on the pioneering work by Clegg (1989) on power in organizations, provides and excellent critique of the filed. However, this work is something of a rarity still, with very limited impact on the information systems discipline. Introna criticizes the conventional approaches to power and information, such as those taken by Keen or Markus, on the grounds that they are limited to a definition of power as something tied to the possession and control of particular resources.

Introna (1997) rejects conceptions which view power as something that (1) is possessed (e.g. by individuals, by a social class, by the people); (2) flows from a centralized source from the top to the bottom (e.g. the law or the state); (3) is primarily repressive in its exercise (i.e. backed by legal sanctions). Instead, he defends power as something that is endemic in human relationships, which can best be described as a network of force relations. Grounded on these foundations, Introna presents a re-assessment of the collapse of the London Ambulance Service Computer Aided Dispatch System which occurred in 1992.

Perspective 4b: The Organizational Learning and Culture Trend

The paper by Markus (1983) referred to above raises another issue of great relevance to IS/IT implementation, i.e. the issue of the clash between cultures within the organization as a result of the introduction of a new information system. On the same topic, El Sawy (1985) suggests that the implementation effort will have a better chance of succeeding if the chances of culture clashes are reduced. This can be achieved if implementation is accompanied by a process of IS/IT 'cultural infusion'. El Sawy reports on a case where a small group of staff was trained on the new system prior to its launching and it was the group's task to introduce the system to their colleagues in the workplace, using formal and informal means. The idea was that the small group should first adopt the appropriate cultural stance towards the new system and then 'infuse' (i.e. *diffuse*, in our terminology) it among their colleagues. The implementation process is reported as having had success.

Ciborra and colleagues (Ciborra and Lanzara, 1989; Andreu and Ciborra, 1994; Ciborra and Lanzara, 1994; Ciborra et al., 1995) have developed some very interesting work in establishing the links between IT/IS effectiveness and IS/IT-related organizational learning and culture. Ciborra and Lanzara (1994:64) start off by making organizational learning the centre of attention for 'the effective adoption of new systems'. Learning is taken to be the competence gained by organizations in 'smoothly turning anomalies and novelties into innovative patterns of behaviour'.

Juxtaposed to the notion of a *learning context*, the locus where learning capabilities originate from, these authors introduce another type of context: the *formative context*. The formative context acts as a kind of counterbalance to the learning context, in the sense that it is the source for the 'limits' of the organization's learning capabilities. This context is formative because 'it may help people see and do things in new ways or, on the contrary, make them stick stubbornly to old ways' (p. 72). Furthermore, Ciborra and Lanzara point out that formative contexts have a double nature: on the one hand they are 'highly stable' and 'inescapable' but, on the other hand, they are also the cultural bed for innovation and change.

Ciborra and Lanzara (1994) apply the action theory which has been put forward by Argyris and colleagues (Argyris, 1977; Argyris et al., 1985; Agyris and Schon, 1978; 1996) to information systems design. They argue that current systems design practice is focused solely on the functional or problem-solving aspects of organizational routines but they fail to take into account how the same routines may 'reproduce or break powerful imageries and institutional bonds at a deeper level' (p. 79). As a solution they propose an alternative approach, which they have called 'designing-in-action'. De-signing-in-action requires the intervention of an outside agent (as is the case with Argyris' approach) who acts as a 'watcher' or 'reflector' of the design activity and helps designers to 'surface conflicts and inconsistencies, to ex-plore deviations from routines and envisage the alternative contexts that they may lead to' (Ciborra and Lanzara, 1994:81). The outcome of such interven-tion, it is claimed, is a new formative context conducive to the implementation of information systems, which are much in tune with the 'real' needs of the organization.

Perspective 4c: The Stages of Maturity and Innovation Trend

In this section we will be looking at two approaches to IS/IT implementation as a process. The first is a well-known attempt to establish the maturity stages which the introduction of IS/IT is presumed to go through in organizations, pioneered by the work of Nolan (1979). The second approach is a stream of research on IS/IT implementation developed by Kwon and Zmud (1987), Cooper and Zmud (1990) and Saga and Zmud (1994) inspired by technical innovation and diffusion theory. Although both approaches conceptualize IS/IT implementation as a process based upon stages of development, they are substantially different as regards both the rationale and the contents of the development stages.

One of the earliest attempts to conceptualize IS/IT implementation as a process of maturity has been carried out by Nolan (reviewed in King and Kraemer, 1984) and comprises six stages: (1) Initiation, (2) Contagion, (3) Control, (4) Integration, (5) Data Administration and (6) Maturity. Nolan's objective was to put forward a predictive model of IS/IT evolution which might be generalizable to organizations of all types. He has postulated that IS/IT evolution in organizations follows two S-shaped learning curves. The first starting with very low levels of learning at the Initiation stage, followed by rapid growth through Contagion, levelling off at the Control and Integration Stages. The second curve starts at the levelling off of the previous curve, has slow growth at first and then more rapid growth through the Data Administration stage, levelling off again at the Maturity stage.

Although Nolan's stages are essentially object-oriented in nature, this work has left an important theoretical contribution, namely, it drew attention to the fact that the growth of organizational computing is related to a process of development of organizational maturity which can be defined in terms of two temporal dimensions: *slack* periods and *control* periods. Huff, Munro and Martin (1988) have reached similar conclusions, but have renamed the dimensions as *expansion* and *control*. Slack or expansion means that the introduction of a new type of technology triggers the need for the organization to learn and to expand, either in terms of knowledge or in terms of computing resources. But after such periods of expansion there is usually a need on the part of management to contain the expenditure and a period of tighter control of the development of computing then follows.

Choo and Clement (1994) express an alternative view of the evolution of ICT in organizations. These authors suggest that IS/IT maturity is a function of the degree of control and influence over computing resources of users versus control and influence over computing resources on the part of IS/IT staff. They suggest further that such control and influence could be ascertained over a number of criteria (e.g. hardware and software acquisition, Information Centre policies, IS training, etc.) that can be used to establish whether an organization is more user-driven or more IS/IT-driven. Although this may sound too simplistic an idea, it does draw attention to the political and sometimes conflictual nature of a *key* element in the process of IS/IT organizational maturity development: the relationship between users and IS/IT specialists.

The last approach on the maturity and innovation trend is based on a stream of research developed by Kwon and Zmud (1987), Cooper and Zmud (1990) and Saga and Zmud (1994) inspired by technical innovation and diffusion theory. This research is also important because it suggests that many of the conclusions that can be drawn about the process of technical innovation can be applied to the process of IS/IT implementation. One contribution is the suggestion that a process of innovation can and should be split up into stages. In discussing the dynamics of implementing innovations, Eveland (1987:313) explains why:

> Putting technology into place in an organization is not a matter of a single decision, but rather of a series of linked decisions and nondecisions. People make these choices and choices condition future choices (...) Researchers have developed the idea of innovation stages as a way of categorizing decisions and defining how this leverage operates, that is, seeing how some decisions of necessity precede and shape later ones (p. 313).

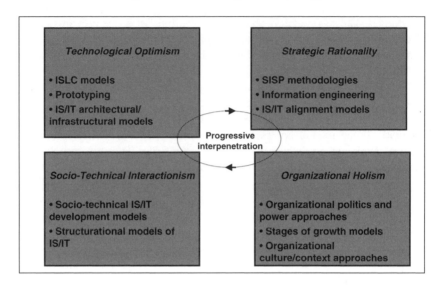

Figure 6.7 The four perspectives of IS/IT implementation: a summary of key features

From the application of the principles of technical innovation to information systems implementation, the following conclusions can be drawn:

1. Given that it is concerned with the introduction of new technologies into the organization, IS/IT strategic development can be conceptualized as a process of technical innovation.
2. In order to be conceptualized as a process of technical innovation, IS/IT implementation must be considered not as an object-oriented process but as an action-oriented process. An object-oriented view of innovation is one where the stages are described in terms of the content of the decisions, rather than in terms of the *actions* taken at each stage of the process.
3. An action-oriented process occurs in sequential stages with imprecise contours at first, and gradually getting an improved definition as the process unfolds.
4. Given that much of the outcome of IS/IT implementation is emergent (Orlikowski, 1992; Walsham, 1993; De Sanctis and Poole, 1994), the sequential stages of IS/IT strategic development must not be conceptualized as being either linear (as in the object-oriented view of technical innovation) or circular, but as a spiral process of continuous change (Slappendel, 1996).

CONCLUSION

In this chapter we have described four perspectives on IS/IT implementation which have evolved over the last three or four decades. Figure 6.6 presents the key features of each of the four IS/IT implementation perspectives. In the research literature, they often appear as separate perspectives in view of the deep fragmentation among the many areas and sub-areas which make up any scientific discipline. Furthermore, each of the perspectives is only partial and cannot encompass the whole problem of the infusion and diffusion of new information technologies in the organization.

We talk of an *Organizational Holistic* approach to implementation of IS/IT because we consider that the effects of implementing information technology artefacts cannot be pinned down to one or two areas in the organization, but are much more pervasive and continuous. Implementation should not be seen as a 'one-off' event which is finished when the information systems development cycle is complete. We see IS/IT implementation as a process more akin to organizational learning and change than to a single step in the methodological frameworks popularized by the technical or the strategic approaches to information systems development. From our point of view, the key issue regarding IS/IT implementation is organizational change which is holistic, complex and non-linear by nature (Burke, 2002). As such, according to this perspective, IS/IT implementation might be defined as a *(never-ending) process of purposefully managed change aimed at the integration of technological artefacts into the social structures and processes of the organization.*

In the adjective *Holistic* it is also implied that none of the remaining approaches is rejected but, on the contrary, that they are all regarded as complementary (see Figure 6.6). Each of the four approaches complements certain aspects where the others seem to be lacking. For example, for the *Technology Optimism* approach IT-related benefits are not necessarily connected to the organization's strategic intent or positioning. Information technology and information systems are expected to evolve in parallel with the organization's strategic objectives but not embedded in such objectives. Also, technology optimists are usually not concerned with the bottom-up factor, that is, with the mutual impacts of new IS/IT to and from existing organizational procedures, practices or values. They are mostly concerned with 'good' IS/IT development methodologies which are put into practice independently of most strategic or organizational concerns.

Some of these issues but not all have been addressed by the *Strategic Imperative* perspective, championed by thinkers from Harvard and the MIT. Building upon the models and frameworks put forward by the *Technology Optimism* perspective in what concerns structured methodologies, prototyping and architectural/infrastructural IS/IT models, IS/IT strategic planners drew attention to the urgent need that exists for the integration between the organization's strategy and IS/IT strategies. In addition to SISP models, the *Strategic Imperative* perspective contributed to the discipline with the IS/IT alignment movement and with the design of the corporate information systems architectures. Bottom-up issues arising from actual on-the-ground implementation are not, however, a concern for IS/IT strategic planners.

Such a shortcoming is dealt with by the *Socio-Technical Interactionist* perspective. Inspired by the early writings on socio-technical systems, this perspective has been an important landmark in the intellectual formation of many IS/IT thinkers since the 1970s. In the 1980s, it gained a new lease of life through the introduction of Giddens's (1984) theory of structuration, brought in from the realms of sociology. The key idea introduced by this perspective is that one can not talk about the impact of IS/IT on the organization without talking about the impact of the organization upon IS/IT. Although some writers claim that this is an organizational perspective (Walsham, 1993), it lacks purposefulness in terms of strategic motivation or orientation.

The *Organizational Holism* perspective results from a recognition that information systems cannot be implemented effectively using exclusively one of the other three perspectives. It is an attempt to complement the top-down technological and planning biases and the bottom-up emergent action focus with other issues of an organizational nature which are, nevertheless, decisive for the final outcome of the implementation exercise. This approach embodies a notion of 'multiple', 'eclectic' or 'mixed' strategies for IS/IT implementation, as discussed by Sullivan (1985), Earl (1989) or de Jong (1994).

De Jong (1994) uses a metaphor entitled *Crossing a River by Searching Useful Stepping Stones on a Sketchy Migration Path* to explain the eclectic approach to IS/IT implementation:

> To cross a river [i.e. to implement IS/IT successfully] first the desired position to reach the other side is roughly determined as well as a rough migration path that seems passable. Directed by the rough migration path, stepping stones are searched to come closer towards the desired position on the other side. On each stone, the choice is made about which step should be taken next, based on the possibilities that arise, the rough migration path that has been chosen, and the experience of the preceding steps. Sometimes, it appears that the rough migration path must be adapted to avoid difficulties or to take advantage of an easy-to-use sequence of stepping stones. It may also appear that another point is more favourable to reach the other side (p. 150).

The eclectic approach, as spelled out by de Jong, highlights not only the need to adopt different postures during the implementation exercise (sometimes a top-down planning stance, other times a bottom-up consolidation concern and occasionally a re-evaluation of the whole exercise) but also the importance of the organizational context. The passage above is an excellent portrait of the emergent and self-organized behaviours which characterize adaptive complex systems and which are particularly useful in explaining the extra-subjective, conceptual or cultural level of organization (see Chapter Four). As pointed out by Ciborra and colleagues, the *formative context* which surrounds an IS/IT implementation exercise *must* be understood and managed in order to ensure a degree of success in the final outcome.

Such emphasis on organizational context makes *Organizational Holism* evocative of the middle-of-the-road approach, embedding *managerial action* as a key foundation of a theory of strategy (see Chapter Five). Managerial action is also strongly implied in the approaches to IS/IT implementation from the point of view of organizational power and politics as well as in the organizational maturity stages approaches. For example, Choo and Clement's (1994) suggestion that IS/IT maturity is a function of the degree of control and influence over computing resources of users versus IS/IT staff reminds us of the strongly political nature of the IS/IT implementation process. Thus, the cultural gap and the unavoidable conflicts between users and IS/IT specialists, as well as the management of IS/IT-related relationships are all crucially important topics in the context of the *Organizational Holism* perspective. Let us delve into them in the chapter that follows.

7. An action-based view of IS/IT strategic alignment

> We human beings are not rational animals; we are emotional, languaging animals that use the operational coherences of language, through the constitution of rational systems, to explain and justify our actions, while in the process and without realizing it, we blind ourselves about the emotional grounding of all the rational domains that we bring forth.
>
> (Humberto Maturana, 1988:787)

INTRODUCTION

In Chapter Two we stated that *IS/IT strategic alignment* is among the major source of dissatisfaction in corporate management. David Norton (2002), one of the creators of the Balanced Scorecard methodology, in expressing the view that after more than two decades of trying the issue of IT alignment has still not been 'solved', asks the question: 'What is it about IT that makes alignment such an elusive, frustrating and career-jeopardizing goal?' (p. 1). In Chapter Six, we discussed briefly the SAM (Strategic Alignment Model) developed by the MIT team led by Scott Morton (1991) and made a reference to a few other papers about *IS/IT strategic alignment*. There is, however, one more model which needs to be mentioned – the OFF (Organizational Fit Framework) created by Earl (1996).

This model, although inspired by the SAM concept, has a few different characteristics. Instead of a construction model, Earl proposes an observation model, the aim of OFF being not to prescribe but to serve as a check list of the items that management has to be aware of, in the toil towards the strategic alignment of IS/IT. The OFF model deals primarily with the components and the imperatives of each of the key strategic domains of the alignment effort.

Whilst agreeing that the articulation of such dimensions and related processes is an important step forward, we question Earl's notion of alignment and especially the translation of such a notion into the real world. Although it has a distinctly more organizational slant than the MIT's SAM, the OFF model is enslaved by a *strategic imperative* perspective of IS/IT implementation, dominated by a worldview of abstract rationality and choice. Alignment or organizational fit cannot be seen as mechanistic notions, but should be regarded as organic, self-organizing and emergent concepts. Alignment is not something that can be planned or charted, neither is it a matter of fitting various types of strategies through linking mechanisms.

In our view, alignment is achieved not by planning linkages between processes but by emphasizing *managerial action.* Managerial action, as we have seen in Chapter Five, is supported by communicational cues embedded in the organization's language which create organizational contexts or a *disposition* favourable to the desired alignment. In his deconstruction of the concept of strategic alignment, Ciborra (1997:70) makes the following observation:

> What happens when we link the boxes of strategy, organization and IT on the [MIT's] diamond diagram? It changes our representation of the interdependencies between some key business variables. We obtain a new geometrical representation that materializes the idea of 'alignment' in front of our eyes (...) When focusing on the geometrical representation of business variables we tend to grant them essence and existence: it is an ideal, perfect world to which the real world has to conform.

Like Ciborra, we believe that the strategic alignment of IS/IT is not about neat geometric models but about a better understanding of a complex (i.e. non-reductionist) issue concerning the formation of organizational contexts, coupled with an improved managerial intervention capability in such contexts. We also concur with Keen (1991:214) when he argues that 'the key to alignment is relationships, not strategy (...) the real problem seems to be the history of relationships or lack of relationships in most organizations'. We believe that contexts influence relationships and relationships between the stakeholders is what makes IS/IT alignment happen, ultimately.

In this chapter we apply some of the theories of managerial action discussed in Chapter Five and the approaches presented under Organizational Holism, in Chapter Six, to *IS/IT strategic alignment.* We argue that alignment cannot be seen as a static proposition that can be strategically engineered, but that it must be regarded as the outcome of an IS/IT-related organizational context shaped by managerial action which, in turn, exerts its influence through IS/IT-related organizational values. Organizational values are the qualitative dimensions of managerial action which take the form of messages or meta-messages (i.e. cues) transmitted or communicated to organizational members explicitly or implicitly about all IS/IT-related issues. Such cues, which might be perceived consciously or which might impinge on perceivers unconsciously or subliminally, shape the perceptions and the behaviour of organizational members (Falcione, Sussman and Herden, 1987).

Following Schneider (1975; 1990) and the idea that climate is a manifestation of the behaviour of a particular occupational group within the organization, then it does make sense to conceptualize a climate or context particular to the IS/IT sub-organization, with its own particular dimensions or organizational values. Mindful of the fact that climates or contexts are organization-specific and that each organization will have its own IS/IT-related context, it is reasonable to assume that some general dimensions can be identified for the IS/IT sub-organization, in the same fashion as has been done for the organization as a whole.

After an initial discussion about the concept of IS/IT strategic alignment, this chapter opens up a novel debate about IS/IT-related contexts, by means of an exercise aimed at converting the language of general corporate governance into the language of IS/IT corporate governance. This is carried out by means of an exposition about context dimensions, where three types of general context dimensions (strategic, attitudinal and structural) are converted into IS/IT corporate governance dimensions. In Chapter Five we touched upon the issue of context dimensions, when the managerial values put forward by Bartlett and Ghoshal (1993) and Ghoshal and Bartlett (1994) – stretch, discipline, trust, support – were discussed. In this chapter, this discussion is broadened to other formulations of context dimensions, including one of the few attempts to pinpoint values or context dimensions in the IS/IT arena. We refer to Ciborra et al.'s (2000) pioneering suggestion of three dimensions specific to IS/IT, namely 'care', 'hospitality' and 'cultivation'.

A COMMENT ON THE OFF MODEL OF STRATEGIC ALIGNMENT

Earl (1989:69) suggests that 'no single IS strategy formulation will work' and argues that strategic development of IS/IT should follow not one but a 'multiple' methodology. Such methodology would be made up of a three-pronged approach: top-down, bottom-up and inside-out. The top-down approach is aimed at clarifying the business strategy in terms of IS needs and policies. The bottom-up method is evaluative in nature and is aimed at understanding current investments in IT and their impacts on the business, in terms of results and use. Finally, the aim of the 'inside-out' approach is to identify opportunities afforded by existing or new information technologies which may bring new strategic options to the business.

Starting from this early foundation of IS/IT strategy formulation, Earl (1996) has put forward the Organizational Fit Framework (OFF) which can be seen in Figure 7.1. OFF uses four major processes which provide the linkages needed in order to create alignment or fit among the corresponding four strategic domains. The strategic domains, which provide the strategic contents, are: Business Strategy, Information Systems (IS) Strategy, Informa-

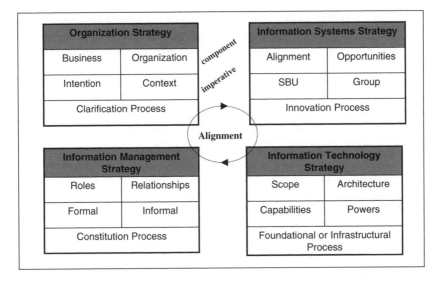

Source: Earl (1996).

Figure 7.1   The Organizational Fit Framework (OFF) alignment model

tion Technology (IT) Strategy and Information Management (IM) Strategy. Each strategic domain is divided up into two key *components*, which are subsets of that particular domain and two *imperatives*, which are important factors that should be taken into account. For example, the components of IT strategy are *scope* and *architecture* and its imperatives are *capability* and *powers*.

Starting with the *Organizational Strategy* domain, this comprises two major components: the business strategic choices as translated into its competitive positioning and the business strategic *intent*, i.e. the organization's 'crystallization of purpose' and its 'criterion in making choices' (Earl, 1996:492). The second component refers to the organization's structural choices, i.e. its hierarchical structure and its control systems, as well as the softer component of its internal *context*, i.e. its management style and its culture. These are components which must be known before embarking on IS/IT strategic development. Hence, knowing and being well informed about the organization's strategy is what Earl calls the *clarification process*.

The second domain is the *IS Strategy*, comprising as its key components, *alignment* and *opportunity*. Alignment is achieved at the level of the strategic business unit, through a variety of techniques, such as critical success factors (Rockart, 1979), or through structural forms such as IS/IT steering committees (Ward and Griffiths, 1996), among others. The objective of the *alignment* component is to keep IT applications aligned with business needs. *Opportunity* refers to the search for more innovative uses of the technology, a task which should be situated at group level. The objective here is to take advantage of the permanent 'push' from the business platforms (Zmud, 1988) in order to identify, in the marketplace, new technology-based enablers of business innovation. The process associated with the IS strategy is the *innovation process*.

The *IT Strategy* encompasses two key elements: *scope* and *architecture*. Scope is concerned with the types of technologies which the organization uses or should use and architecture is concerned with the framework which shapes and controls the IT infrastructure. The imperative related to scope is the capability or the skills, knowledge and activities needed to exploit the technology competently. As regards the architecture, the imperative is the organizational powers needed to implement and control the infrastructure. The process associated with the IT strategy is the *foundation process*, in the sense that the organization's IT architecture lays the technological foundations for all other IT/IS-related activities. This process is a joint consequence of the *inside-out* and of the *bottom-up* approaches to IS strategy, discussed by Earl (1989) in his earlier work.

Finally, the *Information Management* (IM) strategy. Earl (1996) argues that the IM strategy is the *keystone* of the information systems strategy framework. This, it is claimed, is due to the fact that 'IM strategy questions never seem to die, partly perhaps because both technology and organization are constantly changing' (ibid., p. 487). The components of IM strategy are *roles* and *relationships*. The former, according to Earl, refer to who has what formal responsibility and authority in managing IS-related resources. The latter, although not explicitly defined, refers to informal interpersonal relationships among the stakeholders involved in the IS/IT governance process. Associated with the IM strategy domain, we find Earl's *constitution process*, which is explained as follows (1996:498):

> The output linkages from the IM strategy domain can be described as the processes of constitution. Instead of organizing and managing IS, people now talk of 'governance' of the IS function, perhaps in recognition of the many stakeholders, including external ones. Constitution is offered as a noun to describe this process. It can influence the setting of the organization's strategy, for example, when tensions or fault-lines in design of the host organization become manifest as IM issues. It can affect the capability and effectiveness of IS strategy-making, for example, in encouraging teamwork and partnership. It can influence the quality of IT strategic decisions, and the subsequent buy-in to them, by education, development and propaganda programmes.

IS/IT corporate governance is a useful concept because it creates a distinction *vis-à-vis* the daily management of IS/IT-related routines, sometimes seen as something detached from the dynamics of the organization. Monks and

Minow (1995:1) define corporate governance as 'the relationship among various participants in determining the direction and performance of corporations'. The primary participants in corporate governance are the shareholders, the management (led by the chief executive officer) and the board of directors, in addition to a second line of participants, made up of employees, customers, suppliers and the community. The key objectives of corporate governance are all concerned with coordination and alignment – 'alignment of information, incentives and capacity to act and alignment of responsibilities and authorities of all the various constituencies to achieve the optimal conditions for growth and renewal' (ibid., p. 257).

Hence, the notion of IS/IT corporate governance must be based, in the first instance, upon the roles and relationships of all the players involved in the process and Earl (1996) deserves credit for bringing this distinction to the realm of IS/IT strategic alignment. While finding the notion of an *IS/IT constitution process* based on IS/IT corporate governance very innovative, we have trouble agreeing with the proposition that we can strategically plan such a process (thus, the 'IM strategy'). Earl claims that the IM strategy and the *constitution process* are made up of roles and relationships. If roles are strictly confined to their formal aspects we may accept the idea of a strategy, but regarding human relationships, how can they be confined to 'a strategy'? And, above all, what is the role for management in Earl's framework? What guidelines can be offered for the action of managers? Is action important?

The problem with Earl's (1996) formulation of the *constitution process*, made up of formal roles and informal relationships, is that it has not been articulated how such roles are formed or what influences such relationships. Roles and relationships do not exist in a cultural vacuum. They are guided and shaped by values. IS/IT-related values are the constitutive forces which jointly establish an IS/IT-related context. Such forces start with the most basic constitutive forces of any social group – language and languaging (von Krogh and Roos, 1995) and emotions and emotioning (Maturana, 1988), and find expression in the relationships embedded in organizational roles. Thus, it follows that it is through managerial action and through the shaping of an IS/IT-related organizational context that alignment can be achieved. Alignment can only happen if a climate of cooperation exists, conducive to the types of relationships needed for the alignment mechanisms to work.

Earl (1996) himself raises doubts about the appropriateness of the current conceptions of IS/IT alignment:

> it is through organizations that strategies are made and thus naïve, mechanistic and simply aligned organization designs may not provide the adaptation, creativity and entrepreneurship that strategy-making requires (ibid., p. 488); if information flows have to cross internal and external boundaries and information resources be shared by all, should some elements of information strategy be

above or somewhat removed from a current conceptualization of alignment? (ibid., p. 490).

In spite of such doubts, Earl's argumentation does not show signs of an action orientation and this is the reason why the *constitution process* is placed on the same level as the other three, in the OFF model. Although useful as check-list headings, the *clarification, innovation* and *foundation* processes are very different in nature to the *constitution process*. The first three emanate from business-led or managerial-choice decisions. In other words, they all result from processes of planning. The constitution process, however, is different because it emanates from socially-based events, i.e. it is a direct consequence of the actions of the people in the organization and their relationships.

The constitution process is both a cause and a consequence of the other three processes, i.e. it has a generating role. Being the *law of all laws*, a constitution should always be in a position to influence all other laws or processes. Thus, placing the constitution process at the centre of the framework and making it interact with the other three processes from a higher level would seem a more appropriate configuration. In Figure 7.2 we suggest an alternative configuration for the OFF model.

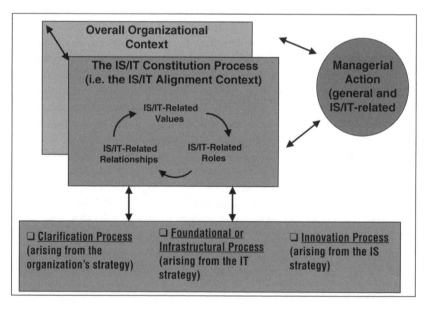

Source: Modified from Earl (1996).

Figure 7.2   A modified version of the Organizational Fit Framework (OFF) alignment model

Moreover, if as suggested by Earl (1996), the *constitution process* is the *cornerstone* of the organization's IS/IT strategy, and if it is to be treated not just as an ordinary process of alignment but as a meta-process with generative capabilities, then we may conclude that the *IS/IT constitution process* not only exerts decisive influence on the organization's alignment capabilities but is also a powerful means of introducing important changes in the organization's overall context or cultural knowledge dimension (see Chapter Four). Hence, the feedback effect from the three strategic processes – clarification, innovation and foundational/infrastructural – on the constitution process and from this back to the overall organizational context, as shown in Figure 7.2.

THE INTERLOCKING OF THE ORGANIZATION'S IS/IT INFRASTRUCTURE AND ITS CULTURAL KNOWLEDGE SUPERSTRUCTURE

In the three dimensional model presented and discussed in Chapter Four we saw that the organization's cultural knowledge is an extra-subjective and self-transcending dimension, made up of rules and resources which go beyond the subjectivity of each individual while governing the collective behaviour of all the individuals in the organization. We also saw that it could be described as a *basho* or a 'platform where [cultural] knowledge is created, shared and exploited, functioning as a medium for the resource concentration of the organization knowledge and of the individuals who own and create such knowledge' (Nonaka et al., 2001:19). A part of the rules and resources that makes up the cultural knowledge dimension has had a new input in the last 30 years or so, in the shape of the IS/IT infrastructure.

The information or IS/IT infrastructure is defined as a bundle of data/ information processing and communication capabilities shared by the large majority of the company's organizational units and usually managed by the information systems/technology department. Such capacities include all the components and imperatives contained within the dimensions of Earl's (1996) model of alignment, namely:

1. the human resources, with the necessary technical and management knowledge and skills as well as the framework of policies, rules, procedures and methodologies which guide their activity (i.e. the Information Management and Organizational Strategy dimensions).
2. the company's data communications networks, its computer equipment, including mainframes, microprocessor-based servers, database management software and all the PCs (i.e. the Information Technology dimension).

3. the applicational infrastructure, that is, the group of software applica-
    tions which address the business needs of the company, as well as the
    data contained in the software applications and its management (i.e. the
    Information Systems dimension).

The IS/IT infrastructure is comparable to a public infrastructure which addresses the community's basic needs for transportation (roads, bridges, railway
lines, etc). As it happens with a country's transport infrastructures, the information infrastructure is built through successive acquisitions of hardware, software,
network equipment and organizing structures. Over time, the information infrastructure becomes structurational regarding the entirety of the organization's
activities. This structurational characteristic applies both ways: either as an
enhancer or as an inhibitor of any new activities in the organization.

Seen from this perspective, the information infrastructure acquires a role
similar to the cultural superstructure, i.e. the invisible force that shapes and
defines each organization. As we have argued in Chapter Four, the *cultural
knowledge dimension* is formed from the bottom up through the interactions
of organizational members, starting from the interpersonal level and evolving
through the intra-group and inter-group levels. In embodying the organizing
process, the organization's members communicate and exchange information
about and through the existing infrastructure of information systems and
technologies. In this way, the technological infrastructure sets the pace for
the organization, not only in terms of the language that is adopted but also in
terms of what is or is not acceptable, in terms of business undertakings. In
other words, the organization's reality construction becomes, unavoidably,
dependent upon all the technological artefacts that it acquires and imple-
ments, throughout its history.

Star and Ruhleder (1996:113) characterize this tight interlocking of the
organization's IS/IT infrastructure and its cultural knowledge superstructure
in the following eight points:

1. Embeddedness. Infrastructure is usually sunk into other structures: so-
    cial or technological.
2. Transparency. Infrastructure is transparent in use in the sense that it does
    not have to be reinvented each time or assembled for each task.
3. Reach and scope, which may be either spatial or temporal. Infrastructure
    has reach beyond a single event or geographical site.
4. Learned as part of membership. Strangers and outsiders encounter infra-
    structure as a target object to be learned about. New participants acquire
    a natural familiarity with these objects as they become members.
5. Links with conventions of practice. Infrastructure shapes and is shaped
    by conventions of a community of practice (e.g. the day-night volumes

of communication flows which affect and is affected by telcos' rates and market needs).
6. Embodiment of standards. Infrastructure tends towards standardization due to the need to interface with other infrastructures and tools.
7. Built on an installed base. Infrastructure does not grow de novo; it has to face the 'inertia of the installed base' and has to live with its strengths and limitations.
8. Visible upon breakdown. Infrastructure is normally invisible but it becomes visible when it breaks down.

Based on the discussion and the arguments presented so far we are in a position to propose, at this juncture, a new definition of IS/IT strategic alignment. As we will see below, it is a definition founded not on descriptive assumptions about strategies, linkages between strategies or strategic implementation order, but on organizational dynamics. Also, it is a definition based on the assumption that that which needs to be aligned – the IS/IT infrastructure – is not an exogenous entity, but an endogenous body totally interwoven into the social fabric of the organization. Lastly, the definition rests on the assumption that alignment is a process of change that evolves with the organization, like so many other processes, such as the introduction of a new product range, the implementation of a new set of human resources policies or the appointment of a new CEO.

> IS/IT strategic alignment is a continuous process of organizational learning and change strongly influenced by IS/IT-related organizational contexts shaped by IS/IT-related managerial values contained within IS/IT-related managerial action and leading to the co-evolution of the organization's strategy and the processes of infusion and diffusion of information technology artefacts into the organization.

At the core of this definition is the notion of IS/IT-related organizational contexts. So, the first step to take in order to operationalize it is to dissect such a notion, starting with organizational contexts in general and then focusing on IS/IT contexts in particular.

ORGANIZATIONAL CONTEXT DIMENSIONS

In Figure 7.2 it is also shown that the IS/IT constitution process is a subsector within the wider organizational context. In view of the fact that IS/IT alignment is one of the key concerns, if not *the* key concern of IS/IT corporate governance in large organizations (Norton, 2002), the context of IS/IT strategic alignment has to have much in common with the context of corporate governance in general. In order to function effectively, IS/IT corporate governance needs, perhaps more so than other functional areas, a context or climate of cooperation. Other functional areas in organizations also have contexts, which can be called constitutive or generative and which become instrumental in their governance. For example, the marketing function tries to instil a context where 'customer is king' as the key value and production tries to create a quality ethos by insisting on messages such as 'right first time'.

IS/IT corporate governance too needs specific IS/IT-related values, which will bring together the various stakeholders around the common aim of strategically aligning IS/IT. This being the case, the managerial action and managerial values associated with the IS/IT strategic alignment context cannot be divorced from the managerial action and managerial values prevalent in the organization as a whole. Thus, it makes sense to start the investigation into the managerial/organizational values associated with IS/IT strategic alignment, from the managerial/organizational values associated with organizations in general.

Organizational context or climate formation are part of a long tradition mainly in the organizational behaviour discipline but also in some sectors of strategic management. The notions of organizational climate and organizational context overlap to a great extent. Authors from industrial economics or strategic management tend to talk of context instead of climate but the contents of the two notions tend to be exactly the same. According to Schneider (1975; 1990) climate is a manifestation of the behaviour of a particular occupational group within the organization, hence *a* climate or *a* context could be taken to be virtually the same as *a* sub-culture. Schneider stresses that climates (or contexts) are an organizational means for *communicating meaning* and Falcione, Sussman and Herden (1987) also emphasize the relevance of communication in explaining the formation of the organization's climate (see also Chapter Four).

In Chapter Five we have also examined organizational values or key dimensions of quality management when discussing the work of Bartlett and Ghoshal (1993) and Ghoshal and Bartlett (1994) on managerial action and organizational context. In the present chapter, we bring together this discussion with the material on context or climate dimensions. What are context dimensions? Context dimensions can be understood as the messages and meta-messages which are transmitted or communicated to organizational members explicitly or implicitly and might be perceived consciously or which might impinge on perceivers unconsciously or subliminally (Falcione, Sussman and Herden, 1987).

The organizational context or climate research tradition has tried to establish the notion of general context dimensions, that is, dimensions that are most likely to induce the creation of a favourable or supportive organizational context for improved organizational performance in most organizational setups. As part of this tradition, Bartlett and Ghoshal (1993) and Ghoshal and Bartlett (1994) have put forward four general context dimensions, i.e. stretch, discipline, trust, support. Falcione, Sussman and Herden (1987) have also suggested a small number of universal context dimensions, i.e. autonomy, [degree of] structure, rewards and consideration, warmth and support.

Looking at both sets of dimensions there seems to be considerable overlap between them, i.e. 'structure' and 'rewards' contains elements of 'stretch'; 'autonomy' and 'consideration, warmth and support' overlap with 'trust' to a certain extent; 'structure' contains elements of 'discipline'; and 'consideration, warmth and support' integrates much of the 'support' dimension. Such overlap holds true when the comparison is extended to organizational climate or context dimensions identified by other authors.

In Table 7.1 we carry out a comparative exercise concerning the work of the seven authors or sets of authors writing about context dimensions or related topics. The first three (Litwin and Stringer, 1968; Likert and Likert, 1976; Falcione, Sussman and Herden, 1987) approach organizational context mainly from a psychological perspective. One author (Norhaug, 1993) takes a human resources outlook and the remaining three (Ghoshal and Bartlett, 1994; Nonaka and Takeuchi, 1995 and von Krogh, Ichijo and Nonaka, 2000) approach context dimensions from a managerial/strategic perspective.

A detailed comparative analysis between the dimensions proposed by each of the seven sets of authors will not be attempted here. In the rows of Table 7.1 a certain degree of matching of dimensions has been attempted, but it is clear how difficult such a task might become if an exact matching was to be attempted. Different authors start from different assumptions and have different definitions of the key dimensions. The result is that each author has his or her slightly different conception of organizational climate or context and of its formation process. Nevertheless, looking at the table one might say that there is some consensus among the seven sets of authors regarding the dimensions' contents as well as three major dimensions types – strategic, attitudinal and structural. The column by Ghoshal and Bartlett (1994) is shaded to indicate that the context dimensions put forward by these authors have been taken as a reference point for some comparative analysis as well as for the translation into IS/IT-related values in the next section.

Nordhaug (1993) has investigated the structural conditions determined by historical factors which facilitate or inhibit learning in organizations. That author makes a distinction between macro- and micro-level barriers to learning in organizations, explaining that micro-level barriers comprise intrapersonal and interpersonal factors. The micro-level barriers are grouped into issues such as current competence, practice opportunities, individual opportunism, relationships between employees and the functioning of groups. Although these factors reflect many of the issues which other authors have discussed

Table 7.1 Organizational context dimensions

Major dimensions identified in the literature		Litwin and Stringer (1968)	Likert (1976)	Falcione, Sussman and Herden (1987)	Nordhaug (1993)	Ghoshal and Bartlett (1994)	Nonaka and Takeuchi (1995)	Von Krogh, Ichijo and Nonaka (2000)
Strategic		Identity Standards Risks	Leadership Goals			Stretch	Intention Fluctuation and creative chaos	Courage
Attitudinal		Responsibility Rewards Conflict Warmth Support	Control Motivation	Rewards Autonomy Consideration/ Warmth/ Support		Discipline Trust Support	Autonomy	Lenience in judgment Mutual trust Active empathy Access to help
Structural		Structure	Communication Decision making	Structure	Macro-level factors		Redundancy of information Requisite variety	

under the 'attitudinal' dimension, they have not been conceived as context dimensions and for this reason they have not been listed.

The same, however, is not the case concerning what Nordhaug calls the macro-level barriers and which have many equivalents in the structural dimensions of organizational context, discussed by four of the other sets of authors, i.e. Litwin and Stringer (1968), Likert and Likert (1976), Falcione, Sussman and Herden (1987) and Nonaka and Takeuchi (1995). Hence, we have retained Nordhaug's macro-level barriers in our table of context dimensions, under the structural dimension category. These macro-level barriers will be detailed below.

Still on the structural dimension, we can see that two sets of authors do not include it in their theories of organizational context (Ghoshal and Bartlett, 1994 and von Krogh, Ichijo and Nonaka, 2000). In our view, the reason why Ghoshal and Bartlett do not mention structure is that their whole theory is geared towards explaining how structure is more informal than formal and how in successful companies structure is replaced by a *matrix state of mind*, i.e. a network of vertical (formal) and horizontal (informal) roles (or processes). This type of new informal structure, enabled by organizational values, is what matters. And if the informal structure works, the formal structure becomes less important. In the case of von Krogh, Ichijo and Nonaka, their objective was to characterize *care* as the key condition for creating enabling contexts. They relate enabling contexts to the concept of *ba* (see Chapter Four) and describe them as something that combines physical space, virtual space (e-mail, internet, etc.) and mental space (emotions, shared experiences, etc.), in a 'network of interactions, determined by the care and trust of participants' (p. 49).

Although writing from different epistemological standpoints, the notions of enabling contexts put forward by Ghoshal and Bartlett (1994) and von Krogh, Ichijo and Nonaka (2000) are quite similar, in the sense that both sets of authors emphasize the extra-subjective component of organizational structure (i.e. a matrix state of mind in the case of Ghoshal and Bartlett and a network of interactions in the case of the second set of authors). As regards the conditions behind the formation of enabling contexts, their thinking is also quite similar. For example, Ghoshal and Bartlett (1994) define *stretch* as 'the attribute of an organization's context that induces its members to voluntarily strive for more, rather than less ambitious objectives' (p. 100), while von Krogh, Ichijo and Nonaka (2000) explain *courage* as an attribute that becomes visible when 'allowing fellow group members or even themselves to experiment' (ibid., p. 54). Although exhibiting different emphases, these two dimensions point in a similar direction and can both be classified as part of a strategic leadership category.

In the strategic category of context dimensions, we also find *intention* and *fluctuation/creative chaos* from the work of Nonaka and Takeuchi (1995) on enabling conditions for organizational knowledge creation. Both are complementary to the *stretch* and *courage* dimensions discussed above. While *intention* is described as 'an organization's aspiration to its goal' (p. 74), *fluctuation* is explained as 'an interruption of our habitual, comfortable state of being' (p. 79), thus occasioning a sense of crisis and increased tension in the organization, referred to as *creative chaos*.

In view of their interest on a new organizational structure (i.e. the hypertext organization), Nonaka and Takeuchi (1995) place more emphasis on structural dimensions than the previous two sets of authors. Hence, they develop the theme of organizational communication through the introduction of the *redundancy of information* dimension put forward as a way of 'promoting the sharing of tacit knowledge because individuals can sense what others are trying to articulate' (ibid., p. 81). Also, they put forward the *requisite variety* dimension, after one of Ashby's laws of systems. Translated into organizational language it is described as a means 'to maximize variety for everyone within the organization, through the fastest access to the broadest variety of necessary information going through the fewest steps' (p. 82, with modifications).

IS/IT-RELATED CONTEXTS AS THE FOUNDATION OF IS/IT STRATEGIC ALIGNMENT

The problem we have now is to see how far such general context dimensions can be appropriately adapted to a new construct: the IS/IT organizational context. In the remainder of this chapter, we propose a new framework for IS/IT management and governance, based on the existing literature on organizational context dimensions and featuring key five dimensions: *IS/IT Intent, IS/IT Discipline, IS/IT Trust, IS/IT Support* and *IS/IT Structural Factors*.

We have assumed that Ghoshal and Bartlett's (1994) three attitudinal dimensions – discipline, trust and support – are general enough to be applicable to any sub-organizational context. Hence, they should also be applicable to the corporate governance of IS/IT, i.e. *IS/IT Discipline, IS/IT Trust* and *IS/IT Support*. In addition, we have assumed that IS/IT context must also be characterized by a strategic dimension, which has been named *IS/IT Intent*, and by a structural dimension, labelled as *IS/IT Structural Factors*. The key attributes of the five IS/IT context dimensions and the corresponding support from the literature are summarized in Tables 7.2 through to 7.6. We start with *IS/IT Intent*.

IS/IT Intent

Table 7.2   IS/IT context dimension: IS/IT intent

IS/IT Context Dimension Attributes

- IS/IT-related strategic visions (Cultivation)
- IS/IT-related collective commitment
- Personal meaning of IS/IT-related issues (Hospitality)
- IS/IT creative chaos (Courage)

Support from the literature		

Grassroots of IS/IT
Ciborra (1994)
● Value bricolage
  strategically
● Design tinkering
● Thrive on gradual
  breakthroughs
 	
IS/IT Managerial Values
Ciborra et al. (2000)
● Care
● Hospitality
● Cultivation
	Intention
	Nonaka and Takeuchi (1995)
	● Organization's aspirations
	● Standards or visions
	● Collective commitment
	
	Creative Chaos
	Nonaka and Takeuchi (1995)
	
	Courage
	Von Krogh, Ichijo and Nonaka
	(2000)
		Stretch
		Ghoshal and Bartlett
		(1994)
		● Shared ambition
		● Collective identity
		● Personal meaning

The IS/IT function at corporate level has strong strategic implications as it has been recognized by many authors, there existing consensus to the effect that the strategic dimension of IS/IT concerns the capability of IS/IT for leveraging the firm's competitive strength (Galliers and Baker, 1994; Ward and Griffiths, 1996; Earl, 1996; Applegate et al., 1999). But the strategic dimension of IS/IT cannot be divorced from the kind of strategic thinking and strategic intent, which exists in the firm in general. Strategic management theorists say that corporate strategic thinking and intent should be widely diffused throughout the organization. Such thinking and intent include many aspects related to the formulation and implementation of the business strategy and each of these aspects has its own strategic angle. For example, marketing or human resources management have strategic dimensions which, while a part of the overall strategic thinking and intent in the firm, also have their own specificities.

Thus, in order to define the contours of an organizational context favourable to IS/IT strategic alignment, we have to start with something akin to strategy, strategic thinking or strategic intent. Strategic thinking can be thought of as something diffused throughout the organization but with an integrating power: 'the outcome of strategic thinking is an integrated perspective of the enterprise, a not-too-precisely articulated vision of direction' (Mintzberg, 1994:108). On the other hand, Hamel and Prahalad (1989) have coined the expression *strategic intent* as a way of overcoming the older and static notion that firms should engage in strategic management in order to obtain 'strategic fit' in relation to the environment. They argue that strategic intent 'establishes the criterion the organization will use to chart its progress' (p. 64). Thus, strategic intent seems to accommodate also the notion of strategic thinking, while giving it a more precise signification.

As information technology applications get more and more infused and diffused throughout the organization and decision making related to IS/IT gets ever more decentralized, corporate strategic thinking will gradually start to encompass also a new type of strategic concern: IS/IT strategic thinking or intent. For the sake of brevity, we will use the shorter form – *IS/IT intent* – as the strategic dimension of IS/IT organizational context. We use the word intent and not intention because the former has a stronger connotation in the management literature with strategy or strategic thinking. However, we do not think that there is much difference in the meaning of intent and intention. Nonaka (1994:17) who takes a more individual-level approach, argues that 'intention is concerned with how individuals form their approach to the world and try to make sense of their environment'. This is not very far from Hamel and Prahalad's (1989:64) notion of intent when applied to the organizational level. What is important is to discover what attributes contribute towards the formation of intent or intention. In their theory of organizational knowledge, Nonaka and Takeuchi (1995:74–5) have identified three attributes of intention as one set of the enabling conditions for the creation of organizational knowledge: the organization's 'aspiration to its goals'; organizational 'standards or visions' and something capable of fostering 'collective commitment'.

Intention as a dimension of organizational context also has some similarities with Ghoshal and Bartlett's (1994) notion of 'stretch'. According to these authors, stretch is composed of three attributes: shared ambition, collective identity and personal meaning. Shared ambition is similar to Nonaka and Takeuchi's organizational aspiration to the organization's goals. Collective identity has similarities with collective commitment and both dimensions are intimately related to organizational purpose. Purpose creates both identity and commitment around a common cause. However, not all such dimensions can be applied to IS/IT corporate governance in a sensible way. It is not realistic to say, for example, that the organization should have a shared ambition or an aspiration in relation to its information technology/systems' goals.

As regards Ghoshal and Bartlett's (1994) stretch dimension we do not consider it to be directly applicable, as a dimension label, to the IS/IT organizational context. Stretch is pitched at a very general level, dealing with the personal aspirations of individuals and, although it is seen as a way of making individuals 'contribute to the overall purpose of the organization' (ibid., p. 100), this dimension lacks, in a more specific environment, a more positive indication of an intent or a feeling of knowing where one wants to be (e.g. in the IS/IT corporate governance context). In other words, by generally building up stretch we may have organizational members who contribute to the overall purpose, but, if we are considering the special case of IS/IT context, we need to be sure that such purpose exists in the first place. Hence, while considering the attributes of shared ambition and collective identity as less relevant in the case of the IS/IT organizational context, the attribute of personal meaning is seen as very relevant.

The content of the *IS/IT intent* dimension also implies that stakeholders should be very clear about the IS/IT-related criterion that the organization will use to chart its progress. IS/IT intent has to do, above all, with the awareness, the understanding, the action and the proaction from all the firm's managers regarding the role of IS/IT in helping to achieve their own business objectives and, ultimately, the firm's strategic aims. According to this definition, in a firm where managers have IS/IT intent, the relationships which characterize the corporate governance of IS/IT will be different from a firm where managers do not have or have less IS/IT intent. Top and senior management should be very clear about the purpose of IS/IT in their particular business (Rockart, 1988; Henderson, 1990). Hence, the suggestion that *IS/IT-related collective commitment* is also an important attribute of IS/IT intent.

The organization's standards or visions are very relevant for the IS/IT organizational context. Keen (1991) argues that it is no longer enough for top managers to be aware or just to have a business vision that links IS/IT and strategic positioning. Now top managers have to do more, i.e. they have to be involved in driving forward the planning of the IS/IT infrastructure. Dutta (1996) reinforces this point by saying that even though IS/IT can be physically outsourced, the management of IS/IT must always be insourced and top managers have to be involved in spite of their lack of familiarity with the new technologies. However, the question of familiarity or knowledge about IS/IT does not seem to be the issue. Rockart (1995) expresses the view that what the CEO knows about IS/IT is not important; what is important is what he or she and other members of the top management team *think* about IS/IT, its role in the organization and their roles in planning and managing it. So, we can say that the *IS/IT-related strategic visions* are an important component of IS/IT intent.

Schein (1992a:93), in a study of the role of the CEO in the management of IS/IT concludes that CEOs find themselves lost in the midst of the increased complexity brought about by IT and reports that they 'acknowledge that future generations of CEOs may be able to take a much more optimistic and proactive stance towards IS/IT'. Building upon the work of Schein, Feeny et al. (1992:14) suggest that the CEO's attitude towards IT can be changed 'through some (planned or unplanned) action, which affects his or her personal experience of IT, his or her perception of the industry relevance of IS/IT and his or her attitude to the needed level of business change'. Thus, it is evident that the role of top management is not only crucial in the management of the IS/IT function, but also that such a role depends very much on top management's attitudes towards IS/IT. One of such attitudes, also related to IS/IT strategic visions, is *cultivation* (Ciborra et al., 2000).

Itami and Numagami (1992), in conceptualizing the interaction between technology and strategy talk about 'strategy cultivating technology' and 'technology driving the cognition of strategy' as the final stages in the evolution of such interaction. In the case of strategy cultivating technology, such evolutionary stage is summed up as the effect of technology accumulation, 'with much greater future potentials than necessary to met current needs' in the 'pursuit of contemporaneous fit between technology and current strategy' (ibid., p. 122). This line of thought in management research is supported by the resource-based approach to strategy, where the major tenet is that current strategy should be formulated with the accumulation of invisible assets and core competencies as basic goals (see Chapter Five). Itami and Numagami's final stage is focused on the effects of current technology upon the collective perception of future strategy. At this stage, strategy cannot be separated from the cognitive processes induced by the technology because technology has become all important and 'not only constrains what the firm can do technically, but frames and drives the way people think' (ibid., p. 131).

The formation of the IS/IT context in an organization depends, to some extent, upon the IS/IT-related personal experience and skills of the top managers who happen to be in charge. Some present-day top managers have had previous experience with IT applications, either as users or as managers and this is usually beneficial to the IS/IT-related responsibilities of the post. IS/IT-related experience is an important contribution to the development of *personal meaning* regarding the role of IS/IT in the business, now and in the future. Personal meaning is also important in view of the special nature of the IS/IT context, regarding its strong technical component. Thus, it seems that there should be some *personal meaning* involved regarding the organizational significance of IS/IT-related issues. Such meaning is reflected in new managerial attitude towards this IT-dominated angle of the organization's corporate governance, an attitude close to hospitability, as discussed by Ciborra et al. (2000). Hence, *IS/IT intent* should include *hospitality*, an attribute which enables managers to host the (IT) stranger and to cope with the ambiguity brought about through the introduction of new IT artefacts in their organization.

Another important attribute which characterizes the strategic dimension of IS/IT-related context is *creative chaos*. Creative chaos is closely related to the requirements put forward by Ciborra (1994) for innovation related to IS/IT strategic development in organizations and which he has called the 'grassroots of IS/IT'. To *value bricolage strategically* means to create the space for trying out creative IT applications embedded in everyday work. To *design tinkering* is an attitude that leads managers to plan and manage the experimentation process, for example, by means of prototyping and closely monitoring the results of utilization of IT applications by end-users. To *thrive on gradual breakthroughs* is a state of mind which should be associated with IS/IT strategic governance. It means to accept and not to reject the deviations, inconsistencies or mismatches to old organizational routines brought about by IS/IT and gradually bring about the necessary reorganization and process reengineering.

These attributes might be collectively named as creative chaos. Creative chaos, in turn, is related to the general dimension of *courage*. As discussed above, courage is an attribute that is related to the costs and benefits of allowing experimentation to take place in the work setting. Other aspects of courage involve exposing oneself to a process of scrutiny and voicing one's opinion in defence of an uncertain proposal for innovation (von Krogh, Ichijo and Nonaka, 2000). Thus, creative chaos, requires courage on the part of managers in view of the highly risky business of experimenting with IT applications.

IS/IT-Related Discipline

Having made an argument in favour of IS/IT intent, now we go back to our starting assumption, i.e. that the other three dimensions – discipline, trust and support – are general enough to be applicable to any sub-organizational context, including the IS/IT corporate governance context. We will work towards this by following mainly Ghoshal and Bartlett's (1994) analysis of the attributes of each of the above dimensions and see how far they can be adapted to the case of IS/IT corporate governance. Whenever we feel that it is appropriate, we will bring in the work of the other authors writing on climate dimensions and to whom we have already referred. Let us start with IS/IT-related Discipline.

According to Ghoshal and Bartlett, the key attributes of discipline are (1) performance measures; (2) fast-cycle feedback and (3) consistent sanctions. Fast-cycle feedback and consistent sanctions do not seem to be applicable to the special case of IS/IT corporate governance. Consistent sanctions is a generic dimension, which applies to human resources management in a very general way, and there is nothing applicable specifically to IS/IT corporate

Table 7.3   IS/IT context dimension: IS/IT-related discipline

---

IS/IT Context Dimension Attributes

- Need to respect IS/IT platform standards
- An understanding of business platform needs on the part of IS/IT
- An understanding of IS/IT development constraints on the part of business units

---

Support from the literature

Discipline	Responsibility	Control
Ghoshal and Bartlett (1994)	Litwin and Stringer	Likert and Likert (1976)
• Performance measures	(1968)	• How concentrated are
• Fast-cycle feedback	• The feeling of being	the control functions?
• Consistent sanctions	'your own boss'	

---

governance. Also, fast-cycle feedback does not apply mainly because there can be no fast-cycle feedback as regards most IS/IT corporate governance decisions. At the corporate level feedback is usually of long-term nature, but on single, one-off IS/IT implementation projects, the questions of feedback are very problematic. Establishing useful evaluation criteria for single IS/IT implementation projects is fraught with difficulties (Remenyi and Sherwood-Smith, 1997).

In trying to apply the 'discipline' dimension to the IS/IT corporate governance context, we should first recall what we said in Chapter Two regarding the first two emerging trends in the information systems function. They were as follows:

1. Building and managing the IT infrastructure, i.e. developing a coherent blueprint for a technology platform responsive to present and future business needs.
2. Building and maintaining partnerships between IT specialists and IS/IT users.

The first point to be made is that for an IT infrastructure to be built up and maintained, 'discipline' and 'control' have to be crucial elements. The literature is filled with examples of organizational members resisting standardization for a variety of reasons, e.g. because the IS/IT department is too slow in responding to the business departments' needs, because the particular application which department X wants to purchase does not fit into the company's IT architectural standards and so on. Thus, the first attribute of the discipline dimension is the *need to respect the standards* (both technical and performance) set as part of the organization's IT infrastructure.

The next issue involves also discipline and control and is one of the main sources of conflict between IS/IT personnel and the line departments. It is the issue of the time delays in the development/implementation of IT applications which all organizations experience or have experienced. This issue is yet another manifestation of the 'cultural gap' between IS/IT and business and, as such, is seen from very different perspectives by these two groups of personnel. Litwin and Stringer (1968) have identified 'responsibility' as one of their eight dimensions of climate. According to these authors, responsibility means 'not having to double-check all your decisions; when you have a job, knowing that it is *your* job' (ibid., p. 81).

Thus, in order to achieve discipline, organizational members must first perceive that they have responsibility. According to Ghoshal and Bartlett (1994:97), discipline 'represents a way of life, a norm applicable to all tasks, rather than compliance with a well-defined set of contracts embodied in a company's strategic and operational control tools'. Likert and Likert (1976) highlight 'control', a dimension of climate also related to discipline. These authors argue that in organizations where the control functions are widely shared, discipline is more likely to flourish. If, on the other hand, the control functions are concentrated in a few points in the hierarchy, individual responsibility is not fostered and discipline cannot ensue.

In IS/IT corporate governance, the problems of responsibility and control are crucial dimensions of discipline but they are usually on a collision course with each other. Both IS/IT and line personnel have responsibility and control over their respective functions, but the responsibility and control of the IS/IT function often interferes with the responsibility and control of the line departments. This situation, which explains the conflict mentioned earlier on, is due to the dependence of the line departments upon the performance of the IS/IT department on highly technical issues, such as IS/IT development or maintenance. Thus, for there to be discipline in IS/IT corporate governance, IS/IT personnel have to be highly aware of the needs of the business units and the personnel from the business units have to be aware of the constraints and limitations of the technical tasks involved in IS/IT development and maintenance.

IS/IT-Related Trust

According to Ghoshal and Bartlett (1994), 'individual-level competence is almost as important for creating an environment of mutual trust as the process attributes of fairness and participation' (ibid., p. 101). For these authors, the key attributes of trust are (1) equity; (2) involvement and (3) competence. Equity or fairness are attributes, which are related to the 'conflict' dimension put forward by Litwin and Stringer (1968:82), i.e. the feeling that problems

Table 7.4   IS/IT context dimension: IS/IT-related trust

IS/IT Context Dimension Attributes

- Involvement in IS/IT planning and policy making
- IS/IT skills and competencies
- IS/IT track record in the organization

Support from the literature

Trust	Mutual trust	**Conflict**
Ghoshal and Bartlett (1994)	Von Krogh, Ichijo and	Litwin and Stringer (1968)
• Equity	Nonaka (2000)	• The emphasis placed
• Involvement		on getting problems
• Competence		out in the open

are dealt with openly and honestly and are not systematically avoided or ignored. Although this is a dimension of climate which can have a role in the shaping of the IS/IT context, there is nothing specific enough to make it an IS/IT context dimension. The same is not true regarding involvement or participation.

The problem of participation is crucial in IS/IT corporate governance in view of its highly technical nature as an organizational function. On the one hand, participation is seen as important but, on the other hand, participation is difficult because the issues are too technical. As a result, decision making in IS/IT corporate governance is often regarded as being easier if there is less participation on the part of all the stakeholders. Opting for not involving managers who do not fully understand all the details involved in an IS/IT-related decision is seen as easier than having to brief and even coach them extensively. However, for there to be trust all managers, especially those who are not directly involved with the planning or operation of IS/IT-related resources but are indirectly affected by the decisions taken about such resources, have to be involved.

The second trust-related attribute, which is relevant for the shaping of the IS/IT ethos, is competence or the perception of competence. In IS/IT corporate governance, we might think of the problem of perception of competence in two parts: (1) the perception on the part of all non-IS/IT managers in relation to the competence of IS/IT managers and IS/IT personnel, on business-related issues and (2) the perception on the part of IS/IT managers and IS/IT personnel in relation to the competence of line managers and line personnel on IS/IT-related issues. As regards the first part, the level of mistrust, which exists in relation to the work of IS/IT personnel, is well known in the IS/IT literature (Markus, 1983; Smith and McKeen, 1992; Wang, 1994,

Ward and Peppard, 1996), especially regarding the timeliness of provision of IS/IT-related services. As regards the second part, the issue stems from the fact that non-IS/IT staff increasingly have to take IS/IT-related decisions. Because this transfer of functional responsibilities to line managers is a fairly recent development, the degree of trust or mistrust is not yet well documented in the literature, but experience in consultancy situations have shown that in fact some mistrust may exist on the part of IS/IT managers. In short, in IS/IT corporate governance, the issue of competence seems to be a source of mistrust both on the part of non-IS/IT personnel and of IS/IT personnel.

IS/IT-Related Support

Table 7.5   IS/IT context dimension: IS/IT-related support

IS/IT Context Dimension Attributes
<ul><li>Autonomy in the use of IS/IT resources</li><li>Need for coherent clarification on policy-related issues</li><li>Need for service orientation on IS/IT-related issues</li></ul>

Support from the literature		
Support Ghoshal and Bartlett (1994)<ul><li>Access to resources</li><li>Autonomy</li><li>Guidance and help</li></ul>	**Active empathy** Von Krogh, Ichijo and Nonaka (2000)	**Autonomy** Nonaka and Takeuchi (1995) **Autonomy** Falcione, Sussman and Herden (1987)

The fourth dimension we propose for the IS/IT context construct is *support*. Ghoshal and Bartlett (1994:103) define this dimension as a managerial value that 'induces [organizational] members to lend assistance and countenance to others' and explain that the mechanisms through which such value is achieved are (1) access to resources available to other organizational actors; (2) freedom of initiative at lower levels and (3) personal orientation from senior managers that 'gives priority to providing guidance and help over exercising authority'.

Thus, according to the first two attributes, support seems to depend mostly on the autonomy that the organization gives to individual organizational members. This is consistent with Nonaka and Takeuchi's (1995) notion of autonomy, as one of the key factors behind the development of individual commitment, and also with autonomy as one of the four psychological 'cues' identified by Falcione, Sussman and Herden (1987) in the formation of the organizations' communication climate. Nonaka and Takeuchi (1995) argue that autonomy 'increases the possibility that individuals will motivate themselves to create new knowledge' and also that 'by allowing them to act autonomously, the organization may increase the chance of introducing unexpected opportunities' (ibid., p. 75).

As regards the formation of an IS/IT context, autonomy may be an important attribute but only in a limited way. There is no difference between the level of autonomy required by the stakeholders in IS/IT corporate governance and the level of autonomy required by the stakeholders in any other organizational function, i.e. the IS/IT manager needs autonomy, just as much as the marketing or the operations managers need autonomy. However, there may be a special case as regards one of the stakeholders in IS/IT corporate governance: the line managers. In view of the changing trends in IS/IT management, reviewed in Chapter Two, many of the traditional tasks of the IS/IT function are moving on to the job descriptions of line managers. But transferring responsibilities and autonomy also means transferring power and influence and such processes are never without difficulties and tend to generate a degree of conflict. The struggle for power and influence over IS/IT-related resources is intimately linked to the autonomy of line managers in relation to those resources. Hence, the degree of autonomy that line managers have in IS/IT-related decision making must be an important attribute of *IS/IT-related support*.

Ghoshal and Bartlett's definition of support has much in common with Litwin and Stringer's (1968) climate dimension, also referred to as support. For the later, support is the 'perceived helpfulness of the managers and other employees in the group; emphasis on mutual support from above and below' (ibid., p. 81). Thus, help and guidance are key components of the support construct at the general organizational level, but not exclusively. Help and guidance are also fundamental attributes in the formation of the IS/IT context. The reason for this is, once again, the highly technical nature of the IS/IT function. Top managers need guidance in understanding the policy implications of new IT applications, middle managers need support in deciding which are the best applications to install and end-users need coaching in using new software tools. Such guidance and assistance must come, of course, from information systems managers and staff, but this is not all. As Earl (1996) has argued, *clarification* is also an important form of help and guidance, which must come from the top of the organization to the information systems manager and to the line managers, so as to enable them to formulate and implement IS/IT-related strategies.

The new role of the information systems managers as 'internal consultants' (Cross et al., 1997) has already been identified and discussed in Chapter Two.

Included in this trend is the need for information systems' personnel to acquire better interpersonal skills (Brown and Ross, 1996) so that such a role of internal guidance and coaching can be fulfilled successfully. It must be noted that when identifying dimensions of a particular context or sub-climate in organizations, such dimensions must not be regarded as static, i.e. dimensions and attributes change as the trends in the management of that particular sector change. So, while the trends in the management of the IS/IT function are changing due to changes in the technology and in the organizational processes, new needs for a more supportive ethos are emerging. This means that if a truly *service orientation* of the IS/IT function was not a particularly important dimension of the IS/IT context in the past, in the future it will be one of its key attributes.

Structural IS/IT-Related Factors

In developing the topic of organizational learning at the strategic management level, Normann (1985:222) asks a fundamental question:

> are there any basic overall properties of organizational structure and management that increase the likelihood of an effective strategic action process?

Interpreted in terms of IS/IT corporate governance, what Normann is saying is that IS/IT-related organizational learning must also be related to IS/IT structural features in the organization. Nordhaug (1993) has taken up this issue and has investigated the structural conditions, determined by historical factors which facilitate or inhibit learning in organizations. That author makes a distinction between macro- and micro-level barriers to learning. Above, the micro-level barriers have already been discussed. As regards the other type of barriers discussed by Nordhaug – the macro-level barriers – they are listed in Table 7.6. They are the structural dimensions of organizational context which authors such as Litwin and Stringer (1968), Likert and Likert (1976), Falcione, Sussman and Herden (1987) and Nonaka and Takeuchi (1995) have also discussed.

Nordhaug's first macro-level barriers or structural factor is the work system. This factor includes job design, job development, the rigidity/flexibility of job boundaries, mobility of jobs across organizational units and the opportunities for the development of multi-skills. Related to the work system is the organizational structure as an important dimension of organizational context, especially in what concerns the way that structure 'allows for contact and interaction across jobs, professions, teams and subunits' (ibid., p. 219). All such considerations regarding the way that the work is organized can be synthesized into one question, i.e. does the organizational structure contain good communication mechanisms?

Organizational knowledge and technology

Table 7.6   IS/IT context dimension: IS/IT-related structural factors

---

IS/IT Context Dimension Attributes

- IS/IT-business integrating mechanisms
- IS/IT-related priorities for human resources development
- IS/IT-related incentive system
- Historical technical quality of IT applications

Support from the literature

Macro-level barriers	**Redundancy & Requisite Variety**	**Communication**
Nordhaug (1993)	Nonaka and Takeuchi (1995)	Likert and Likert (1976)
• Work system		
• Incentives system		**Structure**
• Human Resources Development priority		Litwin and Stringer (1968)
• Organizational structure		**Structure**
• Organizational culture		Falcione, Sussman and Herden (1987)

Communication as a dimension of climate had already been supported in the writings of Likert and Likert (1976), Falcione, Sussman and Herden (1987) and Nonaka and Takeuchi (1995). Thus, as the most horizontal of all functional areas, IS/IT corporate governance needs a variety of *structural overlays* (e.g. IT advisory committee, cross-functional job transfers, joint project management) in order to improve communication and achieve integration between the needs of the IT platform and the needs of the business platform (Zmud, 1988; Brown and Ross, 1996).

Other important structural factors, according to Nordhaug (1993), are the priorities for human resources development and the incentives system. Both factors are crucial in terms of IS/IT corporate governance. Being an area with a strong technological slant, the IS/IT function needs to give special attention to the issue of *human resources development*, not necessarily regarding purely technological skills, but regarding hybrid skills in the technology-business interface (Earl, 1989). In relation to the incentives system, Nordhaug (1993) argues that 'in addition to the career system, the compensation system plays a central part concerning acquisition, exchange and application of individually held competencies' (ibid., p. 213).

The *incentives system* too is a special problem for IS/IT corporate governance, again in view of the fact that the IS/IT function has a strong technological slant. Although there may be a trend for this to be less and less a 'special problem', historically IS/IT staff have earned more than other staff in comparable hierarchical positions and, in fact, this situation has contributed towards the 'cultural gap', which we have discussed in Chapter Two (Ward and Peppard, 1996). However, because the incentives system has been a dividing factor, the IS/IT corporate governance in many organizations has tried to reverse this situations by putting a 'freeze' on the salaries of IS/IT staff. Clearly, this has had both positive and negative consequences in terms of the formation of the IS/IT organizational context.

Finally, Nordhaug (1993) includes as a structural factor the organization's culture. While this inclusion may be debatable because culture can be thought of as the consequence and not the cause of these macro-level barriers, Nordhaug makes a point which may be crucial when translated into IS/IT corporate governance terms. He argues '[culture] is itself a repository of past learning and a means through which this learning as well as new knowledge are communicated between individual employees' (ibid., p. 216). This is perhaps more a situational factor than a structural one, but the point which Nordhaug is trying to make is that situational factors can become structural with the passing of time.

Turning now to IS/IT corporate governance, Land (1992) argues that the perceptions in the organization about the technical quality of an IT application is a key factor for the successful outcome of its implementation. Land is referring to a single IT implementation project, but as time passes and the organization builds up knowledge about the 'usual' technical quality (or lack of it) of successive implementation projects, such collective perceptions become part of the organization's culture. Hence, we may say that the *technical quality of IT applications* is a structural factor contributing to the organization's IS/IT ethos which, at first, may be situational but, eventually, becomes structural.

CONCLUSION

IS/IT-related values are not normally considered a relevant part of IS/IT corporate governance and are not usually associated with IS/IT strategic alignment. Traditionally, IS/IT strategic alignment is seen as something that can be planned or charted, by putting forward a rational theory of alignment and then fitting the various types of strategies through the detailing of the required alignment mechanisms. We contend, however, that there is not much value in detailing alignment mechanisms *a priori*. There are so many organizational variables involved, stretched over such a long period of time, that any type of mechanistic framework is virtually impossible to control.

Instead of designing rational alignment frameworks we should concentrate on the organizational context where the alignment is to take place. The operative word, as suggested by Angell and Smithson (1991), would be to achieve an organizational *disposition,* that is an ethos which would be conducive to the desired alignment. In our view, alignment is achieved not through rational planning but by emphasizing action and, especially, managerial action. Ciborra et al. (2000:30) make the following comment:

> Our research shows that the driving force behind alignment in action, as opposed to the one on paper, is a great amount of caring performed by the various actors involved in the design, implementation and use of IT infrastructures (…) Care itself has a structure linked to how we are-in-the-world, articulated in perception, circumspection and understanding processes.

The 'structure' of care that Ciborra is referring to is featured in the model of IS/IT-related context dimensions presented in this chapter. The listing of values or context dimensions which we have put forward forms the structure of the sub-context (the IS/IT sub-context) in the organization where IS/IT alignment is due to take place. The IS/IT-related values or context dimensions which have been described and discussed are meant as a contribution towards the shaping of an attitude of 'care' on the part of managers and in relation to the issue of IS/IT strategic alignment.

Thus, IS/IT alignment is something which is formed by forces which are constitutive or generative, rather like organizational climates or contexts. Such forces are, primarily, shaped by IS/IT-related values, conveyed through IS/IT-related managerial action and materialized by IS/IT-related roles and relationships. Acting through values in the daily execution of organizational functions are the foundations of organizational leadership, according to Schein (1980). Rather than the behaviour of an individual leader, leadership is considered to be *a distributed set of functions.* Such functions can be the articulation and transmission of a basic purpose, the monitoring of progress, supporting, clarifying, testing consensus, rewarding, punishing and so forth. Likewise, IS/IT-related leadership should be seen as a distributed set of IS/IT-related functions, executed in accordance with a set of IS/IT-related values. Functions and values, in turn, strongly influence the roles and the relationships of the stakeholders involved.

8. Notes on IS/IT strategic development

Can we expect 'frameworks' and 'methodologies' to show anything other than the palest shadow of organizational complexity? This dynamic and ambiguous complexity of an organization's future just cannot be reduced to such simplistic data structures, which imply a tidy and convenient homogeneity in organizations that is just not there.

(Angell and Smithson, 1991: 35–6)

INTRODUCTION

In 1991, at the height of the of the Porterian strategic planning era, a book entitled *Information Systems Management: Opportunities and Risks* by Angell and Smithson was published. In it the authors state: 'the myth of "being in control", so readily demonstrated in many failed applications of information technology, illustrates the related folly of believing in rigidly proactive management' (p. 47). The message did not attract much attention at the time and the thinking from Harvard and the MIT on strategic planning of IS/IT has prevailed as the dominant paradigm till now.

But 12 years later, what do we have? More cost-effective use of IS/IT resources? Less IS/IT-related failures in managerial terms? A more friendly attitude towards IS/IT in general, from the managerial cadre? The answer seems to be no to all three questions. The experience of consultancy projects in IS/IT strategy, planning and implementation, at least outside the context of US companies, does show that the results from a great many investments in IS/IT are still very disappointing. The area still lacks credibility in the eyes of decision makers and the main reason for such a state of affairs is the huge gap that remains in place between theory and practice, between tech-oriented and organization-oriented views of systems implementation and between mechanist and organic perspectives of organizational change.

Angell and Smithson suggest, as an alternative strategy for the development of IS/IT, a strategy based on keeping small because small is flexible and small is controllable. The problem, however, is that very often it is not possible to keep small. Constant mergers and acquisitions still make sense in terms of the economics of competitiveness and large public bureaucracies are strongly averse to downsizing and slow to change. The fact of the matter is that although small and flexible is ideal, in the real-life world of management, we have to live with both oversize and lean, flexible organizations. So, the key problem does not seem to be one of organizational size but one of methodological approach. Information systems implementation is a longitudinal issue, not a cross-sectional one which can be solved just with planning methodologies. Information systems need to grow and be developed with the organization, both from a strategic and an operational point of view and this implies a new praxis, not only in IS/IT governance but in corporate governance as well.

In this chapter we hope to contribute towards such new praxes by introducing a new perspective which we have named *IS/IT strategic development (ISSD)* and which is founded upon the various intellectual and academic propositions we have been discussing since Chapter One. The notion of IS/IT strategic development can be given many different interpretations, so it is important that we clarify firstly the premises upon which such a notion is based, from our vantage point.

1. The first premise comes from the definition of 'information system' suggested by various authors for whom the *integration* of the technical and the social components of an information system is the definition's central idea and the crux of the issue (see, for example, Symons' (1991) definition in Chapter One). For IS/IT strategic development the notions of *integration* or *embedding*, implying action over time, continuity, change, learning and growth, are also the *raison d'être* of all IS/IT-related managerial activity.

2. Managerial action, the trend emphasized in Chapter Five as part of a *middle-of-the-road* approach in the spectrum of the strategic management schools of thought, is our second premise. IS/IT strategic development is strongly influenced by such a mid-level approach, reflected in adjectives such as 'multiple', 'eclectic' or 'mixed' to qualify the strategies for IS/IT development and implementation, as highlighted in Chapter Six. *Organizational Holism* is the IS/IT implementation perspective which better accommodates such labels in an attempt to complement a deterministic top-down planning bias and a diffuse bottom-up emergent action trend with a real-life organizational leadership emphasis.

3. The third premise comes from our discussion about the resource-based approach to business economics and strategy in Chapter Five and from the application of this approach to IS/IT strategy and management (Mata et al., 1995). Thus, IS/IT strategic development is founded upon the idea that, unlike the advice from the *Strategic Rationality* school of thought of IS/IT implementation, the key to the attainment of improvements in the effectiveness of organizational processes does not lie in any external

factors but in the building up of internal IS/IT-related managerial competencies (Sambamurthy and Zmud, 1997). Hence, for IS/IT strategic
development, although the external environmental factors are not ignored, the key strategic issues lie in the development of internal IS/
IT-related resources.

THE COMPONENTS OF IS/IT STRATEGIC DEVELOPMENT

Figure 8.1 shows the major components of IS/IT strategic development. In
the remainder of the chapter, each component will be detailed and discussed.
It must be emphasized, however, that the objective of this chapter is not to
supply a detailed description of the methodologies and approaches which
make up ISSD, but to present some theoretical notes towards the implementation of the new idea.

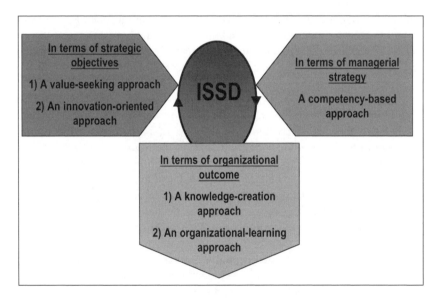

Figure 8.1   The components of ISSD

IS/IT STRATEGIC DEVELOPMENT AS VALUE CREATION

The desired outcome of effective IS/IT strategic development can be thought
of as the ultimate adding of value of IS/IT and its associated internal organi-

zation to the organization's overall effectiveness and strategic objectives (Sprague and McNurlin, 1998). But what does 'adding of value' mean?

One way to approach the question of value is through the concept of the value chain, proposed by Porter (1980; 1985) and which has been applied to IS/IT planning by authors mainly affiliated to the Harvard Business School (Cash et al., 1992; Applegate et al., 1999). This approach, however, is only marginally useful as the basis of a planning methodology and can only work under ideal circumstances. The ideal circumstances refer to the fact that it is virtually impossible to find an organization where the IS/IT infrastructure can be set up from scratch or drastically modified so as to fit with the frequent changes occurring in the value chain and imposed by environmental fluctuations. Besides, such methodologies offer very little in the way of management control. In other words, there is no obvious way to link the recommendations made under the IS/IT plan and the measures of success or failure regarding the technologies and the systems implemented under such a plan.

The lack of a strategic management control tool has been greatly overcome by widespread adoption of the Balanced Scorecard (BSC) methodology. As pointed out in Chapter Two, BSC has arisen as a consequence of a development in strategic management thinking which highlights the company's intellectual capital as the main source of competitive differentiation. Edvinsson and Malone (1997) explain that 'intellectual capital is the possession of the knowledge, applied experience, organizational technology, customer relationships and professional skills that provide Skandia with a competitive edge in the market' (ibid., p. 44). In other words, intellectual capital is made up of the hidden value contained in the host of investments made by the company in human resources development, in the improvement of relations with clients, in the streamlining of its work flows through the optimization of its horizontal process, as well as in its development and innovation efforts which were not necessarily turned into new products. One of the invisible assets which is behind the organization's intellectual capital, and which can be visible through the application of the BSC methodology, is IS/IT strategic development.

Figure 8.2 shows intellectual capital as part of a hierarchy explaining the process of formation of the market value of companies. Intellectual capital is made up of human capital and of structural capital. Human capital is constituted by the knowledge, the attitudes and the competence of the individuals who work in the company and, although it can be considered the raw material of any organization, on its own human capital does not add value. When someone begins to work in a company his or her input in relation to the objectives of the organization is nonexistent. It is only when the person starts to get into the task and to contribute to the work routines that one can say that some human capital exists. One way of thinking about human capital is as the

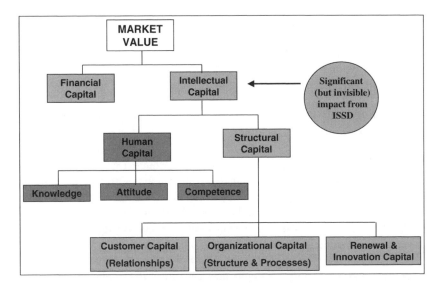

Figure 8.2   The market value hierarchy

result of the amplification of the knowledge created by individual organizational members when they have the opportunity to interact with other individuals in undertaking group work, as has been suggested by Nonaka and Takeuchi (1995). However, for group work to take place some form of organizational structure is needed.

Human capital cannot exist without structural capital. Edvinsson and Malone (1997) suggest that human capital can be compared to the core of a tree trunk while structural capital can be thought of as the layers of timber which grow around the core. With the passing of time, the overlapping layers around the core give the tree firmness and improve its capacity to deal with all kinds of weather. Likewise, structural capital defines the organization's resilience in the form of its capacity for improved effectiveness, competitiveness and survival. It includes the hardware, software, databases, organizational structure, organizational processes procedures and routines, internal innovations, patents, trademarks as well as the relationships with customers. Hence, structural capital (sometimes also known as organizational capital) can be thought of as the ensemble of the invisible assets embedded in the organization's skills, competencies, structures and processes, including all the supporting IS/IT infrastructure.

The goals of the intellectual capital (IC) activity at Skandia, as identified by Edvinsson and Malone (1997), are very closely linked to IS/IT management activity and they are as follows:

1. to identify and enhance the visibility and measurability of intangible assets.
2. to capture such assets, support their packaging and enhance their accessibility by the use of information-sharing technology.
3. to cultivate and channel IC through the development of human resources and IT networking.
4. to promote the adding of value through faster knowledge creation by capitalizing on IC.

The achievement of these goals is controlled through a set of IC indicators which are grouped under the four or five BSC categories: financial, customers, processes, innovation and development, and human resources (in some BSC systems, human resources indicators are left out). The scorecard methodology is essentially a strategic management tool, hence very encompassing in scope. It is meant as a device to communicate organizational results in a very integrated way, meaning that scorecard projects can be adapted to support most kinds of both strategic and operative discussions in modern organizations. The method starts with the sketching of a rough *strategy map* which is no more than a cause-and-effect diagram, inspired by systems thinking (Senge, 1990) and by soft systems methodology (Checkland and Holwell, 1998). An example of a high-level strategy map can be seen in Figure 8.3.

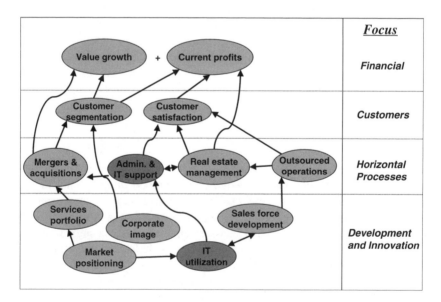

Figure 8.3   The logic of BSC: a strategy map

From this higher-level map, other maps are drawn at business unit or departmental level, to include the IS/IT department.

From a broad definition of the mission and of the vision for IS/IT, the methodology requires that the strategic objectives be broken down into the four or five BSC categories. Each objective is then analysed in terms of critical success factors and further broken down into specific targets and control metrics. The next step is to draw up the action plans which are needed to reach the targets and the metrics. Table 8.1 below furnishes some examples of IS/IT targets.

Table 8.1   IS/IT targets

Scorecard Focus	Broad targets for IS/IT in business strategy	Broad targets for IS/IT as a service department
Financial	How IS/IT contributes to business value	How IS/IT provides value for money for internal clients
Customer	How IS/IT assists in focusing customers	How customer relationship management by managers and staff is supported by IS/IT services
Processes	How we work smarter thanks to IS/IT	How IS/IT systems, procedures and routines contribute to rapid and agile internal systems
Innovation and Development	How IS/IT improves competence and climate	Improving IS/IT skills and competencies

Hence, scorecards can be used not only in determining IT/IS strategy but also in controlling the implementation of the IS/IT plan. The adoption of the BSC methodology as an evaluation tool for IS/IT strategic development over the long term has, as its key benefit, the possibility of rendering visible the value that is created by intangible and hard-to-understand investments in IT/IS. Such a situation would contribute significantly towards changing a situation where IS/IT investments are still mostly treated as current expenses and not as enablers of current and future business success.

IS/IT STRATEGIC DEVELOPMENT AS A PROCESS OF INNOVATION

As we have seen in Chapter Six, one of the perspectives on IS/IT implementation is *The Stages of Maturity and Innovation* trend (see Sub-Perspective 4c of *Organizational Holism*). Under this perspective some authors have suggested that the process of information systems implementation can be paralleled to a process of technical innovation.

Among the authors writing on technical innovation there seems to be fairly wide consensus about the incremental nature of the multi-stage process of technical innovation, also regarded as the outcome of continuous interaction between individuals, the organization and the structural factors of the technology (Nelson and Winter, 1982; Roberts, 1987; Cohen and Levinthal, 1990; Slappendel, 1996). According to Eveland (1987), technical innovation must be seen as an action-oriented process of 'gradual shaping of a general idea, which can mean many different things to different people, into a specific idea that most people understand to mean more or less the same thing' (ibid., p. 313).

Eveland (1987) has suggested five action-oriented stages in a process of technical innovation: (1) Agenda-Setting (2) Matching (3) Redefining (4) Structuring (5) Interconnecting. We propose that with due adaptation these five stages could provide an adequate view of IS/IT strategic development as a process of technical innovation.

1. Agenda-setting – The stage of IS/IT strategic reflection and policy formulation or reformulation, in terms of the organization's known and emerging strategic options.
2. Matching – The stage of drawing up implementation plans for establishing or updating the organization's information systems architecture and technology platforms. It is a three-way interactive process, where requirements from the top of the organization are matched with potentially appropriate new technology to be imported from the outside and with bottom-up organizational realities, regarding both the technological legacy and the human issues emerging from past experiences with the technology (Galliers, 1994).
3. Redefining – The stage of operationally implementing new or modified systems, including the evaluation and implementation of organizational changes involving both technical and human aspects. The word 'redefining' carries a socio-technical meaning whereby both the social and the technical aspects redefine each other or, in structurationist terms, structure and restructure each other (Orlikowski, 1992).
4. Structuring – Once the structures of the technological and the social sides of the organization have redefined each other at the local level as a conse-

quence of a single implementation exercise, the path is set for structuring and restructuring at the organizational and inter-organizational levels. As a result of the new implemented system, new organizational structures start to emerge and new needs are created on the technological front.

5. Interconnecting – The stage where it is no longer possible to set apart the social structures in the organization from the structures emerging from the implemented technology. IS/IT has become embedded in the social fabric of the organization and new needs are created for interconnecting with other organizations. At this point IS/IT strategic development reaches beyond the internal organization and stretches out to new connections between the organization and its environment (i.e. the extended organization). This stage does not stop at a given point but goes on evolving continuously, until it is re-evaluated under the next strategic formulation exercise (Agenda Setting).

The IS/IT strategic development cycle as a process of technical innovation is represented in the outer circle of Figure 8.4. In the inner circle, the traditional information systems development cycle is also represented as a set of small spirals featuring the traditional phases of development – systems scoping,

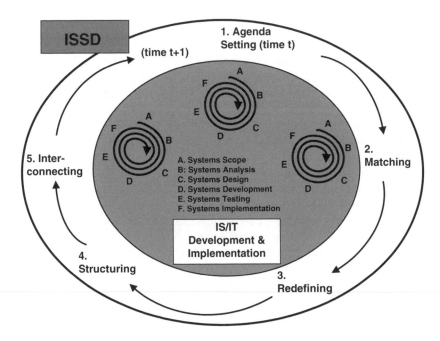

Figure 8.4 ISSD as a process of innovation

requirements specification, systems design, testing and implementation. The figure is also intended to show the differences in the life spans between the two cycles. Whereas the strategic development cycle can last several years, the information systems development cycle usually lasts a few months. In line with the emphasis on action which we have tried to highlight throughout this book, the next question that should be addressed is 'how can the IS/IT strategic development cycle be materialized in practice?'

Given its mixed or eclectic nature, we believe that IS/IT strategic development needs an intervention model which accommodates simultaneously notions such as lengthy organizational change, learning and growth and the need for rapid technological change brought about by changes in the environment. In Chapter Seven we discussed the OFF model of strategic alignment (see Figure 7.1) and, with some adaptations, we believe that this model will serve as an appropriate guideline for the IS/IT strategic development cycle.

The first adaptation we propose concerns the four domains, represented by the four strategies – Organizational Strategy, Information Systems Strategy, Information Technology Strategy and Information Management Strategy. According to Earl (1996), the author of the OFF model, IS/IT strategic alignment is the result of the linkages between these four domains. While doubting that any concrete linkages can be found to bring together such abstract domains, we agree that the managerial processes related to each of the domains can play a very useful role.

The second proposed adaptation to the OFF model concerns the process tied to the Information Management Strategy, which Earl has labelled as the Constitution Process. In Chapter Seven we have presented an argument against the use of such a label for a process which is supposedly on the same level as the other three processes. We have further suggested that the Constitution Process has to be seen as something placed at a higher level and exerting a formative (or constitutive) influence over the other processes. However, we do envisage the need for a fourth managerial process in order for the model to be complete, a process not of an ontological nature but of a more operational nature. We suggest that the fourth process should be called *Process of Organizational Change*. This suggestion is in line with the recommendation made by many of the authors writing under the Organizational Holism perspective (see Chapter Six) to the effect that the purposeful management of change is a key part of the process of IS/IT implementation.

IS/IT-Related Organizational Change

In Chapter Two we have suggested that the *need for a new organizational change orientation* is one of the spin-offs of the web of causes and consequences of the merger of organization and technology. Organizational change has been recognized by an increasing number of authors as one of the core areas of the information systems discipline and it is also one of the corner-stones of the managerial action theory which underpins the notion of IS/IT strategic development. Hence, a managerial process of organizational change must have a place in any framework for long-term development of IS/IT.

The IS/IT-related organizational change process has three major character-istics:

1. An orientation towards people (values, roles and relationships), leader-ship and organizational contexts.
2. An emphasis on key organizational change factors (reorganization of processes or structures, organizational politics, training, communication, etc.).
3. A focus on coaching or process consultation.

The third characteristic of the organizational change process mentioned above – coaching or process consultation – concerns the nature of the inter-vention. Organizational change ought to be regarded by managers not as something that happens occasionally but as a permanent event which needs to be followed and coached. Effective managers are those who are perceived as being able to get the job done, but also those who are able to build and develop their human resources at the same time. A good manager is a coach or a facilitator of efficient and effective processes. Under this role, the man-ager helps to integrate, to coordinate and to blend the know-how of others in order to get things done. In a consultancy situation, such a role is very similar to the process consultant whose aim is to establish a collaborative relation-ship with his or her client in such a way as to enable the client to diagnose, to understand and to solve the problem through his or her own means (Coghlan, 1993).

Figure 8.5 shows the ISSD managerial processes framework. The subject content of each managerial process is fairly straightforward and is in line with the description made in Chapter Seven of the three related areas of strategy – Organizational, Information Systems and Information Technology. What remains to be discussed is the nature of the managerial processes which make up the framework.

IS/IT-Related Managerial Processes

Like a managerial role, a managerial process is a notion which cannot be functionally described because it is an interpretive concept, i.e. it is the behaviours and actions associated with each managerial role that 'collec-tively define the social structure of a company within which its management

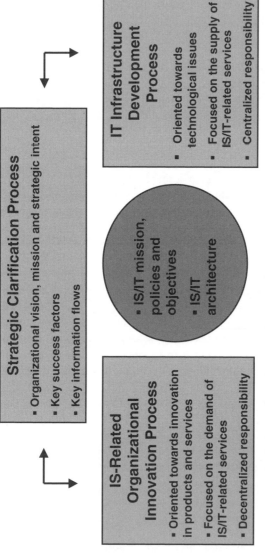

Strategic Clarification Process
- Organizational vision, mission and strategic intent
- Key success factors
- Key information flows

IS-Related Organizational Innovation Process
- Oriented towards innovation in products and services
- Focused on the demand of IS/IT-related services
- Decentralized responsibility

IS/IT mission, policies and objectives
IS/IT architecture

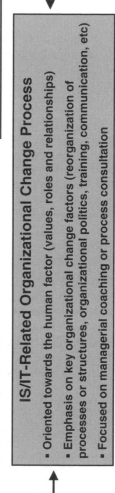

IT Infrastructure Development Process
- Oriented towards technological issues
- Focused on the supply of IS/IT-related services
- Centralized responsibility

IS/IT-Related Organizational Change Process
- Oriented towards the human factor (values, roles and relationships)
- Emphasis on key organizational change factors (reorganization of processes or structures, organizational politics, training, communication, etc)
- Focused on managerial coaching or process consultation

Figure 8.5   A managerial process approach to ISSD

processes are embedded (Bartlett and Ghoshal, 1993:41)'. Management processes are the interlocking behaviours, the relationships or the interactions of managers with the organization in performing their daily activities. They are the managers' key tasks, as seen by themselves. Hence, managerial processes are very much tied to the organization's context. Formal functional roles dictate, in a more or less rigid and vertical manner, what managers have to do. But most functional roles also have an horizontal component in so far as they have to be executed in accordance with the needs imposed by the organization's horizontal (end-to-end) processes. So, it is appropriate to say that every organization has its key managerial process and that the contents of such invisible processes depend upon the overall organizational context.

The three core managerial processes proposed by Ghoshal and Bartlett are the Renewal, the Integration and the Entrepreneurial process. They are 'core' processes because each of them is present in the key managerial roles (top management, middle management and front-line management). In accordance with the view of organizations as 'networks of roles and relationships' Bartlett and Ghoshal (1993:44) argue that

> Each of the three core processes is structured around a specific set of relationships across these three roles (...) In this way, we have defined the structure of the organization not in terms of how subunits are composed and decomposed but as clusters of statuses and associated roles that collectively define the social structure of a company within which its core management processes are embedded.

Bartlett and Ghoshal's and Ghoshal and Bartlett's (1994) notion of managerial processes can be applied to IS/IT strategic development, by linking them to the three key processes discussed by Earl (1996) – the Infrastructural (or Foundation), the Innovation and the Clarification processes. Together with the fourth process proposed earlier – Organizational Change – these can be said to contain all the emerging trends in IS/IT functional management discussed in Chapter Two (see Table 2.1). IS/IT managerial processes can only be described in terms of activities, so in Table 8.2 we present at attempt at matching the four IS/IT managerial processes with the emerging trends in IS/IT management.

The purpose of the table below is to show how IS/IT strategic development as an innovation-guided approach might be carried out in the daily life of an organization. By aligning the actions of the various managers involved with such a shared framework of managerial processes, it is possible to achieve ever improved levels of efficiency and effectiveness in the integration of IS/IT applications and organizational processes.

However, descriptive processes do not, on their own, accomplish better efficiency and effectiveness in the integration of IS/IT applications. The IS/IT managerial processes we have just described have to be enabled by IS/IT-

Table 8.2   Managerial processes for IS/IT strategic development

IS/IT Managerial Processes	IS/IT Functional Management	Senior Line Management	Top Management (Board Member in Charge of IS/IT)
Strategic Clarification	Filtering new developments from the external IT market and translating them into the organization's language	Converting business needs and objectives into well-researched IS/IT proposals	Translating the corporation's intent and purpose into IS/IT corporate objectives through personal involvement in the strategic management of IS/IT
Infrastructure Development	Managing the corporate IT infrastructure and the IT's sourcing strategy working towards rapid achievements of technical progress	Actively contributing towards the maintenance of an IT infrastructure by having a grasp of the technology-related opportunities and constraints	Embedding an IS/IT ethos into the organization and championing IS/IT issues at Board of Directors' level
Organizational Innovation	Serving as internal consultants on IS/IT issues (including business process innovation) in line with the business needs	Searching for IS/IT-based innovative solutions (including those coming out of good local IS/IT initiatives) and linking them with business targets	Facilitating the achievement of a balance in the centralization vs. decentralization issue in line with business objectives
Organizational Change	Striving towards a better understanding of the business-IS/IT interface and actively working on the building of relationships with the line departments	Building communication bridges between IS departmental demand and central IT supply	Enabling the rapid development of the IS/IT workforce especially in terms of the acquisition of strong hybrid competencies

related individual and organizational competencies. Hence, it is important now to glance at the next component of the ISSD framework: the individual competencies issue.

IS/IT STRATEGIC DEVELOPMENT AS A COMPETENCY-BASED ISSUE

Looking at the information systems implementation literature, we can see how much of it has been influenced by industry analysis or 'product-based' models. Some examples are McFarlan's (1981) portfolio approach to information systems management which is inspired on the BCG growth/share matrix, Porter and Millar's (1985) information intensity matrix, Ives and Learmonth's (1984) customer resources life cycle and Wiseman's (1988) strategic option generators.

The approach taken by many researchers in information systems, perhaps by the majority, is to treat information technology applications as products which are placed in organizations to fulfil a function. This approach ignores or overlooks the resources which make up such products, when it is the resources that make a difference to the effectiveness of the organization in the long term. In information systems, resources can be thought of as all the inputs which go into the organizational implementation of an information system, as opposed to a notion of implementation where information systems are treated purely as products, as is the case in the majority of strategic information systems planning (SISP) frameworks and methodologies (see Figure 8.6).

Mata et al. (1995) have applied the resource-based approach to IS strategy and management and have analysed four types of IS/IT attributes in relation to their potential for creating competitive advantage. The IS/IT attributes are capital requirements, proprietary technology, technical IT skills and managerial IS/IT skills. From this research, it was concluded that capital requirements, proprietary technology and technical IT skills were not the kinds of resources which might bring any form of advantage to firms. However, the building up of *IS/IT-related managerial skills* was found to be crucial for an improvement of the effectiveness of organizational implementation of IS and, therefore, for helping companies to achieve sustained advantage over their competitors in the long term. Those authors further explain that unlike technical IT skills, history plays a role in managerial IS/IT skills. These are developed over the longer term and are used in organizations to help the technical IT staff fit into the organization's culture, understand the organization's policies and procedures and learn to cooperate with the rest of the organization on IS/IT-related projects.

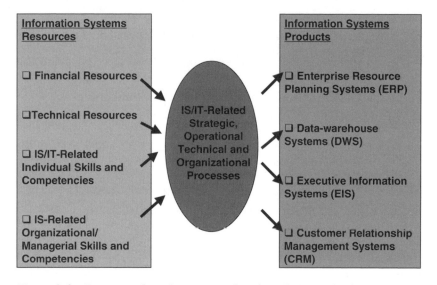

Figure 8.6   Resources-based versus product-based views of information systems

Mata et al. (1995) define IS/IT-related managerial skills as those which include 'management's ability to conceive of, develop and exploit IT applications to support and enhance other business functions' (p. 498). The following examples of IS/IT-related managerial skills are suggested:

1. the ability of IT managers to understand and appreciate the business needs of other functional managers, suppliers and customers.
2. the ability to work with these functional managers, suppliers and customers to develop appropriate IT applications.
3. the ability to coordinate IT activities in ways that support other functional managers, suppliers and customers.
4. the ability to anticipate the future IT needs of functional managers, suppliers and customers'.

There are many models and definitions of competence and competence building. Prahalad and Hamel (1990) and Hamel and Prahalad (1994), who have launched the concept of core competencies, define a competence as 'a bundle of skills rather than a single discrete skill or technology' (1994:202). As regards core competencies, they are defined as 'the sum of learning across individual skill sets and individual organizational units [which] is very unlikely to reside in its entirety in a single individual or small team' (1994:203). Teece (quoted in Conner and Prahalad, 1996) reinforces this view by saying that 'It is not only the bundle of resources that matter, but the mechanisms by which firms learn and accumulate new skills and capabilities, and the forces that limit the rate and direction of this process' (p. 494).

Von Krogh and Roos (1996) have operationalized the concept of competencies by means of a simple model (see Figure 8.7) aimed at illustrating the transformation processes of individual skills into organizational competencies, taking into consideration the forces that limit or enhance the pace of such processes. The model is also very useful in clarifying the terminology in an area where concepts are rather dispersed and not very rigorous.

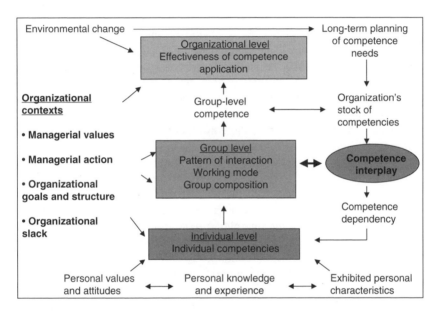

Source:　Modified from von Krogh and Roos (1996).

Figure 8.7　The process of organizational competencies formation and application

Von Krogh and Roos (1996) start off by defining individual competence as being made up of an individual's knowledge, experience, attitudes and exhibited personal characteristics. A distinction is made between knowledge, competence and skills in the following manner: 'while knowledge is about specific insights regarding a particular topic, competence is about the skills to carry out work' (ibid., p. 106). Individual competencies are rarely used in isolation, as most work tasks involve some degree of group involvement. At the group level there is an interplay of individual competencies which, ultimately, gives rise to a degree of group-level competence. The transformation from the individual to the group-level of organizational competencies is mediated by a mechanism named *competence interplay*.

The construct *competence interplay* is crucial for understanding how collective competence or task-specific organizational knowledge is formed. It is described as a group process, characterized by 'a set of fixed and dynamic working modes and patterns of interaction between group members and also by group composition and the extent to which the knowledge of group members is complementary or overlapping' (ibid., p. 108). Competence interplay has two properties: uniqueness and latency. Uniqueness is a result of the unique patterns of interaction and work modes demonstrated by groups in any particular organization. This is obviously unique to the organization. Latency means that the level competence of a particular group may not always be active, but may be evoked if there is a need for it. Thus, group-level competence may be restored at any time, depending on factors such as the task at hand, the availability of earlier group composition, earlier patterns of interaction and earlier work modes.

Competence interplay can be thought of as the outcome of each discrete group-level event, which contributes towards the formation of the organization's overall group-level competence. Group-level competence, in turn, influences the level of effectiveness of competence application at the organizational level as the outcome of the competence interplay of many groups and of many events in time. In other words, one thing is the contribution to a collective competence of the interplay of one group working towards a particular task and another thing is the overall organizational capacity for effectively applying its stock of competencies. Such capacity is restricted by 'group-level competence' which can also be thought of as the level of capacity that organizations develop for team work or other forms of group work to take place. *Competence interplay* gives rise to an emergent consequence, named 'competence dependency'. This means that group-level competence often becomes dependent upon one or more individuals and this dependency, in turn, will inevitably affect the individual level.

All levels of competence formation are conditioned by the organizational context. For example, formal organizational structure can enhance or inhibit the identification, formation and implementation of groups and the existing level of organizational slack can have a bearing on the level of effectiveness in competence application. Organizational slack refers to the pressures which exist in the organization, either in terms of time or of financial resources. The organization's context can also place restrictions on knowledge sharing between organizational members. When interacting among themselves, individuals have a certain mindset regarding what information to share with others and what information not to share. Finally, environmental change, in the long run, is another determining factor of the effectiveness of competence application, both through a direct effect (i.e. sudden changes in the conditions of the market may render some competencies ineffective, at least in the short term) and through a process of evaluation of competence needs and human resources planning to fulfil such needs.

Competence Interplay in IS/IT Corporate Governance

We have seen in Chapter Two that the traditional functions of IS/IT departments are undergoing majors changes due to a variety of factors, which might be divided into two major categories: (1) changes from within the organization, where a combination of more user-friendly technologies and users more knowledgeable about IT can, in some ways, replace the work of traditional IS/IT specialists, and (2) changes from outside the organization, where all kinds of new computer services are being offered, making it more cost-effective for many companies to outsource rather than insource some of the IT-related services. All such changes are creating a need for new types of relationships in the organization or, in other words, a new context comprising the new technologies and the accompanying new roles and relationships is being formed.

Such a new context may be adequately described as one of information systems *governance*, as opposed to the context associated with traditional information systems *management*. Information systems governance is an expression introduced by Michael Earl (1996) but left largely undefined by that author. In using the term, we believe Earl had intended to highlight the involvement of a variety of stakeholders in the process of formulation of IS/IT strategy. However, we sense that IS/IT governance could become a very useful concept if given a wider coverage and made to encompass not only strategy formulation but also strategic and operational implementation and the daily management of IS/IT-related routines, not only within the organization but reaching the *extended organization* as well.

Monks and Minow (1995:1) define corporate governance as 'the relationship among various participants in determining the direction and performance of corporations'. The primary participants in corporate governance are the shareholders, the management (led by the chief executive officer) and the board of directors, in addition to a second line of participants, made up of employees, customers, suppliers and the community. The key objectives of corporate governance concern coordination and alignment – 'alignment of information, incentives and capacity to act and alignment of responsibilities and authorities of all the various constituencies to achieve the optimal conditions for growth and renewal' (Monks and Minow, 1995:257). Thus, we might define IS/T corporate governance as *the ensemble of the roles played*

*by all the stakeholders intervening in the process of IS/IT strategic develop-
ment, the relationships and the interdependencies among such roles.*

If we bring together this definition of governance with the concept of
competence interplay, we might picture IS/IT governance as a set of overlapping triangles featuring the interplay of various IS/IT-related roles. Each
triangle is defined by three or more IS/IT-related roles (see Figure 8.8). There
are two main triangles drawn in full lines. The first [*triangle (a)*] is made up
of the roles of top management, IS/IT management and senior line management and the second [*triangle (b)*] is formed by the roles of senior line
management, middle management and non-managerial end users. There are
two more secondary triangles, the first [*triangle (c)*] comprising the roles of
top management, IS/IT management, senior line management and institutional stakeholders and the second [*triangle (d)*] encompassing all the actors
involved in IS/IT corporate governance. In the corners of *triangle (d)* we
have, in addition to the other already mentioned roles, the suppliers of IS/IT
products and services, a key group of stakeholders in IS/IT governance.

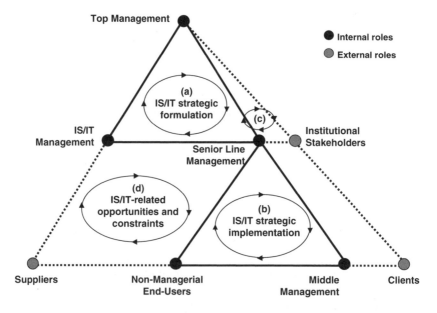

Figure 8.8   Interlocking roles and learning loops of IS/IT governance

The notion of IS/IT governance as a set of overlapping processes has been
explored in the information systems literature by Swanson (1988) who has
suggested a learning model for IS/IT implementation, explaining that learning takes place at two levels: (1) a 'within system' level, where communication

between user and systems developer creates a learning loop in the systems development process, and (2) an 'among systems' level, where the historical dimension of systems development in a particular organization is highlighted. Also, Lucas, Ginzberg and Schultz (1991) have split up their conceptual model of IS/IT implementation into two sub-models: the manager model and the user model, each sub-model having its own causal variables. In the organizational learning literature we find a similar distinction between lower-level and higher-level organizational learning (Fiol and Lyles, 1985). The learning occurring in the upper levels of the organization can lead to the development of new organizational climates and cultures, through a spiral effect spanning the entire organization, while at the lower levels learning is more focused, occurring through repetition at the routine level of operation.

The competence interplay resulting from the permanent interaction of the human agents at each corner of the triangles causes a learning effect. So, although each triangle has a specific purpose, all the triangles jointly contribute to the development and growth of the system as a whole, in terms of IS/IT-related knowledge. Thus, IS/IT governance can be said to constitute a process of learning or, better said, an ensemble of learning processes with the emphasis on the actions of the key types of stakeholders involved. In the figure above, four interacting learning processes (or loops) are depicted.

Triangle (a) is the conceptual space where managerial learning takes place at the strategic level, thus determining the conditions for the success or failure of the remaining process of IS/IT governance. It is the area where IS/IT-related strategic clarification occurs, influencing the overall conditions for the effective implementation/operation of the IT infrastructure and of the emergence of IS-related innovation. Senior line managers, who have been increasingly demanding functional responsibilities in the area of IS/IT governance, are the common element between *triangles (a)* and *(b)*, thus fulfilling a dual role, i.e. linking the top-down managerial choices with the bottom-up efforts for integration of local IS/IT initiatives.

Triangle (b) contains the space where tactical and operational IS/IT-related learning takes place and where the ultimate criteria for implementation success or failure can be found, in terms of business or organizational results. It is the area where IT infrastructure building and IS/IT-related innovation actually occur, involving the matching of top-down implementation of managerial choice and of bottom-up identification of business/innovation needs. In addition to the senior line managers, *triangle (b)* is also formed by the middle managers, who establish the link between senior managers and the end-users and who constitute the first line of contact with IS/IT-related constraints. In the third corner of *triangle (b)*, there are the non-managerial end-users, whose local IS/IT-related learning is a key element in IS/IT governance, both as a constraint and as an opportunity.

The stakeholders who form *triangles (a)* and *(b)* dominate all internal IS/IT-related decision making, strategic formulation and strategic implementation. In *triangle (a)* top managers, information systems managers and senior line managers jointly learn about IS/IT strategy formulation while working on IS/IT managerial decisions, such as outsourcing, selection of major software packages or restructuring of the IS/IT function at corporate level. The loop which develops within *triangle (b)* is where most of the learning directly concerned with IS/IT-related innovation actually occurs. This is so in view of the fact that the non-managerial end-users are, in most organizations, not only the largest group but also the group with the closest contact with clients. It is through the contact with clients that much of IS/IT-related innovation comes about, firstly through the detection of information-related needs and secondly through the innovative use of the tools made available by the organization's IT platform. The middle managers form a crucial link between the outcome of the IS/IT strategic decision-making processes, conveyed by the senior line managers, and of the activity of non-managerial end-users.

Triangle (c) encompasses the institutional stakeholders, in addition to the internal stakeholders from *triangle (a)*. Institutional stakeholders are the individuals or organizations which in one way or another exert an influence on the internal governance of IS/IT. Often, such influence is of a political nature and applies mostly to large publicly funded organizations. Political influence, however, can play a major role both as a facilitator or as an inhibitor of new IS/IT-related initiatives, especially when they involve large capital investments. IS/IT managers or directors, therefore, have to learn how to play the micro-political games which are imposed upon the organization via the institutional stakeholders but this is not a one-way process. Institutional stakeholders can also derive gains from learning about the inner workings of large IS/IT-related initiatives, for example, through personal or institutional prestige or reputation. Hence, a learning loop about IS/IT-related opportunities and constraints is also established at this level.

The fourth triangle – *triangle (d)* – involves all external stakeholders as well as all the internal stakeholders. In addition to the stakeholders who have already been mentioned, *triangle (d)* features also the suppliers of IS/IT-related products and services and the organization's clients. Nowadays the large majority of clients are linked to the organization via the internet which is used not only for conveying information about the organization's products and services, but also for purposes of distribution. The role of the clients in *triangle (d)* is, essentially, to serve as the yardstick for the opportunities which might be presented by IS/IT applications. By constantly assessing the needs of the clients, managers are able to identify the most appropriate applications that the organization should invest in. But the part of the learning loop which involves the clients is not only used to identify opportunities.

It is also used to identify constraints as, for example, in a customer relationship management (CRM) system which consistently carries the wrong information about clients and which becomes a liability for the organization.

Suppliers of IS/IT-related products and services are also key stakeholders in the IS/IT opportunities and constraints learning loop. Their role starts with the overwhelming influence that the marketing power of the players from the IS/IT marketplace exert on each and every individual internal stakeholders in the organization. Such influence can be very harmful if the organization does not have appropriate IS/IT governance structures in place but it can also be extremely beneficial if the internal stakeholders have a good grasp of both opportunities and constraints placed by the new technological offerings. Increasingly, the suppliers of IS/IT-related products and services are considered as partners and not just as vendors, thus assuming a participative role in the governance of IS/IT in organizations. If such a role is accepted as legitimate by the internal stakeholders, then the conditions are set for the suppliers to become part of the organization's communities of knowledge.

The discussion about IS/IT strategic development as a competency-based issue can be narrowed down further by exploring the sets of competencies that each major stakeholder should have. A matrix formed by the key IS/IT governance stakeholders and the four IS/IT managerial processes presents an excellent foundation upon which to base such an exploration. It will not be attempted in this book but it is left here as a suggestion for further research.

IS/IT STRATEGIC DEVELOPMENT AS KNOWLEDGE CREATION

In Chapter Four we have introduced Nonaka and Takeuchi's (1995) theory of knowledge creation. This theory features a central model where the various elements of knowledge creation are interrelated in a dynamic whole, which incorporates four modes and the four processes (see Figure 8.9). The modes are Externalization, Combination, Internalization and Socialization and the processes are Dialogue, Networking, Learning by Doing and Field Building. Externalization is triggered by dialogue or collective reflection. Combination is triggered by networking of newly created or of existing knowledge from different parts of the organization. Learning by doing is the key process in the facilitation of the internalization mode. Finally, socialization starts with the building of a field of interaction, which enables the sharing of experiences and mental models among organizational members.

In the context of ISSD, we submit that IS/IT applications can greatly enable or enhance the four modes and processes of knowledge conversion and suggest that there is great value in analysing the impact of the organiza-

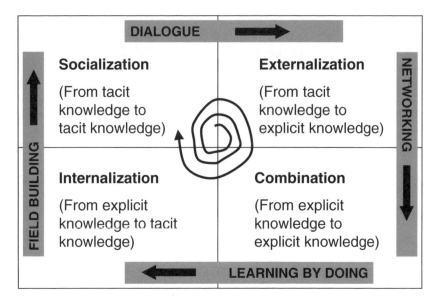

Source: Nonaka and Takeuchi (1995).

Figure 8.9   Modes and processes of knowledge creation

tion's key IS/IT applications in the light of Nonaka and Takeuchi's (1995) knowledge cycle. In Chapter Two we had already made a reference to knowledge outcomes as the third stage of the organizational growth cycle of IS/IT (see Figure 2.2).

Let us start with the knowledge contained in products or services available in the market and which complement, substitute or compete with the products or services of the organization in question. Such knowledge, a crucial part of any organization's intelligence gathering, is tacit knowledge and must be made explicit in order to be used within the organization's internal processes. This holds true regarding any other form of intelligence gathering. Thus, the first step in the knowledge conversion cycle starts in the *externalization* quadrant, with the conversion of tacit knowledge (coming either from the external environment or from within the organization) into explicit knowledge.

The process of intelligence gathering has been greatly enhanced by free text database (financial, business, scientific and technical) available commercially on- or off-line. With the launching of Telerate, the first on-line information service, in 1969, the offer of this kind of service has never ceased to grow. According to Schwuchow (1988), in the ten years between 1978 and 1988 the number of databases commercially available worldwide rose from about 400 to 3700, with the number of database hosting services growing from 59 to 555 in the same period of time. Thus, through database technology which allows information to be retrieved often through the internet, it has been possible for companies to enlarge exponentially their access to external sources of tacit knowledge.

However, for tacit knowledge to be converted into explicit knowledge a process of *dialogue* must be present. So, clearly, externalization does not happen solely on account of more or better IT applications. Externalization happens through face-to-face dialogue, for example, in a brainstorming situation, a form of a formalized dialogue among a group of people voicing ideas or opinions about a central topic. Although brainstorming must be carried out by human beings, the processes which mediate the communication among the members of a brainstorming session can be enhanced by IT, for example, in a teleconferencing environment or through a groupware application.

The second key area of impact is that of *combination* of explicit knowledge with other explicit knowledge which is achieved through *networking*. In terms of the activity of any organization, combination is at the heart of the main production processes, thus taking up a large proportion of all the knowledge conversion activity. In terms of IT applications combination happens, for example, whenever a transaction is processed and the company's back office system is updated. Whether the transaction is the sale of a good, the purchase of a stock item or the payment of a salary, the system is combining explicit knowledge, in the form of data.

The types of information system which support the organization's back office are the so-called ERP (Enterprise Resource Planning) packages. Due to their design, these packages require work to be carried out by processes and most of them embody workflow technologies allowing horizontal processes to be followed through, as in the case of an order being processed, for example. Workflow is also at the heart of IT applications generically known as groupware systems, which have had a major impact not just in the way that each person carries out his or her task, but also in the way that people work together. All of these systems have brought with them major changes to the organization's work processes and therefore to the level of combination and networking which it is possible to achieve.

But in the networking area, the IT applications likely to provoke great changes in internal networking are the intranets, internal communication networks based upon internet hypertext technology. Intranets are easy to use tools mainly due to the fact that most people are quite familiar with internet screens and symbols. When considered as communication tools intranets already have an important role in the way that people share non-structured information (for example, in noticeboards), but when considered as a means of access to business critical applications where structured information can be shared, they reveal their real potential as strategic applications. Intranets enable also the creation of discussion groups and of countless ways of improving and enlarging cooperation and collective learning.

The third key area of impact is that of *internalization*. Internalization means converting explicit knowledge into tacit knowledge and is enabled by processes of *experiential learning* (learning by doing). Internalization and experiential learning are associated with the impact of IS/IT in the organization by means of the phenomenon coined and described by Zuboff (1988) as *informate*. As we have seen in Chapter Two, such phenomena are tied to the representational qualities of IT and to the increasing *textualization of information* in the workplace. The work becomes more abstract and the notion of *learning by doing* assumes special relevance. Many skills of IT use cannot be acquired through traditional training but have to be learned experientially. The question of *learning by doing* is also affected by new work processes often imposed by software applications, new communication patterns forced by local area networks (LANs) or new forms of relationship with clients through the internet.

The fourth area of impact is *socialization*, a mode of knowledge growth where tacit knowledge is exchanged with other tacit knowledge. Here, the process of knowledge conversion suggested by Nonaka and Takeuchi (1995) is *field building*, a concept similar to climate formation, such as presented in Chapter Seven and in relation to the formation of IS/IT-related contexts or fields. In other words, for IS/IT-related tacit knowledge to be exchanged between individuals, a certain type of organizational climate is needed, for example a climate where there is trust and understanding between IS/IT managers and line managers.

IS/IT STRATEGIC DEVELOPMENT AS ORGANIZATIONAL LEARNING

In the preceding chapter, we have proposed that the key ingredient for the process of IS/IT strategic alignment is an environment of facilitation achieved through IS/IT organizational contexts supportive of cooperative and partnership-building relationships between IS/IT specialists and IS/IT users. However, we have also seen throughout the book the history of information systems in organizations shows that the formation of such contexts is filled with obstacles:

> the barriers (…) are generally not knowledge or budgets or technology, but the politics of ambiguity, [i.e.] the lack of clarity about the new role of IS/IT given its historical role and its distance from centrality in the organization, the insularity of IS/IT in its relationships and contacts across the organization, and the insularity of management in its handling of the business implications of IS/IT (Keen, 1988:41)

This conflicting relationship between IS/IT and the business side of the organization stems from the unresolved debate between the centralized versus the decentralized control of IS/IT resources or the 'push-pull dilemma' (Zmud, 1988). The dilemma can be described as follows: in order to facilitate technological innovation in the business platform, 'need pull' and 'technology push' are required and, in order to facilitate technological innovation in the technology platform, 'technology pull' and 'need push' are needed. It is a delicate balance between the push from the technology platform backed by the forces from the IT market on one hand and the organizational absorption capacity of the business platform on the other hand.

Brown and Ross (1996) reinforce the 'push-pull' dynamics by pointing out that organizations strive constantly towards the maintenance of a balance between the development of an IT infrastructure and the building of partnerships between IS/IT staff and IS/IT users. A centralized corporate IT infrastructure brings benefits such as a more cost-effective utilization of computing resources, the synergistic effects of having such resources under a common management structure and all the operational benefits of having standard technology platforms (von Simson, 1990). On the other side of the coin, strong IS/IT staff–users partnerships create other benefits, such as an IS/IT management style which is more responsive to local business needs, a shared understanding of IS/IT capabilities and business unit needs and information systems which are directly targeted at customer needs (Henderson, 1990).

The attainment of a balance between the 'push-pull' forces in the organization is crucial because it means potential success for IS/IT-related innovation. Brown and Ross (1996:59) suggest that 'ultimately, the goal is to have IS/IT-business partnership and IT infrastructure development thinking so enmeshed in the organization's culture as to be self-sustaining regardless of the IS/IT organizational structure'. So, how can the move from structure to culture suggested by Brown and Ross, be achieved? We suggest that such a move is an outcome of information systems strategic development, in the form of IS/IT-related learning. Let us recap some key concepts about organizational learning and knowledge creation in organizations.

According to von Krogh and Roos (1995), organizational learning is the collective capability that organizations have acquired and which enables them to create new knowledge. Such collective capability can be understood as a set of organizational and managerial skills, which can be developed and which allow the organization not only to adapt more effectively to the course of events but actually increase the organization's capacity to innovate, in terms of both process and outcome (Normann, 1985).

Organizational and managerial skills can be task-related or value-related. Both task-related and value-related managerial action shape organizational contexts which, in turn, exert a strong influence on organizational members' predisposition towards initiative, creativity, collaboration and learning (Bartlett and Ghoshal, 1993; Ghoshal and Bartlett, 1994). In accordance with Nonaka and Takeuchi (1995:59), organizational knowledge creation is a process that takes place 'within an expanding community of interaction which crosses intra- and inter-organizational levels and boundaries, amplifying the knowledge created by individuals and crystallizing it as part of the knowledge network of the organization'.

Cohen and Levinthal (1990) argue that cross-functional absorptive (i.e. learning) capacities are a crucial part of the overall organizational effort to build more and better learning capabilities. This is in line with Ghoshal and Bartlett's (1994:107) proposition that collective learning is 'a result of the combination of distributed initiative and mutual cooperation' and also behind Nonaka and Takeuchi's (1995) notion of 'networking knowledge' as the final stage of the process of organizational knowledge creation. In the information systems field, Henderson (1990) has advanced the notion of networking IS-related knowledge and Boynton, Zmud and Jacobs (1994) have described the concept of IT absorptive capacity as embodying concepts such as managerial IT knowledge and IT management process effectiveness.

So, how can the concept of organizational learning be applied to IS/IT strategic development? Organizational learning is both an organizational *process* and an organizational *outcome*. As a process, it is about applying IS/IT task-related knowledge (know what) and value-related knowledge (know how) to work. As an outcome, organizational learning can be regarded as the additions to the organization's stock of knowledge, expressed as the added collective capacity to enhance all types of organizational action and to exert change in the effectiveness of existing IS/IT-related organizational processes. In this sense, we might say that the final aim of IS/IT strategic development is to reach higher levels of IS/IT organizational maturity, those levels where 'management is comfortable *managing* the use of IT and employees are comfortable *using* the technology' (Sprague and McNurlin, 1993:43).

Table 8.3 shows a number of attributes typical of the move towards higher levels of IS/IT-related organizational maturity and learning. The opposite attributes listed in the two columns highlight the changes which would be needed in the collective stock of knowledge of the organization in order to enable one to say that IS/IT-related organizational learning (and IS/IT strategic development) has occurred in that organization.

Table 8.3   Characterizing the final outcome of ISSD, i.e. a move towards higher levels of IS/IT-related organizational maturity and learning

Low level of IS/IT-related organizational maturity and learning, i.e. IS/IT corporate governance relies on IS/IT organizational structural mechanisms	Higher level of IS/IT-related organizational maturity and learning, i.e. IS/IT corporate governance goals have been absorbed into the organization's culture
IS/IT specialist has no change responsibilities beyond building technology	Facilitator promotes change by helping increase clients' capacity for change
IS/IT department determines service levels	Constant negotiation takes place in order to determine effective level of support
Users are involved mostly at the 'requirements' stage in the planning of new information systems	Shared goals are present throughout the planning of new information systems
Formal communication paths between IS/IT and line departments staff	There is mutual understanding of each other's roles
Individual IS/IT projects are justified in terms of return on investment criteria (ROI)	IS/IT evaluation and control is incorporated into the firm's business planning mechanisms
Multiple IT standards. IT infrastructure is built up piecemeal	Firm-wide commitment to an IT infrastructure, which increases flexibility and decreases cycle time
Pockets of IS/IT expertise	Learning approach to IS/IT corporate governance

Sources: Brown and Ross (1996); Markus and Benjamin (1997).

9. Conclusion

> A new view of the world is taking shape in the minds of advanced scientific thinkers the world over, and it offers the best hope of understanding and controlling the processes that affect the lives of us all. Let us not delay, then, in doing our best to come to a clear understanding of it.
>
> (Ervin Laszlo, 1996:viii)

As conveyed at the outset, this book is the result of a series of intellectual challenges related to academic, managerial and consulting activities in the areas of business information, information technology, strategy, organizational development and change management, which have presented themselves to the author over the years. Throughout the book we have tried to build an argument in favour of a more action-oriented (as opposed to a planning-dominated) approach to information systems management.

We have started off by arguing that although there is a strong relationship between the growth of IS/IT in organizations and the emergence of the knowledge economy, it is not possible to establish clear cause-and-effect links between the two phenomena. The impact of information systems and technology in organizations is much more complex and widespread than some schools of thought seemed to believe in the early days of the information revolution. One of the outcomes of such an awareness has been the emergence of the information systems discipline, which has succeeded in highlighting the relevance of many strategic and organizational issues related to the organizational transformations brought about by IS/IT. In this work, we have selected and discussed only a few such topics, i.e. organizational knowledge as a competitive market pressure, new IS/IT strategic alignment needs, new needs for integration of the IS/IT function and the role of the management of IS/IT-related change.

These topics can all be grouped under a large umbrella which academics and practitioners have brought to the forefront of the debate of organizational strategy, i.e. the issue of the knowledge imperative. Another of the challenges we have proposed to tackle in this book has been to show that the knowledge imperative in business and organizational development can only be attained if organization and information systems are treated as one integrated topic and not as two separate ones. As a result of scientific reductionism and the fragmentation of the academic disciplines, the texts on organization theory do not factor in information systems as a key variable. In a similar fashion, the works on information systems/technology usually treat organizations as a given which someone else will take care of, independently. Although this is a generalization, we believe, it is a fair one.

In order to deal with these challenges and to come up with some innovative proposals, we have entered into a number of academic and scientific fields, in a multidisciplinary way, characteristic of the information systems discipline. The outcome of such incursions makes up the analytic contents of the book. In this concluding chapter, we will try to present the synthesis.

COMPLEXITY, ENACTED COGNITION AND AUTOPOIESIS APPLIED TO ORGANIZATIONS

The topic of organizational knowledge is central to our approach to the integration of organization and information systems. A discussion on organizational knowledge, on the other hand, inevitably leads to the debate on human knowledge and cognition and these, in turn, depend on the stance in relation to scientific epistemology and methodology. In other words, where does knowledge primarily come from? From our mind, thoughts, ideas, etc? Or does it come from our body, our action, our behaviour? In order to explain the depth and breadth of these issues, we have introduced some brief epistemological considerations regarding the origin and evolution of human and social cognition. In view of its relevance and impact on scientific epistemology in general, such considerations were framed within a broader discussion about the Complexity archi-paradigm.

Since the publication of Herbert Simon's (1945; 1997) work *Administrative Behaviour*, the academic debate about organizational knowledge and learning has been strongly influenced by a theoretical stance on human (and organizational) cognition known as representationism or cognitivism. After a few decades of research and publishing on organizational knowledge and learning under this theoretical stance, the field does not seem to have evolved a great deal in terms of helping organizational effectiveness or improving managerial practice. Meanwhile, in the cognitive sciences, the debate about the appropriateness of the representationist or cognitivist hypothesis as a basis for explaining human cognition has been going on for many years and alternative explanations have started to emerge (Maturana and Varela, 1980). Maturana and Varela argue that human cognition is not achieved through representations of the environment in the brain, but that cognition is achieved through an 'enaction' of the environment and that in such enaction the whole body is involved, not just the brain.

Hence, the key argument coming out of Chapter Three (Complexity and the new epistemological foundations of organization) was that the notion of embodiment of action is crucial for an understanding of all issues related to the nature of knowledge. As we have seen throughout that chapter, enacted cognition and autopoiesis theories defend a 'constitutive' ontology (as opposed to a 'transcendental' ontology) for the construction of reality. We find the following passage by Merleau-Ponty about the primacy of action, noteworthy:

> Since all movements of the organism are always conditioned by external influences one can, if one wishes, readily treat behaviour as an effect of the milieu. But in the same way, since all stimulations which the organism receives have, in turn, been possible only by its preceding movements which have culminated in exposing the receptor organ to external influences, one could say that behaviour is the first cause of all stimulations (quoted in Varela et al., 1991:174)

The process of embodied cognition is very similar to Giddens' (1984) process of structuration. Giddens' theory argues that it is not possible to separate our subjective dimension from 'reality's' objective dimension. Reality, according to structuration theory, emerges from the dialectic interplay of forces of structure and meaning, i.e. structural regularities are created from subjective meanings and, through socialization processes, structure feeds back upon meanings held by individuals. Central to this process is the notion of duality of structure, explained as the structural properties of social systems, which are both medium and outcome of the practices they recursively organize. It is argued that structure is not 'external' to individuals; 'as memory traces, and as instantiated in social practices, it is in a certain sense more "internal" than exterior to their activities' (Giddens, 1984:25).

Although Giddens did not use autopoiesis theory in shaping his thinking on structuration, Giddens' dynamic conception of social systems is similar and in parts complementary to the formation of social groups in autopoiesis. For example, in both cases the production and reproduction of systems is placed at the centre of the theoretical argumentation and both stress the primary nature of action as involved, practical activity in the world and do not try to divorce thought and language from body (or emotion in the case of autopoiesis). Also, both draw a clear distinction between that which is observable (structure for autopoiesis and system for structuration) and that which is only implicated in the constitution of the system (organization for autopoiesis and structure for structuration) (Mingers, 1995).

Although it still needs further work towards becoming a fully-fledged paradigm for organizational analysis, autopoiesis is a very attractive approach because it offers explanations that are much closer to the 'reality' of organizations than, for example, open systems theory. The open systems orthodoxy in management research has difficulty in explaining, for example, why success is the 'worst enemy' of successful companies and why there are so many cases of very successful companies, which suddenly founder. The paradigmatic example of this is the case of IBM in the early 1990s (Lloyd, 1994; Mills and Friesen, 1996). In drawing attention to the autonomous, operationally closed and self-referential nature of organizational systems, autopoiesis theory brings new explanations to this type of phenomenon. If organizations are essentially closed to new information (as opposed to data) their internal growth in terms of knowledge and learning has to come from within. The environment as provider of new knowledge in the form of a constant flow of inputs into the system loses much of its previous relevance.

These sub-themes from the complexity paradigm help to establish the notion of the constructed organization, i.e. the organization as an artefact constructed though the action of its members. So it might be said that, in terms of application to organizations, the complexity paradigm melts together three organizational metaphors: organizations as cultures, organizations as systems of power and organizations as flux and transformation (Morgan, 1997). The key conclusions that can be derived from such a melting pot are as follows:

1. Transformation, emergence and self-organization are a permanent state of affairs in organizations and the idea that organizations as social systems tend towards stability and equilibrium is largely a misconception.
2. Permanent transformation means that organizations are made up of a wide diversity of political interests, negotiation and conflicts with actors permanently jockeying for influence.
3. The view of organizations as informal networks of power helps to dispel the myth of classical organization theory that formal hierarchical is capable of achieving any form of control.
4. If the micro-management of everyday transactions is not feasible, the art of managing and changing contexts becomes all the more important.
5. Members construct their own reality and their own systems of meaning, regarding both their internal and their external organizational environments.
6. Organizational change and transformation is always a source of unrest in the organization's internal politics; in such a context the legitimacy of the leader becomes a stabilizing factor.
7. Legitimacy is constructed through managerial action and exerts its influence upon the behaviour of organization members through symbolic means.
8. The construction of the organization's external environment in a self-referential manner by the organization's members has very relevant consequences for the management of relationships with the external stakeholders.

MANAGERIAL ACTION AND THE FORMATION OF CONTEXTS OR CULTURAL KNOWLEDGE IN ORGANIZATIONS

A central part in our discussion has revolved around the issue of organizational paradigms. We have attempted to show that the machine organization, the dominant paradigm throughout the last century, is losing ground for a new type of paradigm which can confidently be named the learning organization. We consider the learning organization as a broad concept encompassing many of the organizational principles of the complexity paradigm, such as highlighted above. In the learning organization the imperative for organizational development and growth is knowledge creation. But the knowledge creation imperative is not just an organizational requirement. As we have seen in Chapter Five, it is also a primary strategic and managerial aim which is causing yet another paradigm change in the managerial world.

Managerial action is the concept which is bringing about a turn in the prevailing managerial paradigm. It is a *middle-of-the-road* approach in the spectrum of the strategic management schools of thought, characterized by a bias towards action, materialized through attitudes, values, roles and responsibilities of managers in implementing strategic and tactical decisions. The managerial action approach goes back to the earlier concerns of management as a discipline, where managerial leadership and context formation were given prominence as the keys to the success of any entrepreneurial initiative.

In Chapter Four we have suggested, as the synthesis of the discussion about the new organizational paradigm, a model of organizational context formation which supports the concept of managerial action. The model assumes that treating the concepts of organizational climate, context, culture and knowledge as separate concepts is unhelpful and even confusing. Organizational knowledge is often used to define a notion related to factual knowledge, while organizational culture (and sometimes climate) tend to be connected with emotions, values and attitudes. As pointed out by Mingers (1995), even before we engage in the use of language and in conversation we are primarily affected by emotions – 'our mood or *emotioning* is an ever-present background to our use of language. It conditions our stance or attitude (are we happy or sad, caring or self-concerned, deferential or confident, angry or upset?) and thereby the course of our conversation' (ibid., p. 79, added emphasis).

In the managerial world we tend to think of logic and rationality as something which can be separated from emotions, but as enacted cognition and autopoiesis show, emotions form the background of the embodiment of all our knowledge and cannot be separated from logic. To understand the role of emotions or emotioning is also crucial for an understanding of the nature of social (and organizational) systems. So, the notion of organizational knowledge cannot be divorced from the notion of organizational culture and this justifies our choice of the expression *organizational cultural knowledge* (Sackmann, 1991), as the unifying concept.

The model of organizational context formation presented in Chapter Four suggests that managerial action is the generative mechanism of organizational contexts. The concept of generative mechanism can be better understood with the help of Morgan's (1997) metaphor 'the whirlpool and the river'. The metaphor is inspired by the distinction originally made by Bohm (1980) between the implicate and the explicate orders in natural phenomena, discussed in Chapter Three. When we see a whirlpool (the implicate order) we see something objective happening in front of us and we can try to explain the phenomenon. But if the river (the explicate order) were to suddenly stop running we would be unable to provide any explanations for the phenomenon. So, in order to explain the whirlpool we need to understand its generative processes, which can only be found in the running river. Furthermore, although it is always the same phenomenon, its shape is continually changing according to the state of the water flow.

Likewise, an understanding of organizational contexts (the implicate order) is only possible if we understand its generative processes which can be found in the action of organizational actors with special emphasis on managerial action (the explicate order). In applying the notion of enacted cognition to organizations, Weick (1995) has made an important contribution towards an understanding of how such generative processes work. Weick talks about the creation or the enaction of an organizational reality through managerial authority. He explains that managers have the ability (granted to them by owners of the firm) to take 'undefined space, time, and action and draw lines, establish categories and coin labels that create new features of the environment that did not exist before' (Weick, 1995:31).

Although it always looks the same and it is mostly taken as a given (like the flow of the water in the river), managerial action is supported by powerful communicational cues (rational and emotional), embedded in the organization's language. Language is the element which allows change to come into the system, by providing an interpretive context against which all new data is checked (through self-referentiality) before eventually becoming structurally coupled to the system in the form of new information. Thus, change and knowledge creation in organizations (i.e. Maturana's 'network') will come about through the innovative use of factual information which is never neutral but always qualified by emotional/value-laden information. This is why managerial action is a powerful generative process of organizational context.

MANAGERIAL ACTION AS A TURN IN THE PREVAILING MANAGERIAL PARADIGM

In line with the evolution in the views of human cognition discussed in Chapter Three, we believe that a similar evolution exists in the field of management, with many parallels between the two. Introna (1997) traces the origins of the word 'management' to the Latin word 'manus' and explains how the Cartesian subject–object dualism has separated the present-day concept of management from its original roots. Just as Descartes clearly separated and demarcated the rational subject (res cogitans) from the objective word (res extensa), management thinkers over the years have also separated the rational manager from the tasks being managed (including the workers). Just as Descartes emphasized laws, theories and models (representations of reality), modern management emphasizes the creations of maps (plans, policies and standards), which must correctly represent the situation of the firm. Introna concludes by saying that '*manus*, the authentic management can only happen when dualism, the inauthentic separation is surpassed' (ibid., p. 90).

The idea that there is a need to surpass the mind–body dualism in management is also strongly argued by Nonaka and Takeuchi (1995). According to these authors, to talk about knowledge in Western organizations is to talk about the explicit and objective aspects of knowledge while the tacit and subjective dimensions are almost completely neglected. They explain this state of affairs as a result of the Cartesian dualism between subject and object or mind and body, still very prevalent in Western thinking.

This one-sided view of strategy has major limitations: firstly, the preoccupation with explicit and quantifiable information has made researchers ignore the creation of new visions or value systems; secondly, the emphasis on top-down strategy implementation has neglected a wealth of knowledge, which exists at lower levels in the organization; and thirdly, the prevailing strategic management concepts have made the whole issue of knowledge not 'respectable' enough to be considered as a source of competitiveness.

As suggested in Chapter Five, the two opposing views of strategy and management, i.e. the Cartesian-Taylorist versus the Action-Oriented view are mirrored in the evolution which has characterized the cognitive sciences over the last 40 years (Varela, 1992). Such an evolution, which embodies the turn from a cognitivist to an emergent/enacted epistemological stance can also be given a reading in terms of the managerial paradigm. Thus, the theories of autopoiesis and self-referential social systems discussed in Chapters Three and Four lend additional support to a gradual turn in managerial thinking. Such is a turn away from a rationalist position, where 'scientific', micro-management methods prevailed, to a more holistic, non-positivist and action-oriented stance, where history, context, heuristic rules, learning and

Table 9.1   The current turn in the managerial paradigm

From: Rational Management	To: Action-Based Management
Task-specific	Creative
Problem-solving	Problem definition
Abstract, symbolic	History, body-bound
Universal	Context sensitive
Centralized	Distributed
Sequential, hierarchical	Parallel
World pre-given	World brought forth
Representation	Effective action
Implemented by design	Implementation by evolutionary strategy
Hierarchy	Network
Command and control	Heuristic rules
Information	Learning
Subordinate	Apprentice
Doing and thinking separate	Doing and thinking together

Sources: Adapted from Varela (1992) and Introna (1997).

implementation by evolutionary strategy are the foci of attention (see Table 9.1).

COMPLEXITY, HOLISM AND INFORMATION SYSTEMS

In Chapter Six we have suggested the expression *Organizational Holism* as an approach to IS/IT development, implementation and management. This approach encompasses all the human and social aspects of the implementation of information systems in organizations in accordance with Walsham (1993), while sharing Swanson's (1988) view that IS/IT implementation is a much broader problem than the systems development process as well as Walton's (1988) belief that IS/IT implementation is a process that includes all the phases (before, during and after systems development), at all organizational levels (strategic, tactical and operational). *Organizational Holism* also contributes to the information systems discipline by feeding directly into the implementation research gap identified by Land (1992) and into the epistemological void on the foundations of organization suggested by Checkland and Holwell (1998).

The *Organizational Holism* perspective can also be characterized as being part of a change management school of thought. Intellectually, change management occupies an intermediate position between the opposing camps of planned versus emergent change (Pettigrew, 2000). In adopting a change management posture it is recognized, on the one hand, that it is important to plan and to maintain a strategic perspective in the long term but, on the other hand, that an undue emphasis on the *knowing what* does not solve the problem. It is equally recognized that the organization's emergent properties are as important as the managerial decisions that support the planned side of change and that the *knowing how* is also a key piece of any type of implementation.

The notion of corporate governance of information systems is also part of the change management school of thought. Corporate governance of IS/IT is a comprehensive and holistic approach, bringing together strategic formulation, technological development and organizational implementation aspects of IS/IT and it is an example of the application of the middle-of-the-road approach to strategic management, to IS/IT. In the information systems literature, the middle-of-the-road approach has appeared under labels such as 'eclectic approach' (Sullivan, 1985), 'multiple strategies' (Earl, 1989) or 'mixed development strategies' (de Jong, 1994). The change management component of *Organizational Holism* is reflected in the managerial process approach to IS/IT strategic development (ISSD) presented in Figure 8.5. IS/IT strategic development is presented, in Chapter Eight, as an intellectual stance which elects the logic of mutual causality between managerial action and organizational contexts as the blueprint for intervening in the management and governance of IS/IT. ISSD is meant as an envelope expression encompassing several methodologies and approaches guided, on the whole, by the application of managerial action theory to IS/IT governance. As emphasized in that chapter, the aim is not to furnish a recipe, but to serve as a source of inspiration, mainly to practitioners, as to the endless new possibilities for managing and governing IS/IT.

All of such advice regarding new approaches and new attitudes, however, places new demands on the organization and in what concerns the skills and capabilities of its IS/IT stakeholders for coordination, motivation and leadership. In order to follow an eclectic approach to IS/IT strategic development, the level of organizational maturity related to IS/IT must be high. Going back to stages of growth models discussed in Chapter Six, an eclectic approach is only possible at the most advanced stages of maturity, where contexts of cooperation, interaction and coordination are present (Galliers and Sutherland quoted in Galliers, 1991). The same is true regarding the new propositions put forward in Chapter Seven, where IS/IT strategic alignment has been defined as *a continuous process of organizational learning and change strongly influenced by IS/IT-related organizational contexts* (...)

In our proposals towards a renewed vision of IS/IT strategic alignment, our aim has been to highlight the overriding importance of organizational context in shaping the informal roles and relationships required for the alignment mechanisms to work in the long term. We have not detailed the 'mechanisms', as other literature has done in the past, due to the fact that we consider them to be subsidiary. In other words, the alignment mechanisms which are interwoven into a myriad of organizational norms and procedures are always a consequence of the behavioural relationships between the stakeholders. Furthermore, the norms and procedures behind the mechanisms are, to a large extent, emergent and self-organized occurrences. That being so, there is not much value in detailing alignment mechanisms *a priori*. Instead, we have put forward, in Chapter Seven, a listing of IS/IT-related context dimensions which we hope will be of consequence in shaping the attitudes of managers towards the issue of IS/IT strategic alignment. Our proposals might also be taken up as topics for validation in an exercise of academic research.

The Complexity archi-paradigm enables a bringing together of many of the concepts, models and theories which make up the foundations of the *Organizational Holism* perspective and which have been put forward from Chapter Six onwards. Complexity also affords a unique opportunity at conferring new legitimacy to a badly needed integrated approach to organizations and information systems. The key specific messages for IS/IT management and governance are as follows:

1. Organizations are complex adaptive systems where efficient, effective and sustainable growth and development depends upon the constant production of new internal knowledge.
2. As in complex adaptive systems, the transformation of organizations often starts from small innovations found at the fringes of the system's central core of activity.
3. Innovations and new knowledge are partly associated with the implementation and management of IS/IT in organizations.
4. IS/IT-related innovations and new knowledge creation are often found at the fringes of the organization's central core of activity.
5. Organizations need to adopt new managerial theories and practices in order to flush out and benefit from the knowledge assets found at their fringes, including IS/IT-related new knowledge.
6. Such managerial theories and practices can only be found in holistic approaches which integrate the realms of organizational knowledge and technology.

THE EPISTEMOLOGICAL PROBLEM

Many of the perspectives put forward and discussed in this book are not novel, either in terms of the management and organization science establishments or even in terms of the information systems literature. So, what prevents them from being taken up? The problem is one of credibility. Most of the notions argued throughout the book (organizational knowledge, learning, culture, contexts, values, roles, relationships, etc) are classified as 'flower power' by a large majority of practitioners and by many researchers. They are considered 'interesting' as debating themes but regarded of little consequence when it comes to actual, hands-on management.

The problem, in our view, revolves around the epistemological foundations which guide both professional activity and academic research. The large majority of research papers accepted for publication, for example in the information systems literature, conform to the description of positivist research (97 per cent according to Orlikowski and Baroudi, 1991). A research design can be considered as positivist when formal propositions, quantifiable measures of variables, hypothesis testing and the drawing of inferences about a phenomenon from a representative sample to a stated population are used. Thus, research designs which do not conform to the norm are still not taken very seriously.

The alternative to positivist research is interpretive research. We can talk of interpretive research when there are no predefined dependent and independent variables but when the focus is on the complexity of human sensemaking captured and interpreted against the contextual background where the situation emerges. Interpretive research in information systems attempts to understand the phenomena through the meanings that people attribute to them, enabling an understanding of the social and organizational issues related to the adoption and integration of IS/IT in organizations. As aptly pointed out by Ciborra et al. (2000:27), the aim of interpretive research is

> to get closer to the 'of course', the obvious dismissal of the intricacies of 'real life' that 'naturally' cannot be captured by a model, to that 'business savvy' to which the caveats implicitly make reference.

We hope that through our work the interpretive research camp may receive a small but heartfelt contribution and that in the near future we may read more about organizational action, collective knowledge and information technology as integrated research topics. Hopefully, that will mean that not only non-positivism methods are taking hold but also that our view of the world is becoming less fragmented, more holistic and certainly more in line with our problems.

Bibliography

Allaire, Y. and M.E. Firsirotu (1984), 'Theories of organizational culture', *Organization Studies*, **5** (3), 193–226.

Andreu, R. and C. Ciborra (1994), 'Core capabilities and information technology', paper presented at the Second SISnet Conference, Barcelona, Spain, 1994.

Andrews, K. (1971), *The Concept of Corporate Strategy*, Homewood, IL: Dow-Jones-Irwin.

Angell, I.O. and S. Smithson (1991), *Information Systems Management*, London: Macmillan.

Ansoff, H.I. (1965), *Corporate Strategy*, New York: McGraw Hill.

Applegate, L.M. (1994), 'Managing in an information age: transforming the organization for the 1990s', in R. Baskerville, S. Smithson, O. Ngwenyama and J. De Gross (eds), *Transforming Organizations with Information Technology*, Amsterdam: North-Holland.

Applegate, L.M., J.I. Cash and D.Q. Mills (1988), 'Information technology and tomorrow's manager', *Harvard Business Review* (Nov.–Dec.), 128–36.

Applegate, L.M., F.W. McFarlan and J.L. McKenney (1999), *Corporate Information Systems Management*, Boston: McGraw-Hill.

Argyris, C. (1977), 'Double loop learning in organizations', *Harvard Business Review* (Sept.–Oct.), 115–24.

Argyris, C., R. Putnam and D.M. Smith (1985), *Action Science: Concepts, Methods and Skills for Research and Intervention*, San Francisco: Jossey-Bass.

Argyris, C. and D.A. Schon (1978), *Organizational Learning: A Theory of Action Perspective*, Reading, MA: Addison-Wesley.

Argyris, C. and D.A. Schon (1996), *Organizational Learning II: Theory, Method and Practice*, Reading, MA: Addison-Wesley.

Ashforth, B.E. (1985), 'Climate formation: issues and extensions', *Academy of Management Review*, **10** (4), 837–47.

Attewell, P. and J. Rule (1984), 'Computing and organizations: what we know and what we don't know', *Communications of the ACM*, **27**, 1184–92.

Avgerou, C. and T. Cornford (1993), *Developing Information Systems*, London: Macmillan.

Avison, D.E. and M. Myers (1995), 'Information systems and anthropology: an anthropological perspective on IT and organizational culture', *Information Technology and People*, **8** (3), 43–56.

Avison, D.E. and A.T. Wood-Harper (1990), *Multiview: An Exploration in Information Systems Development*, Oxford: Blackwell.

Bakos, J.Y. and M.E. Treacy (1986), 'Information technology and corporate strategy: a research perspective', *MIS Quarterly* (June), 107–19.

Barnard, C.I. (1938/68), *The Functions of the Executive*, Cambridge, MA: Harvard University Press.

Barney, J.B. (1986), 'Organizational culture: can it be a source of sustained competitive advantage?', *Academy of Management Review*, **11**, 656–65.

Barney, J.B. (1991), 'Firm resources and sustained competitive advantage', *Journal of Management*, **17**, 99–120.

Bartlett, C. and S. Ghoshal (1990), 'Matrix management: not a structure, a frame of mind', *Harvard Business Review* (Jul.–Aug.), 138–45.

Bartlett, C. and S. Ghoshal (1993), 'Beyond the M-Form: towards a managerial theory of the firm', *Strategic Management Journal*, **14**, 23–46.

Bartlett, C. and S. Ghoshal (1994), 'Changing the role of top management: beyond strategy to purpose', *Harvard Business Review* (Nov.–Dec.), 79–88.

Becker, B.E., M.A. Huselid and D. Ulrich (2001), *The HR Scorecard*, Boston, MA: Harvard Business School Press.

Benyon, D. (1990), *Information and Data Modelling*, Oxford: Blackwell.

Bohm, D. (1980), *Wholeness and the Implicate Order*, London: Routledge.

Boje, D.M. (1995), 'Stories of the storytelling world: a postmodern analysis of Disney as "Tamara Land"', *Academy of Management Journal*, **38** (4), 997–1035.

Boje, D.M., D.E. Fitzgibbons and D.S. Steingard (1996), 'Storytelling at *Administrative Science Quarterly*: warding off the postmodern barbarians', in D.M. Boje, R.P. Gephart and T.J. Thatchenkery (eds), *Postmodern Management and Organization Theory*, Thousand Oaks, CA: Sage.

Boland, R. (1987), 'The in-formation of information systems', in R.J. Boland and R.A. Hirschheim (eds), *Critical Issues in Information Systems Research*, Chichester, UK: Wiley.

Boland, R.J. and R.V. Tenkasi (1995), 'Perspective making and perspective taking in communities of knowing', *Organization Science*, **6** (4), 350–72.

Bostrom, R.P. and J.S. Heinen (1977), 'MIS problems and failures: a sociotechnical perspective', *MIS Quarterly* (Sept.), 17–32.

Boulding, K.E. (1956), 'General systems theory: the skeleton of science', *Management Science*, **2**, 197–208.

Bowditch, J.L. and A.F. Buono (1997), *A Primer on Organizational Behaviour*, New York: Wiley.

Boynton, A.C., R.W. Zmud and G.C. Jacobs (1994), 'The influence of information technology management practice on information technology use in large organizations', *MIS Quarterly*, **18** (Sept.), 299–316.

Bradley, S.P. (1993), 'The role of IT networking in sustaining competitive advantage', in S.P. Bradley and J.A. Hausman (eds), *Globalization, Technology and Competition*, Boston: Harvard Business School Press.

Broekstra, O. (1998), 'An organization is a conversation', in D. Grant, T. Keenoy and C. Oswick (eds), *Discourse and Organization,* London: Sage.

Brown, A.D. (1995), 'Managing understandings in IT implementation', *Organization Studies*, **16** (6), 153–69.

Brown, C.V. and J.W. Ross (1996), 'The information systems balancing act: building partnership and infrastructure', *Information Technology and People*, **9** (1), 49–62.

Brown, J.S. and P. Duguid (1991), 'Organizational learning and communities of practice', *Organization Science*, **2**, 40–57.

Brynjolfsson, E. (1993), 'The productivity paradox of information technology', *Communications of the ACM*, **36** (12), 67–77.

Buckley, W. (2001), 'A dynamic systems model', in F. Geyer and J. van der Zouwen (eds), *Sociocybernetics: Complexity, Autopoiesis and Observation of Social Systems*, Westport, CT: Greenwood Press.

Burn, J. (1997), 'A professional balancing act: walking the tightrope of strategic alignment', in C. Sauer and P.W. Yetton (eds), *Steps to the Future*, San Francisco: Jossey-Bass.

Burns, T. and G.M. Stalker (1961), *The Management of Innovation*, London: Tavistock Publications.

Burke, W.W. (2002), *Organization Change: Theory and Practice*, Thousand Oaks, CA: Sage.

Campbell, H. (1996), 'A social interactionist perspective on computer implementation', *Journal of the American Planning Association*, **62** (1), 99–107.

Cash, J.I. and B.R. Konsyski (1985), 'IS redraws competitive boundaries', *Harvard Business Review*, **62** (March–April), 134–42.

Cash, J.I., F.W. McFarlan and J.L. McKenney (1992), *Corporate Information Systems Management*, Boston: McGraw-Hill.

Casti, J. (1997), *Would Be Worlds*, New York: Wiley.

Chakravarthy, B. (1997), 'A new strategy for coping with turbulence', *Sloan Management Review* (Winter), 69–82.

Chandler, A.D. (1962), *Strategy and Structure*, Cambridge, MA: MIT Press.

Checkland, P. and S. Holwell (1998), *Information, Systems and Information Systems: Making Sense of the Field*, Chichester, UK: J. Wiley.

Child, J. (1972), 'Organizational structure, environment and performance: the role of strategic choice', *Sociology*, **6** (1), 1–22.

Child, J. (1984), *Organization*, London: Harper and Row.

Choo, C.W. and A. Clement (1994), 'Beyond the stage models for EUC management', *Information Technology and People*, **6** (4), 197–214.

Ciborra, C.U. (1994), 'The grassroots of IT and strategy', in C. Ciborra and T. Jelassi (eds), *Strategic Information Systems*, Chichester, UK: J. Wiley.

Ciborra, C.U. (1997), 'De profundis? deconstructing the concept of strategic alignment', *Scandinavian Journal of Information Systems*, **9** (1), 67–82.

Ciborra, C.U. and G. Lanzara (1989), 'Change and formative contexts', in H. Klein and K. Kumar (eds), *Systems Development for Human Progress*, Amsterdam: North-Holland.

Ciborra, C.U. and G. Lanzara (1994), 'Formative contexts and IT: understanding the dynamics of innovation in organizations', *Accounting, Management and Information Technology*, **4** (2), 61–86.

Ciborra, C.U., G. Patriotta and L. Erlicher (1995), 'Disassembling frames on the assembly line: the theory and practice of the new division of learning in advanced manufacturing', paper presented at the Information Technology and Changes in Organizational Work Conference, Cambridge, UK, 1995.

Ciborra, C.U. et al. (2000), *From Control to Drift*, Oxford: Oxford University Press.

Clegg, S.R. (1989), *Frameworks of Power*, London: Sage.

Clemons, E.K. (1993), 'Information technology and the boundary of the firm: who wins, who loses, who has to change', in S.P. Bradley and J.A. Hausman (eds), *Globalization, Technology and Competition*, Boston: Harvard Business School Press.

Coase, R.H. (1937), 'The nature of the firm', *Econometrica*, **4**, 386–405.

Coghlan, D. (1993), 'In defense of process consultation', in C. Mabey and B. Mayon-White (eds), *Managing Change*, London: Paul Chapman Publishing.

Cohen, W.M. and D.A. Levinthal (1990), 'Absorptive capacity: a new perspective on learning and innovation', *Administrative Science Quarterly*, **35**, 128–52.

Conner, K. (1991), 'A historical comparison of resource-based theory and five schools of thought within industrial organization economics', *Journal of Management*, **17**, 121–54.

Conner, K.R. and C.K. Prahalad (1996), 'A resource-based theory of the firm: knowledge versus opportunism', *Organization Science*, **7** (5), 477–501.

Cooper, R. and R.W. Zmud (1990), 'Information technology implementation research: a technology diffusion approach', *Management Science*, **34** (2), 123–39.

Cooprider, J.G. and J.C. Henderson (1990), 'Technology-process fit: perspectives on achieving prototyping effectiveness', *Journal of Management Information Systems*, **7** (3), 67–87

Cornford, A. (1995), *Computer-Based Information Systems*, University of London External Programme Guides, London: University of London.

Cross, J., M.J. Earl and J.L. Sampler (1997), 'Transformations of the IT function at British Petroleum', *MIS Quarterly* (December), 401–23.

Curley, K.F. and P.J. Pyburn (1982), 'Intellectual technologies: the key to improving white collar productivity', *Sloan Management Review* (Fall), 31–9.

Cyert, R.M. and J.G. March (1963), *A Behavioral Theory of the Firm*, Englewood Cliffs, NJ: Prentice-Hall.

D'Aveni, R. (1994), *Hypercompetitive Rivalries*, New York: The Free Press

Dahlbom, B. (2000), 'Postface: from infrastructure to networking', in C.U. Ciborra, and Associates, *From Control to Drift*, Oxford: Oxford University Press

Damasio, A.R. (1994), *Descartes' Error*, New York: Putnam.

Davenport, T. (1994), 'Saving IT's soul: towards human-centred information management', *Harvard Business Review* (March–April), 119–31.

Davenport, T.H. and D.A. Marchand (2000), 'Is KM just good information management?', in D.A. Marchand, T.H. Davenport and T. Dickson (eds), *Mastering Information Management*, London: Financial Times/Prentice Hall.

Davenport, T.H. and J.E. Short (1990), 'The new Industrial Engineering: information technology and business process redesign', *Sloan Management Review*, **31** (4), 11–27.

Davies, G.B. and M.H. Olson (1985), *Management Information Systems: Conceptual Foundations, Structure and Development*, New York: McGraw-Hill.

De Jong, W.M. (1994), *The Management of Informatization: A Theoretical and Empirical Analysis of IT Implementation Strategies*, Groningen: Wolters-Noordhoff.

De Lone, W.H. and E.R. McLean (1992), 'Information systems success: the quest for the independent variable', *Information Systems Research*, **3** (1), 60–95.

De Marco, T. (1979), *Structured Analysis and Systems Specification*, New York: Yourdon Press.

Dertouzos, M. (1997), *What Will Be: How the New World of Information Will Change our Lives*, London: Piatkus.

De Sanctis and M.S. Poole (1994), 'Capturing the complexity of advanced technology use', *Organization Science*, **5** (2), 121–47.

Drucker, P. (1955), *The Practice of Management*, Oxford: Butterworth-Heinemann.

Durkheim, E. (1938), *The Rules of Sociological Method*, New York: Free Press.

Dutta, S. (1996), 'Linking IT and business strategy: the role and responsibility of senior management', *European Management Journal*, **14** (3), 255–66.

Earl, M.J. (1989), *Management Strategies for Information Technology*, Hemel Hempstead, UK: Prentice-Hall.

Earl, M.J. (1996), 'Integrating IS and the organization: a framework of organizational fit', in M.J. Earl (ed.), *Information Management: The Organizational Dimension*, Oxford: Oxford University Press.

Earl, M.J. (ed.) (1996), *Information Management: The Organizational Dimension*, Oxford: Oxford University Press.

Eason, K.D. (1988), *Information Technology and Organizational Change*, London: Taylor and Francis.

Eccles, R.G. (1991), 'The performance measurement manifesto', *Harvard Business Review* (Jan.–Feb.), 131–7.

Eccles, R.G. and N. Nohria (1992), *Beyond the Hype: Rediscovering the Essence of Management*, Boston, MA: Harvard Business School Press.

Edvinson, L. and M.S. Malone (1997), *Intellectual Capital*, London: Piatkus.

El Sawy, O.A. (1985), 'Implementation by cultural infusion', *MIS Quarterly*, **9** (2), 131–40.

Elam, J.J., M.J. Ginzberg, P.G.W. Keen and R.W. Zmud (eds) (1988), *Transforming the IS Organization*, Washington, DC: International Center for Information Technologies.

Eveland, J.D. (1987), 'Diffusion, technology transfer and implementation', *Knowledge: Creation, Diffusion, Utilization*, **8** (2), 303–22.

Falcione, R.L., L. Sussman and R.P. Herden (1987), 'Communication climate in organizations', in F.M. Jablin, L.L. Putnam, K.H. Roberts and L.W. Porter (eds), *Handbook of Organizational Communication*, Newbury Park, CA: Sage.

Fayol, H. (1949), *General and Industrial Management*, London: Pitman.

Feeny, D., B. Edwards and K. Simpson (1992), *Understanding the CEO/CIO Relationship*, Oxford: Oxford Institute of Information Management.

Feeny, D.F. and L.P. Willcocks (1998), 'Re-designing the IS function around core capabilities', *Long Range Planning*, **31** (3), 354–67.

Finkelstein, C. (1989), *An Introduction to Information Engineering: From Strategic Planning to Information Systems*, Sydney: Addison-Wesley.

Fiol, C.M. (1991), 'Managing culture as a competitive resource: an identity-based view of sustainable competitive advantage', *Journal of Management*, **17** (1), 191–211.

Fiol, M.C. and M.A. Lyles (1985), 'Organizational learning', *Academy of Management Review*, **10** (4), 803–13.

Follett, M.P. (1924), *Creative Experience*, New York: Longmans Green.

Forester, T. (1980), *The Micro Electronics Revolution*, Oxford: Blackwell.

Freeman, W.J. (1999), *How Brains Make Up Their Minds*, London: Phoenix, Orion Books.

French, W.L. and C.H. Bell (1995), *Organization Development: Behavioural Science Interventions for Organizational Improvement*, Englewood Cliffs, NJ: Prentice-Hall.

Galbraith, J. (1973), *Designing Complex Organizations*, Reading, MA: Addison-Wesley.

Galliers, R.D. (1991), 'Strategic information systems: myths, realities and guidelines for successful implementation', *European Journal of Information Systems*, **1** (1), 55–64.

Galliers, R.D. and B.S.H. Baker (eds) (1994), *Strategic Information Management: Challenges and Strategies in Managing Information Systems*, Oxford: Butterworth-Heinemann.

George, J.F., S. Iacono and R. Kling (1994), 'How do office workers learn about computing?', *Information Technology and People*, **6** (4), 249–70.

Geyer, F. and J. van der Zouwen (2001), 'Introduction to the main themes in sociocybernetics', in F. Geyer and J. van der Zouwen (eds), *Socio-cybernetics: Complexity, Autopoiesis and Observation of Social Systems*, Westport, CT: Greenwood Press.

Ghoshal, S. and C.A. Bartlett (1994), 'Linking organizational context and managerial action: the dimensions of quality management', *Strategic Management Journal*, **15**, 91–112.

Ghoshal, S. and C.A. Bartlett (1998), *The Individualized Corporation: A Fundamentally New Approach to Management*, London: Heinemann.

Ghoshal, S. and P. Moran (1996), 'Theories of economic organization: the case for realism and balance', *Academy of Management Review*, **20** (1), 58–71.

Giddens, A. (1984), *The Constitution of Society: Outline of the Theory of Structuration*, Cambridge: Polity Press.

Grant, R.M. (1991), 'The resource-based theory of competitive advantage: implications for strategy formulation', *California Management Review*, **33** (Spring), 114–35.

Guedes, F.C. (1999), *Economia e Complexidade*, Coimbra, Portugal: Livraria Almedina.

Gutek, B.A., T.K. Bikson and D. Mankin (1984), 'Individual and organizational consequences of computer-based information technology', in S. Oskamp (ed.), *Applied Social Psychology Annual: Applications in Organizational Settings*, Beverly Hills, CA: Sage.

Haeckel, H.H. and R.L. Nolan (1993), 'Managing by wire', *Harvard Business Review* (Sept.–Oct.), 122–32.

Hall, G., J. Rosenthal and J. Wade (1993), 'How to make reengineering really work', *Harvard Business Review* (Nov.–Dec.), 119–31.

Hamel, G. and C.K. Prahalad (1989), 'Strategic intent', *Harvard Business Review*, **67** (May–June), 63–76.

Hamel, G. and C.K. Prahalad (1994), *Competing for the Future*, Boston, MA: Harvard Business School Press.

Hammer, M. and J. Champy (1994), *Reengineering the Corporation: A Manifesto for Business Revolution*, London: N. Brealey.

Handy, C. (1978), *Gods of Management*, London: Souvenir Press.

Hansen, G.S. and B. Wernerfelt (1989), 'Determinants of firm performance: the relative importance of economic and organizational factors', *Strategic Management Journal*, **10**, 399–411.

Hedberg, B. (1981), 'How organizations learn and unlearn', in P. Nystrom and W. Starbuck (eds), *Handbook of Organizational Design*, Vol. 1, New York: Oxford University Press.

Hedlund, G. (1994), 'A model of knowledge management and the N-Form Corporation', *Strategic Management Journal*, **15**, 73–90.

Henderson, B.D. (1970), *The Product Portfolio*, Boston: Boston Consulting Group.

Henderson, J.C. (1990), 'Plugging into strategic partnerships: the critical IS connection', *Sloan Management Review* (Spring), 7–18.

Henderson, J.C., J.B. Thomas and N. Venkatraman (1992), 'Making sense of IT: strategic alignment and organizational context', working paper, Sloan School of Management – MIT: C.I.S.R.

Hill, W.F. (1997), *Learning: A Survey of Psychological Interpretations*, New York: Longman.

Huber, G.P. (1984), 'The nature and design of post-industrial organizations', *Management Science*, **30**, 928–51.

Huber, G.P. (1990), 'A theory of the effects of advanced information technologies on organizational design, intelligence and decision making', *Academy of Management Review*, **15** (1), 47–71.

Huber, G.P. (1991), 'Organizational learning: the contributing processes and the literatures', *Organization Science*, **2** (1), 88–115.

Huff, S.L., M.L. Munro and B.H. Martin (1988), 'Growth stages of end-user computing', *Communications of the ACM*, **31** (5), 61–74.

Ilharco, F. (2003), 'Clausewitz on knowledge: a phenomenological analysis of *On War*'s explicit and implicit accounts of knowledge', paper presented at the 4th International Conference on Organizational Knowledge, Learning and Capabilities, IESE, Barcelona, April, 2003.

Introna, L. (1997), *Management, Information and Power*, London: Macmillan.

Itami, H. and T. Numagami (1992), 'Dynamic interaction between strategy and technology', *Strategic Management Journal*, **13**, 119–35.

Ives, B. and G.P. Learmonth (1984), 'The information system as a competitive weapon', *Communications of the ACM*, **27** (12), 1193–1201.

Jackson, M. (1983), *Systems Development*, Englewood Cliffs, NJ: Prentice-Hall.

Joyce, P. and A. Woods (1996), *Essential Strategic Management: From Modernism to Pragmatism*, Oxford: Butterworth-Heinemann.

Kakabadse, A. and N. Kakabadse (1999), *Essence of Leadership*, London: International Thomson Business Press.

Kaplan, R.S. and D. Norton (1996), *The Balanced Scorecard*, Boston: Harvard Business School Press.

Kappelman, L.A. and E.R. McLean (1994), 'User engagement in information systems development', in L. Levine (ed.), *Diffusion, Transfer and Implementation of Information Technology*, Amsterdam: North-Holland.

Katz, D. and R.L. Kahn (1966), *The Social Psychology of Organizations*, New York: Wiley.

Keen, P.G.W. (1981), 'Information systems and organizational change', *Communications of the ACM*, **24** (1), 24–33.

Keen, P.G.W. (1988), *Competing in Time*, Cambridge, MA: Ballinger.

Keen, P.G.W. (1991), *Shaping the Future: Business Design through Information Technology*, Boston: Harvard Business School Press.

Kelly, M. (1994), 'Productivity and IT: the elusive connection', *Management Sciences*, **40** (11), 1406–25.

Kenney, M. (2001), 'The temporal dynamics of knowledge creation in the information society', in I. Nonaka and T. Nishiguchi (eds), *Knowledge Emergence*, New York: Oxford University Press.

King, J.L. and K.L. Kraemer (1984), 'Evolution of organizational information systems: an assessment of Nolan's stages model', *Communications of the ACM*, **27** (5 May), 466–75.

Kraemer, K.L., J.L. King, D.E. Dunkle and J.P. Lane (1989), *Managing Information Systems: Change and Control in Organizational Computing*, San Francisco, CA: Jossey-Bass.

Kuhn, T. (1970), *The Structure of Scientific Revolutions*, Chicago: Chicago University Press.

Kwon, T.H. and R.W. Zmud (1987), 'Unifying the fragmented models of information systems implementation', in R.J. Boland and R.A. Hirscheim (eds), *Critical Issues in Information Systems Research*, Chichester, UK: Wiley.

Lacity, M. and R. Hirscheim (1995), *Beyond the Outsourcing Bandwagon*, Chichester, UK: Wiley.

Land, F. (1985), 'Is an information theory enough?', *The Computer Journal*, **28** (3), 211–15.

Land, F. (1992), 'The management of change: guidelines for the successful implementation of information systems', in A. Brown (ed.), *Creating a Business-Based IT Strategy*, London: Chapman-Hall.

Land, F. (1994), 'The new alchemist: or how to transmute base organisations into corporations of gleaming gold – key note address', paper presented at the Transforming Organizations with Information Technology Conference, University of Michigan, Ann Arbor, 1994.

Land, F., N. Detjejaruwat and C. Smith (1983), 'Factors affecting social control: the reasons and values – part 1', *Systems, Objectives, Solutions*, **3** (3), 155–64.

Land, F., N. Detjejaruwat and C. Smith (1983a), 'Factors affecting social control: the reasons and values – part 2', *Systems, Objectives, Solutions*, **3** (4), 207–26.

Land, F., P. Le Quesne and I. Wijegunaratne (1989), 'Effective systems: overcoming the obstacles', *Journal of Information Technology*, **4** (2), 81–91.

Landauer, T.K. (1995), *The Trouble with Computers: Usefulness, Usability and Productivity*, Cambridge, MA: MIT Press.

Large, P. (1984), *The Micro Revolution Revisited*, London: Francis Pinter.

Lave, J. and E. Wenger (1991), *Situated Learning: Legitimate Peripheral Participation*, Cambridge, UK: Cambridge University Press.

Laszlo, E. (1996), *The Systemic View of the World*, Cresskill, NJ: Hampton Press.

Leavitt, H.J. and T.L. Whisler (1958), 'Management in the 1980s', *Harvard Business Review*, **38** (6), 41–8.

Lederer, A.L. and V. Sethi (1988), 'The implementation of strategic information systems planning methodologies', *MIS Quarterly* (Sept.), 445–61.

Lee, Alan S. (1991), 'Architecture as a reference discipline for MIS', in H.-E. Nissen (ed.), *The Information Systems Research Arena of the '90s*, Amsterdam: North-Holland.

Lewin, A.Y. and J.W. Minton (1986), 'Determining organizational effectiveness: another look and an agenda for research', *Management Science*, **32** (5), 514–38.

Lewin, K. (1947), 'Frontiers in group dynamics I', *Human Relations*, **1**, 5–40.

Lewin, K. (1947), 'Frontiers in group dynamics II', *Human Relations*, **1**, 147–53.

Lewin, R. (1993), *Complexity: Life on the Edge of Chaos*, London: Phoenix Paperbacks.

Lewin, R. and B. Regine (2000), *Weaving Complexity and Business: Engaging the Soul at Work*, New York: Texere.

Likert, R. and J.G. Likert (1976), *New Ways of Managing Conflict*, New York: McGraw-Hill.

Litwin, G.H. and R.A. Stringer (1968), *Motivation and Organizational Climate*, Boston: Harvard University.

Lloyd, B. (1994), 'IBM: decline or resurrection?', *Management Decision*, **32** (8), 5–10.

Lucas, H.C. (1975), 'Performance and the use of an information system', *Management Science*, **20**, 908–19.

Lucas, H.C. (1990), *Information Systems Concepts for Management*, New York: McGraw-Hill.

Lucas, H.C., M. Ginzberg and R. Schultz (1991), *Implementing Information Systems: Testing a Structural Model*, Norwood, NJ: Ablex.

Luhmann, N. (1986), 'The autopoiesis of social systems', in F. Geyer and J. van der Zouwen (eds), *Sociocybernetic Paradoxes: Observation, Control and Evolution of Self-Steering Systems*, London: Sage.

Luhmann, N. (1995), *Social Systems*, Stanford, CA: Stanford University Press.

Lundberg, C.C. (1984), 'Strategies for organizational transitioning', in J.R. Kimberly and R.E. Quinn (eds), *New Futures: The Challenge of Managing Corporate Transitions*, Homewood, IL: Dow-Jones-Irwin.

Lyotard, J.F. (1984), *The Post-Modern Condition: A Report on Knowledge*, Minneapolis: University of Minnesota Press.

McFadden, F.R. and J.A. Hoffer (1994), *Modern Database Management*, Reading, MA: Addison-Wesley.

McFarlan, F.W. (1981), 'Portfolio approach to information systems', *Harvard Business Review*, **59** (Sept.–Oct.), 142–50.

McFarlan, F.W. (1984), 'Information technology changes the way you compete', *Harvard Business Review*, **62** (May–June), 98–103.

McFarlan, F.W. and R.L. Nolan (1995), 'How to manage an IT outsourcing alliance', *Sloan Management Review*, **36** (2), 9–23.

McGregor, D. (1960), *The Human Side of Enterprise*, New York: McGraw-Hill.

McNurlin, B.C. and R.H. Sprague (1998), *Information Systems Management in Practice*, Upper Saddle River, NJ: Prentice-Hall.

Macdonald, H. (1991), 'The strategic alignment process', in M. Scott Morton (ed.), *The Corporation of the 1990s*, New York: Oxford University Press.

Magalhães, R. (1998), 'Organizational knowledge and learning', in G. von Krogh, J. Roos and D. Kleine (eds), *Knowing in the Firm: Understanding, Managing and Measuring Knowledge*, London: Sage.

Magalhães, R. (1999), *The Organizational Implementation of Information Systems: Towards a New Theory*, unpublished PhD thesis, London School of Economics.

Mahoney, J.T. (1995), 'The management of resources and the resource of management', *Journal of Business Research*, **33**, 91–101.

Malone, T.W. and J.F. Rockart (1993), 'How will information technology reshape organizations? Computers as coordination technology', in S.P.

Bradley and J.A. Hausman (eds), *Globalization, Technology and Competition*, Boston: Harvard Business School Press.

March, J.G. and H.A. Simon (1958), *Organizations*, New York: Wiley.

Markus, M.L. (1983), 'Power, politics and MIS implementation', *Communications of the ACM*, **26** (6), 430–44.

Markus, M.L. and R. Benjamin (1997), 'IT-enabled organizational change', in C. Sauer and P.W. Yetton (eds), *Steps to the Future*, San Francisco: Jossey-Bass.

Markus, M.L. and D. Robey (1988), 'Information technology and organizational change: causal structure in theory and research', *Management Science*, **34** (5), 583–98.

Martin, J. (1989), *Strategic Information Planning Methodologies*, Englewood Cliffs, NJ: Prentice-Hall.

Mason, R.O. (1993), 'IS technology and corporate strategy', in A.J. Rowe, R.O. Mason, K.E. Dickel, R.B. Mann and R.J. Mockler, *Strategic Management: A Methodological Approach*, Reading, MA: Addison-Wesley.

Mata, F.J.F., W.L. Fuerst and J.B. Barney (1995), 'Information technology and sustained competitive advantage: a resource-based analysis', *MIS Quarterly*, **19** (4), 487–505.

Maturana, H. (1988), 'Reality: the search for objectivity or the quest for a compelling argument', *Irish Journal of Psychology*, **9** (1), 25–82.

Maturana, H.R. and F.J. Varela (1980), *Autopoiesis and Cognition: The Realization of the Living*, Dordrecht, Holland: D. Reidel Publishing.

Maturana, H.R. and F.J. Varela (1987/1992), *The Tree of Knowledge*, Boston, Shambhala.

Mills, D.Q. and G.B. Friesen (1996), *Broken Promises: An Unconventional View of What Went Wrong at IBM*, Boston: Harvard Business School Press.

Mingers, J. (1995), *Self-Producing Systems: Implications and Applications of Autopoiesis*, New York: Plenum Press.

Mingers, J. (2001), 'Information, meaning and communication: an autopoietic approach', in F. Geyer and J. van der Zouwen (eds), *Sociocybernetics: Complexity, Autopoiesis and Observation of Social Systems*, Westport, CT: Greenwood Press.

Mintzberg, H. (1990), 'The design school: reconsidering the basic premises of strategic management', *Strategic Management Journal*, **11** (3), 171–95.

Mintzberg, H. (1994), 'The fall and rise of strategic planning', *Harvard Business Review* (Jan.–Feb.), 107–14.

Mintzberg, H. and J.B. Quinn (1991), *The Strategy Process: Concepts, Contexts, Cases*, Englewood Cliffs, NJ: Prentice-Hall.

Monks, R.A.G. and N. Minow (1995), *Corporate Governance*, Oxford: Blackwell.

Morgan, G. (1997), *Images of Organization*, Thousand Oaks, CA: Sage.

Morieux, Y.V.H. and E. Sutherland (1988), 'The interaction between the use of information technology and organizational culture', *Behaviour and Information Technology*, **7** (2), 205–13.

Mumford, E. (1983), *Designing Human Systems*, Manchester: Manchester Business School Publications.

Mumford, E. (1996), *Systems Design: Ethical Tools for Ethical Change*, Basingstoke, UK: Macmillan.

Mumford, E. and M. Weir (1979), *Computer Systems in Work Design: The ETHICS Method*, London: Associated Business Press.

Nelson, D.L. (1990), 'Individual adjustments to information-driven technologies', *MIS Quarterly*, **14**, 79–98.

Nelson, R.R. and S. Winter (1982), *An Evolutionary Theory of Economic Change*, Cambridge, MA, Harvard University Press.

Nicolis, G. and I. Prigogine (1989), *Exploring Complexity*, New York: W.H. Freeman.

Nolan, R. (1979), 'Managing the crisis in data processing', *Harvard Business Review*, **57** (2), 115–26.

Nonaka, I. (1988), 'Creating organizational order out of chaos', *California Management Review*, **30** (Spring), 57–73.

Nonaka, I. (1994), 'A dynamic theory of organizational knowledge creation', *Organization Science*, **5** (1), 14–37.

Nonaka, I., N. Konno and R. Toyama (2001), 'Emergence of *ba*', in I. Nonaka and T. Nishiguchi (eds), *Knowledge Emergence*, New York: Oxford University Press.

Nonaka, I. and H. Takeuchi (1995), *The Knowledge Creating Company: How Japanese Companies Create the Dynamics of Innovation*, New York: Oxford University Press.

Nordhaug, O. (1993), *Human Capital in Organizations: Competence, Training and Learning*, Oslo/London: Scandinavian University Press/Oxford University Press.

Normann, R. (1985), 'Developing capabilities of organizational learning', in J.M. Pennings et al. (eds), *Organizational Strategy and Change*, San Francisco: Jossey-Bass.

Norton, D. (2002), 'The alignment enigma', *CIO Insight*, Special Issue 2002, Ziff Davies Media Inc., editors@cioinsight.com.

Olve, N.-G., J. Roy and M. Wetter (1999), *Performance Drivers*, Chichester, UK: Wiley.

Orlikowski, W.J. (1992), 'The duality of technology: rethinking the concept of technology in organizations', *Organization Science*, **3** (3), 398–427.

Orlikowski, W.J. and J.J. Baroudi (1991), 'Studying information technology in organizations: research approaches and assumptions', *Information Systems Research*, **2** (1), 1–28.

Orlikowski, W.J. and D.C. Gash (1994), 'Technological frames: making sense of information technology in organizations', *ACM Transactions on Information Systems*, **12** (2), 174–207.

Parsons, G.L. (1983), 'Information technology: a new competitive weapon', *Sloan Management Journal* (Fall), 3–14.

Parsons, T. (1952), *The Social System*, London: Tavistock.

Parsons, T. and N.J. Smelser (1956), *Structure and Process in Modern Society*, New York: Free Press.

Pascale, R.T., M. Millemann and L. Gioja (2000), *Surfing the Edge of Chaos*, London: Texere.

Penrose, E. (1959/1995), *The Theory of the Growth of the Firm*, Oxford: Oxford University Press.

Pentland, B. (1995), 'Information systems and organizational learning: the social epistemology of organizational knowledge systems', *Accounting, Management and Information Technologies*, **5** (1), 1–21.

Petrozzo, D. (1995), 'Restructuring the purpose of IT in an organization', *National Productivity Review*, **14** (3), 17–26.

Pettigrew, A. (1987), 'Context and action in the transformation of the firm', *Journal of Management Studies*, **24** (6), 649–70.

Pettigrew, A. (2000), 'Linking change processes to outcomes', in M. Beer and N. Nohria (eds), *Breaking the Code of Change*, Boston: Harvard Business School Press.

Pettigrew, A., R. Whipp and R. Rosenfelt (1989), 'Competitiveness and the management of strategic change', in A. Francis and P. Tharanken (eds), *The Competitiveness of European Industry*, London: Routledge.

Pettigrew, A. and R. Whipp (1991), *Managing Change for Competitive Success*, Oxford: Blackwell.

Polanyi, M. (1973), *Personal Knowledge: Towards a Post-Critical Philosophy*, London: Routledge & Kegan Paul.

Pondy, L.R. and I. Mitroff (1979), 'Beyond open systems models of organization', in B.M. Staw (ed.), *Research in Organizational Behavior – Vol.1*, Greenwich, CT: JAI Press.

Porter, M. (1980), *Competitive Strategy*, New York: The Free Press.

Porter, M. (1985), *Competitive Advantage*, New York: The Free Press.

Porter, M. (1991), 'Towards a dynamic theory of strategy', *Strategic Management Journal*, **12** (Winter), 95–117.

Porter, M. (1996), 'What is strategy?', *Harvard Business Review* (Nov.–Dec.), 61–78.

Porter, M. and V.E. Millar (1985), 'How information gives you competitive advantage', *Harvard Business Review*, **63** (4), 149–60.

Prahalad, C.K. and G. Hamel (1990), 'The core competence of the corporation', *Harvard Business Review* (May–June), 79–91.

Prigogine, I. and I. Stengers (1985), *Order out of Chaos*, London: Fontana Paperbacks.

Quinn, J.B. and M.N. Baily (1994), 'Information technology: increasing productivity in services', *Academy of Management Executive*, **8** (3), 28–47.

Remenyi, D. and M. Sherwood-Smith (1997), *Achieving Maximum Value from Information Systems*, Chichester, UK: Wiley.

Roberts, E.B. (1987), 'Managing technological innovations: a search for generalizations', in E.B. Roberts (ed.), *Generating Technological Innovation*, New York: Oxford University Press.

Robey, D. (1977), 'Computers and management structure: some empirical findings re-examined', *Human Relations*, **30**, 963–76.

Robey, D. (1981), 'Computer information systems', *Communications of the ACM*, **24** (10), 679–87.

Robey, D. (1995), 'Theories that explain contradiction: accounting for the contradictory organizational consequences of Information Technology', paper presented at the International Conference on Information Systems, Amsterdam, 1995.

Robey, D. and A. Azevedo (1994), 'Cultural analysis and the organizational consequences of IT', *Accounting, Management and Information Technologies*, **4**, 23–37.

Rockart, J.F. (1979), 'Chief executives define their own data needs', *Harvard Business Review*, **57** (2), 81–93.

Rockart, J.F. (1988), 'The line takes the leadership: IS management in a wired society', *Sloan Management Review*, **29** (Summer), 57–64.

Rockart, J.F., M.J. Earl and J.W. Ross (1996), 'Eight imperatives for the new IT organization', *Sloan Management Review*, **38** (Fall), 43–55.

Rockart, J.F. and J.E. Short (1989), 'IT in the 1990s: managing organizational interdependence', *Sloan Management Review*, (Winter), 7–17.

Ross, J.W., C.M. Beath and D.L. Goodhue (1996), 'Develop long-term competitiveness through IT assets', *Sloan Management Review*, **38** (Fall), 31–42.

Rowan, J. (1976), *Ordinary Ecstasy: Humanistic Psychology in Action*, London: Routledge & Kegan Paul.

Rumelt, R. (1984), 'Towards a strategic theory of the firm', in R. Lamb (ed.), *Competitive Strategic Management*, Englewood Cliffs, NJ: Prentice-Hall.

Sackmann, S. (1991), *Cultural Knowledge in Organizations: Exploring the Collective Mind*, Newbury Park: Sage.

Saga, V.L. and R.W. Zmud (1994), 'The nature and determinants of IT acceptance, routinization and infusion', in L. Levine (ed.), *Diffusion, Transfer and Implementation of Information Systems*, Amsterdam, Holland: North-Holland.

Sambamurthy, V. and R.W. Zmud (1997), 'At the heart of success', in C.

Sauer and P.W. Yetton (eds), *Steps to the Future*, San Francisco: Jossey-Bass.

Schein, E. (1980), *Organizational Psychology*, Englewood Cliffs, NJ: Prentice-Hall.

Schein, E. (1992), *Organizational Culture and Leadership*, San Francisco: Jossey-Bass.

Schein, E. (1992a), 'The role of the CEO in the management of change: the case of information technology', in T.A. Kochan and M. Useem (eds), *Transforming Organizations*, New York: Oxford University Press.

Schneider, B. (1975), 'Organizational climates: an essay', *Personnel Psychology*, **28**, 447–79.

Schneider, B. (1990), 'The climate for service: an application of the climate construct', in B. Schneider (ed.), *Organizational Climate and Culture*, San Francisco: Jossey-Bass.

Schwuchow, W. (1988), 'The development of the international market for online information services', Proceedings of the 14th FID Conference, Helsinki, September, 1988, 166–78.

Scott Morton, M. (ed.) (1991), *The Corporation of the 1990s: Information Technology and Organizational Transformation*, New York: Oxford University Press.

Selznick, P. (1957), *Leadership in Administration*, New York: Harper & Row.

Semler, R. (1994), 'Why my former employees still work for me', *Harvard Business Review* (Jan.–Feb.), 64–74.

Senge, P. (1990), *The Fifth Discipline: The Art and Practice of the Learning Organization*, London: Century Business.

Simon, H. (1945/1997), *Administrative Behavior*, New York: The Free Press.

Slappendel, C. (1996), 'Perspectives on innovation in organizations', *Organization Studies*, **17** (1), 107–29.

Smith, H.A. and J.D. McKeen (1992), 'Computerization and management: a study of conflict and change', *Information and Management*, **22**, 53–64.

Sprague, R.H. and B.C. McNurlin (eds) (1993), *Information Systems Management in Practice*, 3rd edn, Upper Saddle River, NJ: Prentice-Hall.

Sprague, R.H. and B.C. McNurlin (1998), *Information Systems Management in Practice*, Upper Saddle River, NJ: Prentice-Hall.

Sproull, L and S. Kiesler (1991), *Connections: New Ways of Working in the Networked Organization*, Cambridge, MA: MIT Press.

Stacey, R.D. (2001), 'Complex responsive processes in organizations', London: Routledge.

Star, S.L. and K. Ruhleder (1996), 'Steps towards an ecology of infrastructure: design and access to large information spaces', *Information Systems Research*, **7** (1), 111–34.

Stein, E.W. and V. Zwass (1995), 'Actualizing organizational memory with information systems', *Information Systems Research*, 6.

Stickland, F. (1998), *The Dynamics of Change*, London: Routledge.

Strassman, P.A. (1985), *Information Payoff: The Transformation of Work in the Electronic Age*, New York: The Free Press.

Sullivan, C.H. (1985), 'Systems planning in the information age', *Sloan Management Review* (Winter), 3–11.

Swanson, E.B. (1988), *Information Systems Implementation*, Homewood, IL: Irwin.

Symons, V.J. (1991), 'Impacts of information systems: four perspectives', *Information and Software Technology*, **33** (3), 181–90.

Teece, D.J. (2000), *Managing Intellectual Capital*, New York: Oxford University Press.

Tenkasi, R.V. and R.J. Boland (1993), 'Locating meaning making in organizational learning: the narrative basis of cognition', in R.W. Woodman and W.A. Passmore (eds), *Research in Organizational Change and Development – Vol. 7*, Greenwich, CT: JAI Press.

Thompson, J. (1967), *Organizations in Action*, New York: McGraw-Hill.

Thurow, L. (1991), 'Foreword', in M.S. Scott Morton (ed.), *The Corporation of the 1990s: Information Technology and Organizational Transformation*, New York: Oxford University Press.

Trisoglio, A. (1995), 'The strategy and complexity seminar', Unpublished Working Paper 1: Managing Complexity, London School of Economics, London.

UK Academy for Information Systems (1997), *UK AIS Newsletter*, Vol. 1, No. 3.

Van der Heijden, K. (1996), *Scenarios: The Art of Strategic Conversation*, Chichester, UK: J. Wiley.

Varela, F.J. (1984), 'Two principles of self-organization', in H. Ulrich and G.J.B. Probst (eds), *Self Organization and Management of Social Systems*, New York: Springer Verlag.

Varela, F.J. (1992), 'Whence perceptual meaning? A cartography of current ideas', in F.J. Varela and J.-P. Dupuy (eds), *Understanding Origins*, Dordrecht, Holland: Kluwer Academic Publishers.

Varela, F.J. , E. Thompson and E. Rosch (1991), *The Embodied Mind*, Cambridge, MA: MIT Press.

Von Bertalanffy, L. (1950), 'The theory of open systems in physics and biology', in F.E. Emery (ed.), *Systems Thinking*, Harmondsworth, UK: Penguin.

Von Eckardt, B. (1993), *What is Cognitive Science?* Cambridge, MA: MIT Press.

Von Krogh, G. and J. Roos (1995), *Organizational Epistemology*, Basingstoke, UK: Macmillan.

Von Krogh, G. and J. Roos (1995a), 'Conversation management', *European Management Journal*, **13** (4), 390–94.

Von Krogh, G. and J. Roos (1996), 'Arguments on knowledge and competence', in G. Von Krogh and J. Roos (eds), *Managing Knowledge: Perspectives on Cooperation and Competition*, London, Sage.

Von Krogh, G., I. Nonaka and K. Ichijo (2000), *Enabling Knowledge Creating Company: How to Unlock the Mystery of Tacit Knowledge and Release the Power of Innovation*, New York: Oxford University Press.

Von Simson, E.M. (1990), 'The centrally decentralized IS organization', *Harvard Business Review* (Jul.–Aug.), 158–62.

Waldrop, M.M. (1992), *Complexity: The Emerging Science at the Edge of Order and Chaos*, London: Penguin Books.

Walsh, J.R. and G.R. Ungson (1991), 'Organizational memory', *Academy of Management Review*, **16**, 57–91.

Walsham, G. (1993), *Interpreting Information Systems in Organizations*, Chichester, UK: Wiley.

Walton, R. (1988), *Up and Running: Integrating Information Technology and the Organization*, Boston, MA: Harvard Business School Press.

Wang, C.B. (1994), *Techno Vision*, New York: McGraw-Hill.

Ward, J. and P. Griffiths (1996), *Strategic Planning for Information Systems*, Chichester, UK: Wiley.

Ward, J., P. Griffiths and P. Whitmore (1990), *Strategic Planning for Information Systems*, Chichester, UK: Wiley.

Ward, J. and J. Peppard (1996), 'Reconciling the IT–business relationship: a troubled marriage in need of guidance', *Journal of Strategic Information Systems*, **5**, 37–65.

Weber, M. (1947), *The Theory of Social Economic Organizations*, London: Oxford University Press.

Weick, K.E. (1991), 'The nontraditional quality of organizational learning', *Organization Science*, **2** (1), 116–24.

Weick, K.E. (1995), *Sensemaking in Organizations*, Beverly Hills, CA: Sage.

Wernerfelt, B. (1984), 'A resource-based view of the firm', *Strategic Management Journal*, **5**, 171–80.

Wernerfelt, B. (1995), 'The resource-based view of the firm: ten years after', *Strategic Management Journal*, **16**, 171–4.

Wheatley, M.J. (1999), *Leadership and the New Science*, San Francisco: Berret-Koehler.

Willcocks, L. (1994), 'Managing information systems in UK public administration: issues and prospects', *Public Administration*, **72** (Spring), 13–32.

Winter, S.G. (1987), 'Knowledge and competence as strategic assets', in D.J.

Teece (ed.), *The Competitive Challenge: Strategies for Industrial Innova-tion and Renewal*, Cambridge, MA: Ballinger Pub.

Wiseman, C. (1988), *Strategic Information Systems*, Homewood, IL: Irwin.

Yetton, P.W. (1997), 'False prophecies, successful practice and future direc-tions in IT management', in C. Sauer and P.W. Yetton (eds), *Steps to the Future*, San Francisco: Jossey-Bass.

Young, T.R. (1991), 'Chaos and social change: metaphysics of the postmodern', *The Social Science Journal*, **28** (2), 289–305.

Yourdon, E. (1989), *Modern Structured Analysis*, Englewood Cliffs, NJ: Prentice-Hall.

Zackman, J. (1987), 'A framework for information systems architecture', *IBM Systems Journal*, **26** (3), 276–92.

Zackman, J. (1997), 'Enterprise architecture: the issue of the century', *Data-base Programming and Design*, February.

Zackman, J. and J. Sowa (1992), 'Extending and formalizing the framework for information systems architecture', *IBM Systems Journal*, **31** (3), 590–616.

Zimmerman, B. and D.K. Hurst (1993), 'Breaking the boundaries: the fractal organization', *Journal of Management Inquiry*, **2** (4), 334–55.

Zmud, R.W. (1988), 'Building relationships throughout the corporate entity', in J. Elam (ed.), *Transforming the IS Organization*, Washington, DC: ICIT Press.

Zuboff, S. (1988), *In the Age of the Smart Machine: The Future of Work and Power*, Oxford: Heinemann.

Zuboff, S. (1991), 'Informate the enterprise: an agenda for the 21st century', *National Forum* (Summer), 3–7.

Zuboff, S. (1995), 'The emperor's new information economy', paper pre-sented at the Information Technology and Change in Organizational Work Conference, Cambridge, UK, 1995.

Index

Academy for Information Systems
  (UKAIS) 2
action 218
  action-based view of strategic
    alignment 158–86
    interlocking of IS/IT infrastructure
      and cultural knowledge
      superstructure 165–7
    IS/IT-related contexts as foundation
      of strategic alignment 172–85
    OFF model 160–65
    organizational context dimensions
      167–72
  designing in 152
  managerial 120–21, 160, 188, 220,
    222–3
  theory of 115, 117–22
    espoused theory of action 90–91,
      115, 116
active perception 52
AGIL 72
Allaire, Y. 81
American Airlines 26
Andreu, R. 39, 145, 151
Andrews, K. 141
Angell, I.O. 186, 187
Ansoff, H.I. 107, 141
Applegate, L.M. 26, 126, 173, 190
architecture of IS/IT 139
Argyris, Chris 11, 90, 91, 111, 112, 115,
  116, 152
Aristotle 52
artificial intelligence 5, 54, 86
Ashforth, B.E. 37
Attewell, P. 18
automation 20
autonomy 182
autopoiesis 43, 55–61, 62, 96, 218–19
Avgerou, C. 137
Avison, D.E. 39
Azevedo, A. 39

ba/basho 80, 86, 92, 165
Baker, B.S.H. 173
Bakos, J.Y. 126, 141
Balanced Scorecards Methodology
  (BSC) 23, 190, 192, 193
Barnard, Chester 11, 111, 112–13, 114,
  117
Barney, J.B. 99, 108, 110
Baroudi, J.J. 129, 226
barriers to learning 183–4
Bartlett, C.A. 11, 37, 111, 114–15, 117,
  118, 119, 120, 160, 168, 169, 171,
  172, 174, 177, 178, 179, 180, 181,
  182, 199, 214
Beath, C.M. 32
Becker, B.E. 98
behaviour
  group 93–4
  interpersonal 93–4
  Model I and Model II 115–16
  organizational 37, 111, 118
Bell, C.H. 116
Benjamin, R. 36
Benyon, D. 137
Bohm, D. 80–81, 221
Boje, D.M. 68, 78, 88, 96, 127
Boland, R. 76–7, 96
Bostrom, R.P. 146
Boulding, K.E. 68, 70
bounded rationality 74, 140
Bowditch, J.L. 118
Boynton, A.C. 38, 214
Bradley, S.P. 26
bricolage 145
Broekstra, O. 86, 87, 97
Brown, C.V. 183, 184, 213
Buckley, W. 48
Buono, A.F. 118
Burke, W.W. 155
Burn, J. 144
Burns, T. 11, 111, 113, 117, 118

Business Process Re-engineering (BPR)
114
Business Systems Planning (BSP) 138

Campbell, H. 137, 146, 148
capital
human 114, 190–91
human capital, human resources
development 184
intellectual 105, 190, 191–2
structural 191
working 105
Cartesianism 42
Cash, J.I. 26, 126, 141, 190
Casti, J. 44
causal ambiguity 108
causes and consequences of IS/IT
16–40
inconclusive search for cause-and-
effect 18–20
key themes 27–39
web of causes and consequences
20–26
Chakravarthy, B. 25
Champy, J. 26
Chandler, Alfred 13, 107, 141
change
cultural 93
IS/IT and 196–7
management of 8, 223–4
need for change orientation 37–9
chaos 10, 42, 47
chaos theory 45
creative 177
Checkland, P. 4, 27, 37, 128, 129, 192,
223
chief executives (CEOs) 175–6
Child, J. 20, 93
choice, managerial 93
Choo, C.W. 22, 153, 157
Ciborra, C.U. 26, 31, 38, 39, 144, 145,
146, 149, 151, 152, 157, 159, 160,
176, 177, 186, 226
clarification 183
classification 48
Clegg, S.R. 150
Clement, A. 22, 153, 157
Clemons, E.K. 26
climate 182
organizational 84–6

closure
operational 51
organizational 58, 63
code of conduct 113–14
cognition 217
autopoiesis theory 43, 55–61, 62, 96,
218–19
cognitivist/connectionist hypotheses
48, 49–51
enacted 43, 217–18
enactive approach to 112
knowledge and 48–9
pragmatist/enaction hypotheses 48,
52–5
Cohen, W.M. 194, 214
colour 53
commitment 175
common sense 52
communication 29, 60, 65, 67, 113,
184–5
conversation 63, 66
language 60–61
communication technologies, convergence with IS/IT 25–6
competencies 181
core 110, 202
interplay 204, 205–09
strategy development as competency-
based issue 201–09
competition
competitive potential 6
compression of competitive time 20
hypercompetition 20, 24, 25
organizational knowledge as competitive market pressure 27–9
strategy and 98
theory of competitive positioning
100–106
complexity 3, 10, 11, 42, 43–8, 68, 81,
86, 217
autopoiesis theory 43, 55–61, 62, 96,
218–19
cognitivist/connectionist hypotheses
48, 49–51
pragmatist/enaction hypotheses 48,
52–5
self-referential social systems 61–7
connectionism 50–51
Conner, K. 99
conservative systems 44–5

constitution 37, 38, 162–5, 196
constraints of IS/IT 17
consumer's market 114
context 117, 151, 221
   action-based view of strategic
      alignment and 167–72
   context-forming organizational model
      88–96
      inter-subjective or dyadic activity
         dimension 90–92
      micro-communities of knowledge
         or role formation dimension
         93–6
      theory of organization or cultural
         knowledge dimension 92–3
   IS/IT-related contexts as foundation
      of strategic alignment 172–85
   organizations as 84–6
control 22, 179
conversation 63, 66
Cooper, R. 153
core competencies 110
Cornford, A. 125
Cornford, T. 137
corporate governance 162–3, 168, 185,
   224
   competence interplay and 205–09
costs of IS/IT 22
coupling, structural 58–9
courage 177
creation of knowledge 78–80
creative chaos 177
critical success factors 27
Cross, J. 183
culture
   knowledge and 92–3, 166–7, 221
   organizational 70–71, 80–84, 110,
      119, 136, 151–2, 185, 221
Curley, K.F. 24
customer resource life cycle framework
   27
cybernetics, socio-cybernetics 62–3
Cyert, R.M. 75

Dahlbom, B. 16
Damasio, A.R. 51
data 5–6
   data modelling 137
   databases 210–11
   fixation on 70

storage 5, 22
D'Aveni, R. 24
Davenport, T. 26, 139, 145
Davies, G.B. 128
De Jong, W.M. 156
De Marco, T. 137
De Sanctis, G. 17, 126, 137, 146, 148
defensive routines 115
definitions of IS/IT 2–4
Dertouzos, Michael 3, 24, 25
Descartes, René 49, 222
design school of strategy 145
designing in action 152
determinism 18, 42, 71–3, 76, 107
   arguments against 19
   soft-line 147–8
diffusion of IS/IT 29, 126, 133–5
discipline 118, 177–9
disposition 186
dissipative systems 44, 45
domination 93
double contingency 65
double-loop learning 116
Drucker, Peter 11, 111
dualism 42, 222
Durkheim, Emile 72
Dutta, S. 175
dyadic activity 90–92
dynamic systems 45

Earl, Michael J. 32, 37, 126, 141, 144,
   158, 160, 161, 162, 163, 173, 182,
   184, 196, 199, 224
Eason, K.D. 147
Eccles, R.G. 20, 87
e-commerce 24
economics, complexity and 47
Edvinsson, L. 23, 190, 191
effectiveness 27, 100, 101
efficacy 27
efficiency 27
El Sawy, O.A. 39, 151
Elam, J.J. 32
emergence 86
   strategy and 98
emotional intelligence 122
enacted cognition 43, 51, 52–5, 217–18
enaction 112
endogeneity of IS/IT 17
Enlightenment 43

Enron 41
Enterprise Resource Planning (ERP) 8, 211
environmental analysis 101
epistemology 10, 43, 54, 226
equilibrium 72
Erlicher, L. 39
espoused theory of action 90–91, 115, 116
Eveland, J.D. 153–4, 194
Executive Information Systems (EIS) 23
expansion 22
experiential learning 212
explicit knowledge 79, 211

Falcione, R.L. 84, 159, 168, 169, 171, 183
feedback 177–8
Feeny, D. 176
Finkelstein, C. 140
Fiol, C.M. 82, 84, 86, 89, 94, 110, 207
fire ants 45–6
Firsirotu, M.E. 81
first-mover advantage 107–08
five forces model 101, 107
flocking 86–7
flux and transformation 136
Follet, Mary Parker 11, 111, 112
Forester, T. 20
Foucault, Michel 52
fractals 46–7
fragmentation 44
Freeman, W.J. 48, 51, 52, 56
French, W.L. 116
Friesen, G.B. 219
Frito-Lay 26

Galbraith, J. 74
Galliers, R.D. 22, 126, 141, 142, 173, 194, 224
Gash, D.C. 126
Gates, Bill 7
Gell-Mann, Murray 86
general systems theory 68
genetic epistemology 54
George, J.F. 145
Gestalt theory 63, 68
Geyer, F. 62
Ghoshal, S. 10, 11, 37, 111, 114–15, 117, 118, 119, 120, 159, 168, 169,
171, 172, 174, 177, 178, 179, 180, 181, 182, 199, 214
Giddens, Anthony 37, 65–6, 126, 147, 149, 156, 218
Ginzberg, M. 207
Goodhue, D.L. 32
Grant, R.M. 99, 107
Griffiths, P. 126, 141, 161, 173
Grindley, K. 33
Guedes, F.C. 42, 43, 47, 68
Gutek, B.A. 20

Haeckel, H.H. 26
Hall, G. 26
Hamel, G. 106, 110, 174, 202
Hammer, M. 26
Handy, Charles 11
Hebb's rule 50
Hedberg, B. 75
Hedlund, G. 79
Heidegger, Martin 52
Heinen, J.S. 146
Henderson, J.C. 32, 107, 144, 175, 213, 214
Herden, R.P. 84, 159, 168, 169, 171, 182, 183
Hill, W.F. 63
Hirscheim, R. 25
Hoffer, J.A. 137
holism 38, 44, 127, 223–5
    organizational holistic perspective on implementation 149–53, 154–6
Holwell, S. 4, 27, 37, 128, 129, 192, 223
hospitality 176
Huber, G.P. 19, 75, 138
Huff, S.L. 22, 153
human capital 114, 190–91
    human resources development 184
Hurst, D.K. 47
hypercompetition 20, 24, 25
hypocrisy 116

IBM 41, 219
Ichijo, K. 11, 169, 171, 177
idealism 49
identity 84, 94, 95
Ilharco, F. 121
imperative, organizational 140
implementation 8–9, 37–8, 125–56
    definition 126

implied implementation strategy
132–3
infusion vs. diffusion focus 133–5
likely outcome 133
methodological approach 128–9
organization metaphors 135–6
organizational holistic perspective
149–53, 154–5
overcoming barriers 98
socio-technical interactionism 144–9,
155
strategic rationality 140–44
technological optimism 136–40, 155
incentives system 184
incrementalism 10
Industrial Revolution 16
information 5
cognition and 49
processing of 74–5, 76
textualization of 20–22
information systems/information
technology (IS/IT) 1, 3
definitions 2–4
as emerging discipline 2–3
endogeneity 17
organization and 19
purpose of book 11–12
research method 12–13
roadmap of book 13–15
views of 16–17
see also individual topics
infusion of IS/IT 27, 29, 133–5
innovation 113, 152–3, 162
strategy development as innovation
process 194–201
integration of IS/IT function 31–6
intellectual capital 105, 190, 191–2
intelligence
development of 19
emotional 122
intensity matrix 27
intent 173–7
interactionism, socio-technical 144–9,
155
interdisciplinarity, *see*
multidisciplinarity
international relations 2, 3
Internet 24
interpretivism 10–11, 129, 226
inter-subjectivity 90–92, 94

Introna, L. 116, 151, 222
Itami, H. 12, 17, 176
Ives, B. 27, 126, 141, 201

Jacobs, G.C. 38, 214
Joyce, P. 10

Kahn, R.L. 73, 94
Kakabadse, A. 117
Kakabadse, N. 117
Kaplan, R.S. 6
Kappelman, L.A. 138
Katz, D. 73, 94
Keen, P.G.W. 25, 33, 151, 159, 175, 212
Kelly, M. 20
Kenney, M. 24
Kiesler, S. 26
King, J.L 152
knowledge 5, 42, 217
cognition and 48–9
as competitive market pressure 27–9
creation of 12, 29, 78–80
strategy development of as 209–12
culture and 92–3, 166–7
development 11
epistemology 10, 43
explicit knowledge 79, 211
knowledge base 5
knowledge economy 6–7
management systems 5
micro-communities of 93–6
organizational cultural knowledge
119, 221
tacit knowledge 79, 95–6, 211
wealth creation and 5–7
Konsynski, B.R. 26, 126, 141
Kraemer, K.L. 38
Kramer, K.L. 152
Kuhn, T. 7
Kwon, T.H. 152, 153

Lacity, M. 25
Land, F. 3–4, 38, 125, 142, 185, 223
Landauer, T.K. 20
language 60–61, 87
culture and 82–3
Lanzara, G. 38, 149, 151, 152
Large, P. 20
Laszlo, Ervin 216
Lave, J. 94

Learmonth, G.P. 27, 126, 141, 201
learning
  barriers to 183–4
  double-loop learning 116
  experiential 212
  Hebb's rule 50
  organizational 24, 70, 75, 90, 140–41,
    151–2, 217
    strategy development as 212–14
  radical 145
  single-loop 115–16
  types of 24
Leavitt, H.J. 20
Lederer, A.L. 141, 142
Lee, Alan S. 139
legitimacy 117
legitimate participation 94–5
legitimation 93
Levinthal, D.A. 194, 214
Lewin, R. 45, 47, 86, 90, 95
life cycle framework 27, 137–8
Likert, J.G. 169, 171, 178, 179, 183, 184
Likert, R. 169, 171, 178, 179, 183, 184
Litwin, G.H. 169, 171, 178, 179, 180,
    182, 183
Lloyd, B. 219
logical compound synthesis 12–13
Lucas, H.C. 128, 207
Luhmann, N. 62, 65, 93
Lundberg, C.C. 13
Lyles, M.A. 207
Lyotard, J.F. 91

MacDonald, H. 144
McFadden, F.R. 137
McFarlan, F.W. 25, 26, 126, 141, 201
McGregor, D. 118
machine organization 70, 135–6, 139
McKeen, J.D. 181
McKesson Drug Co. 26
McLean, E.R. 138
McNurlin, B.C. 31, 32, 139, 190, 214
Magalhães, R. 13, 77
Mahoney, J.T. 99, 111
Malone, M.S. 23, 190, 191
Malone, T.W. 26
management 222
  automation and 20–22
  Balanced Scorecards Methodology
    (BSC) 23

change management 8, 223–4
chief executives (CEOs) 175–6
choice 93
complexity and 47
implementation programmes and 8–9
interpretivism and 10–11
IS/IT-related management processes
    197–201
managerial action 120–21, 157, 188,
    220, 222–3
managerial rationalism 141
new forms of control 22–3
new modernist type of 10, 99, 111
power of 91–2
scientification of 42
strategy as managerial action 98–124
  basic concepts of theory of
    competitive positioning
    100–106
  middle-ground 99, 111–17
  resource-based approach 106–11
  towards a theory of managerial
    action 117–22
theory development in 13
March, J.G. 74, 75
Markus, M.L. 36, 137, 140, 146, 151,
    181
Martin, B.H. 22, 153
Mason, R.O. 129
Mata, F.J.F. 188, 201, 202
materialism 48
Maturana, Humberto 53, 55, 56, 57, 59,
    60, 61, 62, 66, 116, 122, 158, 217
maturity, stages of 152–3
meaning
  formation of 94
  personal 176
memory, organizational 77
Merleau-Ponty, Maurice 52, 218
metaphors, organizational 135–6
methodology 10, 12–13, 43
Millar, V.E. 27, 126, 141, 201
Mills, D.Q. 26, 219
Mingers, J. 43, 57, 59, 62, 65, 67, 89,
    93, 218, 220
Minow, N. 163, 205
Mintzberg, Henry 98, 100, 145, 174
mismatch with models 41
Mitroff, I. 76
Model I and Model II behaviour 115–16

models, mismatch with 41
Monks, R.A.G. 162, 205
Moran, P. 10, 118
Morgan, G. 70, 80, 81, 135, 139, 140, 149, 219, 221
Morieux, Y.V.H. 39
multidisciplinarity 2, 3
  theory-building and 12–13
Mumford, Enid 146
Munro, M.L. 22, 153
Myers, M. 39

narrative 96
Navigator model 23
Nelson, R.R. 108, 194
Netscape 24
networks
  autopoietic 56–7
  combination of knowledge and 211
  human 29
new economy 6–7
new modernism 10, 99, 111
new organizational paradigm 71
  emergence, self-organization and language 86–8
  knowledge creation 78–80
  open systems theory 68, 73–4
  organizations as climates or contexts 84–6
  organizations as living cultures 80–84
new science 9–10, 42
Nicolis, G. 44
Nohria, N. 87
Nolan, R. 22, 25, 26, 153
Nonaka, Ikujiro 11, 29, 42, 78, 79, 80, 86, 165, 169, 171, 172, 174, 177, 182, 183, 184, 191, 209, 210, 212, 214, 222
non-linear behaviour 42, 44, 47
non-profit organizations 101
Nordhaug, O. 169, 183, 184, 185
Normann, R. 37, 117, 183, 213
Norton, David 6, 158, 167
Numagami, T. 12, 17, 176

old organizational paradigm
  determinism and equilibrium 70, 71–3
  information processing metaphor 74–5
  verdict on 76–7

old science 43–4
Olson, M.H. 128
Olve, N.-G. 23
Olympic Games 41
open systems theory 68, 73–4
operational closure 51
optimism, technological 136–40, 155
organization
  closure 63
  constitution 38
  IS/IT and 19
  learning in 70
  new paradigm, open systems theory 73–4
Organizational Fit Framework (OFF) model 159–64, 196
organizational technologies, *see* information systems/information technology (IS/IT)
Orlikowski, W.J. 17, 38, 126, 129, 147, 148, 194, 226
outsourcing 25
overcapacity 114

paradigm changes 7–11, 222
  new organizational paradigm 71
    emergence, self-organization and language 86–8
    knowledge creation 78–80
    open systems theory 68, 73–4
    organizations as climates or contexts 84–6
    organizations as living cultures 80–84
  old organizational paradigm
    determinism and equilibrium 70, 71–3
    information processing metaphor 74–5
    verdict on 76–7
Parsons, Talcott 72
participation 180
  legitimate 94–5
Pascale, R.T. 23, 43, 45, 47, 149
Pattriota, G. 39
Penrose, E. 108
Pentland, B. 141
Peppard, J. 36, 181, 185
perception, active 52
personal meaning 176

Petrozzo, D. 20
Pettigrew, A. 107, 134, 224
Phillips 66 26
Piaget, Jean 54
Plato 49
Polanyi, Michael 79
political power 150–51
Pondy, L.R. 76
Poole, M.S. 17, 126, 137, 146, 148
Porter, Michael 27, 93, 98, 100, 101,
    104, 105, 106, 107, 123, 126, 141,
    190, 201
positioning, theory of competitive
    positioning 100–106
positivism 129, 226
poverty 41
power 91–2
    organizational 116–17, 150–51
    political 150–51
pragmatist/enaction hypotheses 48, 52–5
Prahalad, C.K. 99, 106, 110, 174, 202
Prigogine, I. 44, 71
processes, managerial 120
processing of information 74–5, 76
products, evolution of 24
purpose 113
Pyburn, P.J. 24

Quinn, J.B. 100

radical learning 145
rationality
    bounded 74, 140
    managerial rationalism 141
    strategic 140–44, 188–9
reductionism 44, 76
redundancy 172
Regine, B. 47, 90
Remenyi, D. 178
rent 106–07
representationism 50, 51, 217
research method 12–13
resources
    embeddedness of 108
    resource-based approach to strategy
        106–11
responsibility 179
Reynolds, Craig 86
Roberts, E.B. 194
Robey, Daniel 19, 39, 137, 140, 146

Rockart, J.F. 26, 27, 32, 161, 175
role, formation of 93–6
Roos, J. 11, 43, 47, 87, 112, 163, 203,
    213
Ross, J.W. 32, 183, 184, 213
routines, defensive 115
Rowan, J. 123
Ruhleder, K. 166
Rule, J. 18
Rumelt, R. 107, 108

SABRE 26
Sackmann, S. 119
Saga, V.L 153
Sambamurthy, V. 189
sanctions 177
Schein, Edgar 81, 82, 86, 175, 176, 186
Schneider, B. 38, 159, 168
Schon, Donald A. 11, 90, 91, 111, 112,
    115, 152
Schultz, R. 207
Schwuchow, W. 210
science 129
    new science 9–10, 42
    old science 43–4
    scientification of management 42
Scott Morton, M. 30, 142, 158
self-organization 10, 42, 86
    fractal geometry and 46–7
self-production (autopoiesis) 43, 55–61,
    62, 96, 218–19
self-reference 58
    social systems 61–7
self-regulation 72
self-steering 42
Selznick, Philip 11, 94, 111, 122
Semler, R. 26
Senge, P. 192
Sethi, V. 141, 142
Sherwood-Smith, M. 178
Short, J.E. 26
signification 93
Simon, Herbert 41, 71, 74, 94, 140, 217
single-loop learning 115–16
Skandia 23, 191
slack 22
Slappendel, C. 194
Smelser, N.J. 72
Smith, H.A. 181
Smithson, S. 186, 187

social systems, self-referential 61–7
socio-cybernetics 62–3
sociology, systems theory and 72
socio-technical interactionism 144–9,
  155
soft-line determinism 147–8
Sowa, J. 138
Sprague, R.H. 31, 32, 139, 190, 214
Sproull, L. 26
stability 72
Stacey, R.D. 47
stakeholders 205–09
Stalker, G.M. 11, 111, 113, 117, 118
standards 179
Star, S.L. 166
Stengers, I. 71
stock market crash (1987) 47
storage of data 5, 22
Strassman, P.A. 20
Strategic Information Systems Planning
  (SISP) 141–2, 201
strategy
  action-based view of strategic
    alignment 158–86
    interlocking of IS/IT infrastructure
      and cultural knowledge
      superstructure 165–7
    IS/IT-related contexts as foundation
      of strategic alignment 172–85
    OFF model 160–65
    organizational context dimensions
      167–72
  definition of 100
  development of 187–215
    as competency-based issue 201–09
    components of 189
    information systems and 12
    as innovation process 194–201
    as knowledge creation 209–12
    as organizational learning 212–14
    as value creation 189–93
  implementation of IS/IT and 126–7,
    129
  implied implementation strategy
    132–3
  strategic rationality 140–44
  as managerial action 98–124
    basic concepts of theory of
      competitive positioning
      100–106

middle-ground 99, 111–17
resource-based approach 106–11
towards a theory of managerial
  action 117–22
new modernist school of 10
strategic alignment 29–31, 142–4
strategic option generator model 27
strategic planning 10
stretch 118, 174–5
Stringer, R.A. 169, 171, 178, 179, 180,
  183
structural capital 191
structural factors 183–6
structuration theory 65–6, 67, 126, 147,
  149, 155, 218
structured systems analysis 137
subjectivity
  generic 94
  inter-subjectivity 90–92, 94
Sullivan, C.H. 27, 29, 32, 224
support 118, 181–3
Sussman, L. 84, 159, 168, 169, 171,
  182, 183, 184
Sutherland, E. 39, 224
Swanson, E.B. 37–8, 206, 223
SWOT analysis 108
Symons, V.J. 4, 137, 142, 146, 148, 188
systems theory 68, 72
  open systems theory 68, 73–4

tacit knowledge 79, 95–6, 211
Takeuchi, H. 11, 29, 42, 78, 79, 80, 169,
  171, 172, 174, 182, 183, 184, 191,
  209, 210, 212, 214, 222
taxonomies 48
technology 7
  constraints of 17
  endogeneity 17
  innovation 113
  strategy and 176
  technological optimism 136–40, 155
  see also information systems/
    information technology (IS/IT)
Teece, D.J. 23, 202
Tenkasi, R.V. 96
textualization of information 20–22
theory
  application in practice 9
  development of 12–13
  multidisciplinarity and 12–13

of organization 92–3
  paradigm changes 7–11
theory X and theory Y 118
Thompson, J. 74
time compression diseconomies 107
Total Quality Management (TQM) 114
Treacy, M.E. 126, 141
Trisoglio, A. 45, 47
trust 118, 180–81

uncertainty 22
Ungson, G.R. 77
universities 101
unpredictability 42

value 105, 117
  strategy development as value
    creation 189–93
  value chain 190
van der Zouwen, J. 62
Varela, Francisco J. 48, 49, 50, 51, 52,
    53, 54, 55, 56, 57, 58, 59, 60, 61,
    62, 63, 112, 217, 222
variety 172
vision 53, 175
von Bertalanffy, L. 71, 73
von Clausewitz, Carl 121, 122
Von Eckardt, B. 48
von Krogh, G. 11, 43, 47, 87, 95, 112,
    163, 169, 171, 177, 203, 213
von Simson, E.M. 213

Waldrop, M.M. 10
Walsh, J.R. 77
Walsham, G. 17, 126, 147, 156, 223
Walton, R. 37, 223

Wang, Charles 36, 181
Ward, J. 36, 126, 141, 161, 173, 181,
    185
warfare 121, 122
wealth, IS/IT and creation of 5–7
Weber, Max 72
Weick, Karl E. 37, 75, 85, 86, 89, 93,
    112, 123, 221
Weir, M. 146
Wenger, E. 94
Wernerfelt, B. 99, 108
Wheatley, M.J. 9, 47
Whipp, R. 107, 134
Whistler, T.L. 20
Willcocks, L. 39
Winter, S. 108, 110–11, 194
Wiseman, C. 27, 126, 141, 201
Wood-Harper, A.T. 140
Woods, A. 10
work ethic 112, 114
work system 184
working capital 105
World Bank 41
World Trade Center attack (11 Septem-
    ber 2001) 41, 47
Worldcom 41

Yetton, P.W. 144
Young, T.R. 42, 44, 46, 47
Yourdon, E. 137

Zackman, J. 138
Zimmerman, B. 47
Zmud, R.W. 32, 38, 152, 153, 162, 184,
    189, 213, 214
Zuboff, Shoshana 20–21, 147, 212